expl

TENERIFE

Tim Jepson

AA Publishing

Front cover: San
Andrés, northeast of
Santa Cruz de Tenerife
Page 2: a colourful
balcony in La Orotava
Page 3: Barranco del
Infierno (Hell's Gorge),
near Adeje
Page 4: a tiled chair in
Santa Cruz de Tenerife
Page 5: (a) fishing at
Las Galletas, Costa del
Silencio; (b) colourful
strelitzia
Page 6: one of nine
statues of Guanche
menceys (leaders) at
Candelaria
Pages 6–7: Valle de
Guimar
Page 7: an attentive
guard dog, La Orotava
Page 8: coastline
scenery near Bajamar
Page 9: lunar-like
landscape, Parque
Nacional del Teide

Written by Tim Jepson
Edited, designed and produced by AA Publishing
Maps © The Automobile Association 1998

The contents of this publication are believed correct at the
time of printing. Nevertheless, the publishers cannot be
held responsible for any errors or omissions or for changes
in the details given in this guide or for the consequences of
any reliance on the information provided by the same.
Assessments of attractions, hotels, restaurants and so
forth are based upon the author's own personal experience and, therefore, descriptions given in this guide
necessarily contain an element of subjective opinion
which may not reflect the publishers' opinion or dictate a
reader's own experiences on another occasion. We have
tried to ensure accuracy in this guide, but things do change
and we would be grateful if readers would advise us of any
inaccuracies they may encounter.
Some material in this book has been previously published
by AA Publishing in various publications.

A CIP catalogue record for this book is available from the
British Library.

ISBN 0 7495 1716 6
Published by AA Publishing (a trading name of Automobile
Association Developments Limited, whose registered
office is Norfolk House, Priestley Road, Basingstoke,
Hampshire RG24 9NY. Registered number 1878835).

Colour separation by Fotographics Ltd
Printed and bound in Italy by Printer Trento srl

Titles in the Explorer series:
Australia • Boston & New England • Britain
Brittany • California • Caribbean • China • Costa Rica
Crete • Cuba • Cyprus • Egypt • Florence & Tuscany
Florida • France • Germany • Greek Islands • Hawaii
Indonesia • Ireland • Israel • Italy • Japan • London
Mallorca • Mexico • Moscow & St Petersburg
New York • New Zealand • Paris • Portugal • Prague
Provence • Rome • San Francisco • Scotland
Singapore & Malaysia • South Africa • Spain • Thailand
Tunisia • Turkey • Turkish Coast • Venice • Vietnam

AA World Travel Guides publish nearly 300 guidebooks to
a full range of cities, countries and regions across the
world. Find out more about AA Publishing and the wide
range of services the AA provides by visiting our Web site
at www.theaa.co.uk.

How to use this book

Mantequilla Danesa HEYMAN

This book is divided into five main sections:

❏ Section 1: *Tenerife Is*
discusses aspects of life and living today, from tourism to art and culture

❏ Section 2: *Tenerife Was*
places the country in its historical context and explores past events whose influences are still felt

❏ Section 3: *A to Z Section*
covers places to visit, arranged by region, with suggested walks. Within this section fall the Focus-on articles, which consider a variety of topics in greater detail

❏ Section 4: *Travel Facts*
contains the strictly practical information that is vital for a successful trip

❏ Section 5:
Hotels and Restaurants
lists recommended establishments in Tenerife, giving a brief résumé of what they offer

How to use the star rating
Most places described in this book have been given a separate rating:

▶▶▶ **Do not miss**

▶▶ **Highly recommended**

▶ **Worth seeing**

Map references
To make the location of a particular place easier to find, every main entry in this book is given a map reference, such as 53C2. The first number (53) indicates the page on which the map can be found; the letter (C) and the second number (2) pinpoint the square in which the main entry is located. The maps on the inside front and inside back covers are referred to as IFC and IBC respectively.

Contents

Quick reference

This quick-reference guide highlights the elements of the book you will use most often: the maps; the introductory features; the Focus-on articles; the walks and the drives.

Tim Jepson's love of travel
began with a busking trip
through Europe, and has
since taken him from the
drowsy calm of the
Umbrian hills to the
windswept tundra of the
Yukon and far North. He
has lived in Italy, but has
plans to leave the warmth
of the Mediterranean for
the Arctic and hidden
mountains of South
America. He has
written several guides for
the AA, including AA
Explorer guides to *Italy,
Florence & Tuscany* and
Canada.

My Tenerife by Tim Jepson

My first thoughts on Tenerife were probably those of
most people who know the island only by reputation.
Here, surely, was a package-holiday destination and no
more, geared solely to visitors who sought a stress-free
week or two under a warm sun. Culture might be there
for those who wanted it; landscapes there must surely
be, but hardly anything worth writing home about.
Besides, who was going to leave the beach or hotel
swimming pool to venture into the great unknown
beyond the pubs, restaurants and clubs?

As ever, reputation and first impressions proved wide
of the mark. Tenerife certainly caters for mass tourism.
The big southern resorts of Los Cristianos and Playa de
las Américas are deservedly popular and perfect for
a cheap and unpretentious holiday in subtropical
surroundings. No one can pretend they offer much in the
way of local colour or culture. And it's these attributes,
together with majestic landscapes and wonderful food
and wine, that make the most lasting impression on
visitors to the island.

Tenerife mixes the culinary and cultural traditions of
Spain, Portugal, Africa, northern Europe and South
America, a heady brew that reaches its climax in the
annual Santa Cruz Carnival, the world's largest. History
and culture can be found in lovely old towns such as
La Laguna and La Orotava, while hints of traditional ways
can still be glimpsed in remote mountain villages,
age-old festivals and the skills of local craftspeople.

For me, though, Tenerife's main appeal lies in its landscapes. For sheer splendour and strangeness, little beats
the volcanic majesty of Mount Teide, the highest
mountain on Spanish territory, or the evocative sight of
the palms, banana plantations and subtropical gardens
that swathe much of the island's lush northern coast. I
could happily devote an entire visit to exploring the
verdant, forest-covered slopes of the Anaga Mountains
or spend a few hours in solitude, walking the laurel
woodlands of La Gomera. Tenerife may have the veneer
of a package-tour heaven, but underneath it has the
charms of a lost island paradise.

TENERIFE IS

■ **Tenerife is one of Europe's most popular holiday destinations, an island of limpid seas, perpetual sunshine and a wealth of leisure and nightlife opportunities. Yet beyond the big resorts lies a land of unexpected beauty, complete with historic old towns, traditional villages, ancient woodlands, pastoral valleys, desolate uplands and spectacular mountains.** ■

Facts Tenerife is one of the Canary Islands, an archipelago of seven large and six small islands close to the African coast. Spain – to which the islands belong – lies 1,120km to the north. The Sahara is just 300km away, while the Tropic of Cancer lies 480km to the south. The islands' latitude – 28° north – is the same as the Bahamas. Tenerife is the archipelago's most popular island, attracting some four million visitors annually. It is also the largest, measuring 130km from east to west and 90km from north to south (an area of 2,057sq km). Its population is around 650,000, with another 20,000 on La Gomera, a small and largely unspoilt island off the southwest coast.

Towns Tenerife's capital is Santa Cruz, a bustling city with a likeable life of its own. Most visitors, though, are more likely to become familiar with one of the island's three major resorts: Puerto de la Cruz, on the north coast, which has been popular with visitors for over a century, and Los Cristianos and Playa de las Américas (on the south coast), the best known of Tenerife's newer package-holiday resorts. These last two – the product of the 1960s and 1970s tourist boom – are places to come for a holiday of guaranteed sunshine, well-ordered surroundings, non-stop nightlife, and – if you want it – virtually no contact with local Tenerife life. Puerto de la Cruz, by contrast – though not without its English pubs, fast-food joints and timeshare touts – preserves traces of its old Spanish-Colonial character, something which tends to attract a slightly older and more discerning tourist. Much the same applies to the towns of Santa Cruz, La Orotava, La Laguna and Garachico, all with appealing old centres, as well as to Los Gigantes and Puerto de Santiago, two smaller and more stylish resorts on the west coast.

❑ 'No place in the world seems to me more likely than Tenerife to banish melancholy and restore peace to a troubled spirit…'
Alexander von Humboldt
(1889) ❑

Left: Tenerife's finest beach, Playa de las Teresitas, is very popular with visitors

Landscapes Tenerife's variety of landscapes is a revelation. Broadly speaking, the island divides into two, with arid, desert-like hills, mountains and coastal plains in the south, and more verdant, fertile and forested valleys and mountains in the north. If truth be told, the south offers little to see, but in the north the lush Valle de la Orotava, the Anaga mountains (in the northeast) and the Teno Massif (in the northwest) offer superb natural scenery, breathtaking panoramas and wonderful walking trails. At the heart of the island, brooding over everything, towers the mighty peak of Mount Teide, the highest point on Spanish territory. Elsewhere the island's scenic patchwork includes

Mount Teide dominates this superb mountain landscape, a feature of central Tenerife

thick pine forests, dank laurel woodlands, romantic gorges, soaring cliffs, bare lunar landscapes, and deep-cut *barrancos*, or canyons, that plunge spectacularly to the sea.

Leisure If walking, touring or exploring old towns doesn't appeal, Tenerife offers an almost limitless range of other leisure activities. All it lacks, oddly, are good beaches, though plenty of alternatives are available to keep holidaymakers happy. You can pursue all manner of watersports, notably sailing, diving, waterskiing, surfing and windsurfing, as well as activities such as golf, tennis, fishing, riding and dolphin-watching.

Waterparks, wildlife centres and other diversions are also springing up. And if the neon nightlife of the resorts begins to pale, the island offers a wealth of enticing local fiestas and festivals.

> ❑ 'The blue sky and all-pervading sun overhead, the delicious warmth but exquisite freshness of the air, all tell us that we have reached the haven of our rest … the Fortunate Islands.'
> Francis Hart, Letter (1887) ❑

■ **Tourism can be a two-headed monster, voracious on the one hand, and bringing wealth and well-being on the other. In few places has it been as rampant as Tenerife, a poor and peripheral island until the 1950s, but in the wake of large-scale development now one of Europe's most visited package-holiday destinations.** ■

Beginnings Tourism in Tenerife is not new. Some of the first visitors – scientists and botanists for the most part – arrived at the beginning of the 19th century. A few years later the growth of the banana industry brought genuine holidaymakers, thanks largely to foreign fruit importers like Fyffes and Yeoward, whose banana boats ferried some of the earliest 'package' tourists to the island. Visitors signed up for a 16-day round trip, beginning at Liverpool and sailing to Tenerife by way of Lisbon, Madeira and Las Palmas. Their arrival led to a hotel-building boom, with luxury hotels springing up in Puerto de la Cruz to accommodate visitors. The two world wars, coupled with recession and dictatorship, stunted further development of the industry, and for 50 years tourism remained a small-scale concern.

The black-sand beach at Las Gaviotas

Boom All this changed in 1957 with the introduction of the first charter flights, a phenomenon which turned Puerto de la Cruz into an international resort. A few years later the island's hotter southern coast began to see the first signs of development, a trend which received a massive boost with the opening of the Reina Sofía Airport in 1978. This led to the mushrooming of Los Cristianos and Playa de las Américas, now two of Europe's largest holiday resorts. Over the next 15 years the vast numbers taking package tours to these and other resorts showed a marked decline. For some the reason was the growth of cheaper long-haul destinations, for others the fact that Tenerife no longer offered such good value for money. For many, though, the reason was disenchantment at the concrete 'jungle' aspect of the island's resorts, and the 'pile-it-high-and-sell-it-cheap' mentality of large-scale, low-cost tourism.

Time-share sales are symbolic of the vast tourist industry

Debate Large-scale developments and low-cost tourism have their advantages, however, not least of which are jobs on an island where unemployment is traditionally high. Public works, hotels and apartments all bring work, while improved roads carry tourists to previously impoverished villages to spend money in restaurants and craft shops. Moreover, much of the work is year round, and not prone to the hardships and vicissitudes of agriculture (Tenerife's traditional employer). Against these advantages, however, can be set the fact that many hoteliers and time-share operators bring in their own staff and exclude locals. Worse, young people often leave villages in search of work, leaving them moribund and depopulated. Tourists often swamp the remaining villages, destroying the character which made them attractive in the first place. Visitors also put pressure on resources and the environment, creating problems of water supply and sewage disposal, and damaging flora and fauna through increased pollution levels.

Change Tenerife's approach has meant more people in the short term, but the cost has been a damaged and unattractive image. The more stylish islands with a more considered approach – notably Lanzarote and Madeira – have consistently attracted a higher-spending clientele, which has proved to be far more profitable over the longer term. Belatedly realising its mistakes, Tenerife has now begun to change, and is clamping down on high prices and poor service. It has also coupled an awareness of the need for environmental protection with a move away from high-rise hotels to better beaches and facilities, and developments more in keeping with local styles. The result has been a renewed upsurge in tourism, with figures for 1994 showing a 15 per cent increase in the number of visitors compared with those for 1993. Whether the changes have come too late, however, and what will be the long-term effects of the previous attitude, are still open to debate.

13

❑ By 1995 an estimated four million tourists a year were visiting Tenerife; in 1950 the figure was 15,000. Tourism contributes an estimated 60 per cent to Tenerife's gross national product (GNP). ❑

■ The image of Tenerife as a tourist destination, occupied only by large hotels and cramped beaches, is belied by the wealth, beauty and variety of its flora and fauna. Parks, gardens and the island's wild outdoors, blessed with a varied and benign climate, support a vast profusion of rare and spectacular trees and flowers. ■

Fecund Tenerife is a veritable paradise for the botanist, amateur gardener, or those who simply enjoy a profusion of flowers, trees and exotic shrubs in their natural setting. The island teems with almost 2,000 different species, around 700 of which are endemic, and can be seen in the island's parks and gardens, or tangled into hedgerows. These include carnations, marigolds, geraniums, purple bougainvillaea, orange nasturtiums and the huge red splashes of hibiscus. Forests contain dark, dank woods of laurel, laburnum and Canary pine, valleys are coated in cork, broom and mimosa, and meadows and heathlands are scented with the heady aroma of honeysuckle, broom and eucalyptus.

Weather There are several factors contributing to Tenerife's floral richness. One of the most important is the climate, for the island lies just off the coast of north Africa, barely 300km from the western Sahara. This provides a greenhouse-like heat which is perfect for growing, but is also hot and inhospitable to vegetation, hence the barrenness of the island's southern margins. On much of the island, however, the subtropical climate is tempered by cool seas and moisture-laden trade winds, whose rainfall provides the green-tinged hills and mountains of the Anaga and Teno massifs (see pages

Flowers bloom even on inhospitable Mount Teide

80 and 134). Tenerife's island status also means its plants have developed in splendid isolation over the millennia. As a consequence, those that have disappeared elsewhere in Europe and north Africa – the result of climatic changes which produced the Ice Ages and the drying-up of the Sahara – have survived unscathed on their island outpost.

Habitats Perhaps the main reason for Tenerife's floral variety is the effect of climate combined with the large differences in altitude across the island. Tenerife's domain ranges from sea level to Mount Teide, which at 3,718m is the highest point on Spanish territory.

Plants have therefore been able to adapt to changing climatic conditions by 'migrating' to different altitudes. Better still, plants of different types and origins – from cacti to alpines – can usually find a home somewhere on the island. You quickly notice the difference between vegetation zones as you travel around. The ground between sea level and about 600m, for example, is the domain of the tropical and sub-tropical species, colonised by banana trees (see page 68), mimosa, palisanders, jacaranda, rubber trees, lilies, roses, poinsettia and countless others. In the drier south the same zone includes cacti, agaves, the date-palm and the ubiquitous prickly pear.

Highlights Highlights of these lower altitudes are the dragon tree, one of the most remarkable of all Tenerife's trees (see page 122), and the graceful *strelitzia*, or bird-of-paradise flower, whose orange-purple petals and distinctive birdlike shape have become the Canary Islands' virtual emblem. Higher up the altitude scale are chestnuts, eucalyptus and various deciduous evergreens, most notably the laurel, which on Tenerife and La Gomera forms some of the world's last *Laurasilva* forests (see page 170). Higher still, above about 1,100m, are tree-heath and pine forests, and between 2,000 and 2,700m, where the number of species growing begins to tail off, the highlights are the huge flowers of the giant bugloss and the widespread *retama*, or Teide broom.

Tenerife supports everything from cacti to alpines

■ Tenerife is far more than bars, beaches and noisy nightlife. Across the island lie several beautiful mountain enclaves, among them two superb national parks, and a wide range of smaller parks, gardens and scenic retreats that offer walks, wildlife, superb views and a peaceful escape from the island's larger towns and resorts. ■

Top: mouflon, *introduced into Tenerife in the 1970s*
Above: a wild cat

Two sides Too many visitors come to Tenerife and leave with the wrong impression. This is particularly true of those who visit the large southern resorts, situated amidst unforgiving desert-like landscapes. If you remain in these resorts, you'll not only fail to see the island's more verdant and beautiful central and northern areas, but you'll also run the risk of missing the island's peaceful and reflective side. As well as two major national parks (Parque Nacional del Teide and Parque Nacional de Garajonay) – Tenerife boasts a wealth of botanical gardens, swathes of unspoilt countryside and two wonderfully scenic mountain areas in the island's northern extremities. All are full of flowers, plants and trees (see page 14), a range of animals, butterflies and birdlife, and a variety of walking and outdoor opportunities.

Retreats Tenerife's scenic jewel is the Parque Nacional del Teide, a national park which protects Mount Teide, Spain's highest mountain, and a wide range of extraordinary volcanic landscapes on and around the peak (see page 126). Thousands of people annually reach Teide's summit, either on foot or by cable car, and many more explore the park's hinterland from the spectacular road which crosses its arid southern margins. Tenerife's other national park, the Parque Nacional de

Garajonay, could hardly be more different (see page 170). Situated at the heart of La Gomera, the island southwest of Tenerife, it consists largely of dank forest, an eerie and magical world of lichen- and moss-covered trees. Much of the forest consists of laurel, one of the last areas in Europe where this type of woodland survives. Almost equally verdant are the forested crags and valleys of the Teno and Anaga mountains, two beautiful upland enclaves on Tenerife's eastern and western tips (see pages 134 and 80).

Diversions Other outstanding areas of natural beauty include the Cumbre Dorsal, best seen in conjunction with Mount Teide (see page 70), the Valle Gran Rey on La Gomera (see page 178) and the Barranco del Infierno close to Playa de las Américas (see page 142). Easy walks and longer hikes are possible in all of these areas (as well as in the mountains and national parks), with maps, guides and background information available from local information centres. Venturing a little way from the package resorts also offers the chance to enjoy Tenerife's fauna. This is not, perhaps, as spectacular as its flora, but among the larger animals embraces creatures such as rabbits, bats, hedgehogs, wild cats and *mouflon*, a type of wild sheep introduced by hunters in the 1970s. At the other extreme are a wealth of insects and spectacularly coloured butterflies. Tenerife has no poisonous snakes or scorpions – but there are mosquitoes.

Birds Birdlife on the island is abundant, with about 200 species including the blue Teide finch, the *picapinos* (a type of woodpecker) and a variety of robin. Occasionally you may also hear the song of the *capirote*, or Canary nightingale, as well as the twittering of the canary, the most famous island bird of all (see panel, page 64). Other common birds include ravens, wild pigeons, chaffinches, bluetits, blackbirds and birds of prey such as buzzards, kestrels, vultures, white eagles and sparrow hawks. Abundant marine life also attracts a wealth of seabirds, among them Cory's shearwater, the little shearwater, the rare Bulwer's petrel and the European and Madeiran storm petrels.

A Cory's shearwater, among the many seabirds attracted to Tenerife's shores

Fiestas and folklore

■ **The people of Tenerife love to celebrate, so much so that it can often seem as if island life is one long round of parties – any excuse will do, including religious holidays, island patron saints' days, saints' days, village saints' days, town foundation days, a day to mark the repulse of a pirate attack, or another to mark the miraculous apparition of the Virgin. ■**

Celebrations It's said that there's a festival somewhere in the Canaries every day of the year. This may be an exaggeration, but it's a fair bet that at some time on Tenerife you'll bump into a fiesta. Celebrations, whatever their origin, usually include processions, one of which is likely to be secular (with marching bands and fancy dress), and the other religious. Often they are a combination of the two. Whatever the event, the streets come alive with musicians, clowns, food sellers, bands and majorettes. Beauty queens drape themselves over decorated floats, and locals (and visitors) of all ages are invited to join in the dancing, singing and other festivities. After a solemn Mass, fireworks often round things off, accompanied by folk events such as Canarian wrestling (see page 19) and noisy, night-long revelries.

Variety There are literally dozens of fiestas across the island throughout the year, details of which can be gleaned from posters or local tourist information offices. By far the most famous are the carnival celebrations in Santa Cruz (February), one of the largest events of its kind (see page 50). These are closely followed by events to celebrate Corpus Christi (May–June), the best known of which are the vast floral carpets laid out in the streets and squares of La Orotava (see panel page 92). Festivities for Semana Santa (Holy Week), from March to

April, are also widespread, and mark – more or less – the start of the rural *romería*, or pilgrimage season. These can be some of the most colourful and rustic celebrations, particularly when the local statue of the Virgin is paraded through the streets on a cart pulled by two heavily decorated bullocks. Two of the best are San Isidro in La Orotava (June) and San Benito Abad at La Laguna (first Sunday of July).

Tradition Whatever the occasion, it will most likely include traditional Canarian folk events. Local dancing, in particular, is striking, featuring both music and traditional dress. The *isa* is a light-hearted dance, while the *folia*, in which a man expresses his feelings for a woman, is a slower and more sombre ritual.

People of all ages take part in Santa Cruz's Carnival

Music often involves traditional instruments, among them *cháracas* (castanets), the *banduria*, a type of mandolin, and the *timple*, a small and simplified guitar. Songs and rhythms usually display the unmistakable influences of South America.

Wrestling One of Tenerife's most fascinating traditional activities is *lucha Canaria* (Canarian wrestling), an ancient sport which probably has its origins in Guanche duels and trials of strength. Today it commands an immense following, both among participants and spectators. *Bregas* (bouts) are sometimes held as featured events during fiestas or *romerías*. Otherwise you can watch televised bouts or attend local matches, details of which are posted on walls or advertised in news-

Fiestas are a fun and integral part of life

papers. Most towns and villages boast a team, each of which consists of 12 men. Matches are held outdoors or in specially constructed *terreros* (halls), and take place in 9m-wide, sand-covered rings, to prevent injury. Combatants are barefoot and wear special shirts and coarse linen trousers. The aim of a bout is to floor one's opponent, though restrictions apply to the methods that can be used. Great technical knowledge is required, and Canarian boys often begin to learn the sport as early as three years old. Belts are worn to denote proficiency, rather like judo and karate: beginners wear white belts, progressing through yellow, orange, green, black, red and blue.

■ Art, culture and architecture on Tenerife owe much to the influence of the Spanish, who bequeathed not only their language, but also much of their Latin outlook to the island and its inhabitants. At the same time, local people have retained their own cultural identity, preserving a rich artistic and intellectual life despite the advent of mass tourism. ■

Tradition The art and culture of the Guanches, Tenerife's earliest inhabitants, are conspicuous by their absence (see pages 26 and 136). Guanche language, dress, religion and customs, not to mention art and artefacts, were largely extinguished by the Spanish *conquistadores*. As a result, modern islanders have little sentimental attachment to their past. Modern culture is largely Spanish –

A craftsman puts the finishing touches to traditional Canarian baskets

islanders look Spanish and speak Spanish – yet many locals prefer to think of themselves as *Canarios* rather than Spanish, whom they describe as *Peninsulares* (people from Tenerife are known as *Tinerfeños*). Part of this has to do with a strong island identity, part with the distance from the Spanish mainland, and part with the alienation and resentment at the degree to which the Canaries were ignored and left to stagnate under the Franco regime.

> ❏ A popular saying claims *'Canarias es tierra de poetas'* – 'the Canaries is a land of poets'. ❏

Culture This is not to say the *Tinerfeños* abhor all things Spanish. Latin culture and temperament are deeply ingrained, with Spanish *joie de vivre* being nowhere more marked than in Tenerife's numerous fiestas. Café life, the siesta, the evening *paseo* (stroll), male machismo, dressing well and football fervour are other shared Spanish traits (flamenco, though often found on the island, is not – it's there for the tourists). Visitors should not be tempted to condescend to locals, or deceived into thinking they lack culture merely on the evidence of the island's apparently soulless resorts. Tenerife's residents enjoy a rich cultural and intellectual life, as a stroll around the bookshops of La Laguna, the island's university town, will prove. Concerts, plays and opera performances are staged in many

main towns, while daily newspapers are full of advertisements for lectures, seminars and courses for self-improvement.

Legacy Modern artists, craftspeople and pioneering architects such as César Manrique (see page 104) provide further evidence of the island's healthy cultural life. But Tenerife, contrary to initial impression, is also an island of past artistic and cultural glories. Genuine artistic masterpieces, it is true, are few and far between. In architectural terms, however, and in the wealth of superb wood carving in churches and old town centres, the island is outstanding. The lack of any damaging wars, coupled with a mild climate, has left many older buildings unravaged by the passage of time. Gothic buildings are rare – the style was past its prime by the time the Spanish invaded and began building. Renaissance buildings, however, abound, as well as buildings displaying the so-called *mudéjar* style, a mingling of Gothic, Renaissance and richly ornamented Moorish-influenced motifs.

Woodwork By the end of the 15th century, the *mudéjar* style had evolved into the Platersque, a style which took its intricacy a stage further. In Tenerife and elsewhere in the Canaries, this decoration largely took the form of wooden ceilings and other intricately carved objects, largely because Canary pine, rather than stone, was the building material closest to hand. Numerous Tenerife churches have glorious carved and painted vaults, while many domestic

houses and noble mansions in towns like La Laguna and La Orotava are graced with beautifully carved wooden balconies. La Laguna's old quarter, in particular, is a showcase of Spanish-Canarian architecture from the 16th and 17th centuries. Many leading churches also boast wooden statues by Luján Pérez (1756–1815), the greatest of the Canarian sculptors.

Examples of Tenerife's wood-carving tradition are found in towns like La Orotava

■ **Most remote islands attract exotic myths, and Tenerife and the Canaries are no exception. Two of the most persistent tales connected with the archipelago are those of Atlantis – the Canaries are considered by some to be the mythical land – and the existence of San Borondón, a mysterious 'eighth Canary Island'.** ■

Atlantis The Canaries have long been associated with myth and mystery. Homer may have been thinking of the islands when he described the 'Elysian Fields' as a land at the 'end of the earth', a land whose inhabitants are 'blessed with an ever tranquil life' and where there is 'no snow, no winter storm, no pouring rain'. Plato, by contrast, in talking of the fabled land of Atlantis, described an island to the west of Gibraltar, a Shangri-la which had been cast to the bottom of the ocean by earthquakes and tidal waves. Only seven mountain tops, he wrote, remained above the waters. There are, of course, seven major islands in the Canary archipelago, a coincidence which has since seen it linked with this venerable island myth.

Borondón Another myth talks of a legendary 'eighth Canary Island', the so-called 'San Borondón', named after St Brendan (or Brandon), a 6th-century Irish monk whose mission in life was to find an island where saints were supposedly reincarnated. After a seven-year quest, he eventually found an island which sailors subsequently described as lying some 200 nautical miles from the Canaries. The legend continues that after seven years on the island, St Brendan and his monks were told to leave by an angel. After sailing for another seven years, and despairing of ever finding land, they spied another island. No sooner had the monks landed, however, than the land began to rumble (a Canary volcano?): beating a hasty retreat, the monks watched the island sink beneath the waves.

St Brendan encounters a giant whale during his journey

Myth and legend

■ **The early history of Tenerife and its first inhabitants is one of almost total myth and mystery. Virtually nothing is known of the island, or of the other Canary Islands, before the arrival of the Spanish** *conquistadores* **in the 15th century. Even the origins of the names 'Tenerife' and 'Canary' are surrounded by controversy.** ■

Conjecture The existence of Tenerife and the Canary Islands has been known since time immemorial. Homer described them as the location of the 'Elysian Fields', while the Greeks referred to them as the 'Isles of the Blessed'. Herodotus, writing in the 5th century BC, called them the 'Garden of Hesperides'. When they were first settled, however, is a matter of conjecture (see below). Phoenician sailors probably came to the islands between 1100 and 600 BC, reputedly to collect *orchilla*, a purple dye used to colour clothes and carpets. Later, the Carthaginians, a north African race, also dispatched boats to the islands. In the 2nd century AD, the Greek geographer Ptolemy marked the Canaries –

The Greek historian Herodotus described the Canaries as the 'Isles of the Blessed'

HPOΔOTOC

though not named as such – on a map of the world. He also placed the prime meridian – then the end of the known world – on the western tip of El Hierro, the archipelago's smallest and most westerly island.

Canine The 'Isla Canaria' first appeared on a Spanish map in 1339, though how the name evolved is a mystery. The 1st-century Roman historian Pliny the Elder alludes to the islands in his 'Natural History', ascribing them names and describing numerous items of geographical information (most of them wrong). He also described how King Juba II of Mauretania dispatched ships to the Canaries around 25 BC to AD 25. On their arrival, the islands were found to be deserted and scattered with the ruins of once-great buildings. The most striking feature, however, were the islands' wild dogs (*canis* in Latin), two of whom were captured and returned to the king. From this the Canaries are said to have taken their name.

Theories This is not the only theory. Some claim the islands took their name from the 'Cape of Canauria', a headland on the African coast (now Cape Bojador). Others favour the idea that the islands were named by the Romans after the singing bird, the canary (*canara* in Latin). Others again allude to the possibility of an 'underworld' connection, for the Romans linked the islands with a kingdom of the dead, a domain which lay to the west of the known world. In Roman and other ancient mythologies the dead were conducted to the underworld by dogs (another link with the Latin

canis). The derivation of the name Tenerife is equally contentious, many people claiming it comes from the language of the Guanches, the island's earliest inhabitants (see page 26). Little is known of this language, though it may be that *tener*, *fe* or *ife* (or all three) meant 'mountain', 'snow' or – the best literal translation – 'snow-covered mountain', an obvious reference to Mount Teide, the island's most conspicuous landmark.

Settlement If accounting for the Canaries' names is difficult, then the question of when the islands were first settled is even more vexing. When the Spanish arrived during the Middle Ages they found a distinct but almost Stone Age culture on the islands (see page 26). How long the inhabitants had been there, however, is a mystery. Some claim the islands were settled in two waves, the first as early as 3000 BC. Others, including many present-day scholars on Tenerife, believe the first inhabitants came ashore around 500 BC. The next best guess is that the first arrivals landed during the 1st and 2nd centuries BC, that they were tall, fair-skinned, blue-eyed and blond-haired, and that they were of Berber and north African origin. Historians have given them the name 'Guanches'.

❏ There is no written evidence of Tenerife's history before the 15th century, apart from indecipherable rock drawings. ❏

A 17th-century map of the Canary Islands

The Guanches

■ For hundreds of years before the arrival of the Spanish in the 15th century, Tenerife and the other Canary Islands were inhabited by the Guanches, a group of primitive but well-organised tribes. Archaeologists are still baffled as to whether they were African or European since their origins remain a mystery. ■

Guanches Strictly speaking 'Guanche' means 'son of Tenerife', from the ancient Canarian *guan*, meaning 'son', and *Achinech* meaning 'Tenerife'. Over the years, however, it has come to be used as the generic name for all the islanders who occupied the Canaries before the Spanish Conquest. But although scholars agree on a name, nobody seems really certain about where the people originated. All anyone can be sure of is that they came from somewhere, for the theory that the Canaries became detached from Africa with a few surviving inhabitants is now discredited. But if they came from across the sea, why have no boats – or pictographs of boats – ever been found? New ideas to explain the conundrum are devised every year, but essentially archaeologists are concerned with two main theories: that the Guanches came from Europe or from north Africa.

Europeans Those championing the European line claim the Guanches were descendants of the megalithic cultures of the French coast and Iberian Peninsula (notably southern Spain). They suggest tribes sailed from these areas around 3000 BC, with tides and trade winds making such a journey far easier in crude boats than the equivalent voyage from Morocco. The early date would also explain why the Spanish found the Guanches such a primitive culture. Like the Stone Age tribes of prehistoric Europe, for example, they had no knowledge, among other things, of metals, the wheel or the

bow and arrow. Close links with European races are also borne out by archaeological evidence, notably the discovery of links between the pottery, religious customs and spiral engravings of the two cultures. Critics who claim that later African

A statue of a Guanche mencey, or chieftain

tribes (see below) shared similar characteristics are answered by the fact that French and Iberian tribes of the period (3000 BC) probably also migrated to north Africa.

Africans Proponents of the African line of enquiry will have none of this. They argue that the Guanches were descendants of north African Berber tribes, and arrived at the earliest around 500 BC, and in all probability much later, around 200–100 BC. It is likely that they travelled in crude reed boats, which then rotted, hence the lack of any remains. Because there were no reeds on Tenerife, they were unable to construct new boats to escape the island, and did not have the technology for more advanced craft. As with the European theory, archaeological evidence – notably ceramics – and linguistic similarities lend weight to the notion, though these factors in themselves are inconclusive. Far more persuasive is the proof gained from carbon dating, the results of which correspond with dates around 200–100 BC. The weight of current opinion is now largely with the 'Africans', though the theory has one

A Guanche sepulchre: the Guanches had a cult of the dead similar to the Egyptians

substantial and unexplained flaw: if the Guanches were 2nd-century BC Berbers, why is it that in crossing the sea they apparently 'forgot' the advances – the plough and bow and arrow to name just two – of their African contemporaries?

Cultured Although the Guanches were primitive, they were far from ignorant. Many 15th-century Spanish accounts praise their cultural and artistic achievements, and the organised and hierarchical nature of their society (see page 136). Each tribe or kingdom was arranged in *mencey-atos* (chiefdoms) and ruled by a *mencey* (king) and council of elders (the Spanish would later conquer the island partly by setting one tribe against another). Next came a class of nobles, and below them the ordinary Guanches: simple farmers and herdspeople who lived largely in caves and wore crude clothes. Cults, chiefdoms and crude weapons, however, would prove no match for the Spanish *conquistadores*.

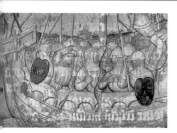

■ The final conquest of Tenerife by the Spanish in the 15th century was preceded by a period of around a hundred years when a succession of European traders and adventurers made tentative sorties to the Canaries. These voyages culminated in the arrival of Frenchman Jean de Béthencourt, the first to subjugate any of the islands by force. ■

Contact African and European traders had probably been visiting Tenerife and the Canaries for hundreds of years before any attempt was made at permanent settlement. Phoenicians and Carthaginians made sorties here in the centuries preceding the birth of Christ; the Romans were occasional visitors (fragments of Roman amphorae have been discovered off the coast); and the Arabs are known to have landed on Gran Canaria in the 9th and 10th centuries. Sporadic links with the outside world are confirmed by further archaeological evidence, notably the Guanches' use of a circular hand-mill, a sophisticated item for grinding wheat and barley.

Slavery Greater attention began to be paid to the Canaries from about the 13th century, when French, Majorcan, Portuguese and Genoese sailors started to put in at the islands. It was a Genoese, Lancellotto Malocello, who 'discovered' Lanzarote in 1312, to which he gave his name in the course of charting its waters. Lancellotto was to remain on Lanzarote until 1330, using the native population for labour, but apparently making no attempt to conquer the island. Fellow Europeans followed for more nefarious purposes, namely the abduction of the Guanches as unwilling tools in the slave trade. Between 1340 and 1342 both the Spanish and Portuguese sent heavily armed fleets to the archipelago, the greater interest in the Canaries being reflected in the claim of Pope Clement VI in 1344 to have authority over 'all lands to be discovered'.

Early Settlement Clement then declared Luís de la Cerda, a leading light of the Castilian (Spanish) royal family, 'King of the Canary Islands'. This was an honorary title, for the archipelago at the time remained in the hands of its original Guanche inhabitants. Towards the end of the 14th century, Cerda was succeeded by Roberto de Bracamonte, though he too was content to retain an honorary title, making no attempt to take the islands by force. This more onerous task was left to Bracamonte's cousin, a Norman baron called Jean de Béthencourt (1359–1425), a key figure in

Jean de Béthencourt, 15th-century conqueror of the Canaries

28

Tenerife's medieval change of fortune. In 1402, Béthencourt set sail from La Rochelle in the company of Gadifer de la Salle (1340–1422), a Spanish nobleman whom he had partnered in a 'crusade' against Tunis in 1390. Their aim was to take Tenerife and Gran Canaria on behalf of Henri III of Castile.

Conquest In the event they sailed first to Lanzarote and Fuerteventura, which Béthencourt, in a flush of delight, respectively named *Alegranza* (Joy) and *Graciosa* (Beautiful), apparently unperturbed by the less than amenable appearance of the islands' bare and rugged landscapes. Lanzarote was quickly captured, earning Béthencourt the title 'King of the Canary Islands' (Gadifer gained no such title, and withdrew in a sulk, taking no further part in the islands' conquest). After returning to Spain for supplies, Béthencourt defeated the Guanches of Fuerteventura in 1405, founding a town which he named Betancuria. El Hierro, then the westernmost point in the known world, was next to fall (Gran Canaria and La Palma, however, held out against his assault). Béthencourt ruthlessly imposed Christianity on the native populations of the conquered islands, and also imported hundreds of peasant colonists from Normandy and Spain. On his retirement he appointed his nephew, Maciot de Béthencourt, viceroy of the islands. This turned out to be something of a misguided promotion, for in 1415 Maciot was forced by the Spanish king to relinquish his title on the grounds of incompetence.

Part of Gadifer de la Salle's 1402 expedition to Tenerife

■ Half a century of confusion followed Béthencourt's Spanish conquest of Lanzarote and Fuerteventura, with Portugal and Spain vying for control of the Canarian archipelago. In 1478, Spain purchased complete sovereignty of the islands, clearing the way for the bloody invasion of Tenerife and La Palma by the infamous Alonso Fernández de Lugo. ■

Confusion The retirement of Jean de Béthencourt to France, and the removal of his nephew due to incompetence, left the status of the half-conquered Canary archipelago in some confusion. The disgraced nephew, Maciot, sold his title (Viceroy of the Canary Islands) to Diego de Herrara, a Spanish envoy. He also offered part shares to Prince Henry of Portugal and Hernán Peraza the Elder, a hard-hearted Spanish count. In 1445 the latter, having moved his base between Fuerteventura, El Hierro and La Gomera, finally established himself as the tyrannical ruler and self-styled Count of La Gomera (see page 166).

Over the next 30 years, Spanish and Portuguese boats sailed to the other islands, both powers, albeit half-heartedly, claiming some degree of sovereignty over the partially conquered archipelago. In 1478, the wrangling was settled once and for all when the Spanish purchased the rights to Fuerteventura, Lanzarote, El Hierro and La Gomera. A year later the arrangement was ratified by the Treaty of Alcáçovas, which recognised the Canaries as Spanish and compensated Portugal with the rights to west Africa and the Atlantic's other off-shore islands.

Attack The way was then open for an all-out attack on the still-unconquered islands. Ferdinand and Isabella of Spain sanctioned the second phase of the conquest, unleashing a force led by Juan Réjon, who landed on Gran Canaria in 1478 and founded what would become Las Palmas. After a series of bitterly fought battles, Gran Canaria's Guanche tribes were defeated in 1483. In 1492 Christopher Columbus, also sailing under the patronage of Ferdinand and Isabella, stopped in the Canaries to take on supplies during his voyage to the New World (see page 166). In the same year, the island of La Palma fell to Spanish invaders, this time under the leadership of Alonso Fernández de Lugo (1456–1525), an ambitious and ruthless Andalucian nobleman whose name remained forever associated with the conquest of the Canaries.

Tenerife In 1495 Alonso turned his attention to Tenerife, landing a force of 1,000 men, all of whom were massacred by a Guanche force at Barranco de Acentejo (the spot is now known as *La Matanza* (the massacre) and is situated 16km east of present-day Puerto de la Cruz). Alonso himself barely escaped, and returned three years later with a larger army. This defeated and massacred a force of 2,000 islanders, as the Guanches had been weakened by in-fighting between rival tribes. The following year Alonso

La Laguna, founded by Alonso Fernández de Lugo in 1499

The Reception of Christopher Columbus by Ferdinand and Isabella, *Eugene Deveria*

founded La Laguna, later to become Tenerife's capital.

Henceforth Tenerife, like La Palma and Gran Canaria, was controlled on behalf of the Spanish crown by *capitanes-generales*, rulers licensed to sell land and water rights (without ownership) to settlers. The smaller islands were made *señorios*, subject to Spanish sovereignty, but made over as fiefdoms to nobles or clerics who levied duties on behalf of themselves and the Crown.

Oblivion The Guanches, of course, had no place in any of these arrangements. Theirs was largely a tale of oblivion, either at the hands of the Spaniards' superior weaponry – mostly cross-bows – or from new diseases, introduced by the invaders, to which they had no resistance. Many were shipped away as slaves, or commandeered as forced labour. It seems that not all were annihilated, as was once thought, since anthropological research has shown that many Guanche racial characteristics survive in modern-day Canarians. Guanche culture, however, was to disappear in less than a century.

■ **Tenerife's position proved to be its fortune in the centuries following the Spanish conquest, its ports providing a staging post for ships travelling between Europe and the Americas. But it was not only the sea trade which prospered, for a succession of commercial ventures on the island itself also produced a measure of economic success.** ■

Slaves Tenerife's position, astride the Atlantic's trading routes to the south and west, had long made it a natural port of call for ships sailing to the Orient and the Americas. As early as 1492, Christopher Columbus had used La Gomera, an island off Tenerife's southern coast, as a staging post for supplies before his pioneering voyages to the New World. Later the Canaries became way stations in the slave trade, and later still the source of products for trade and gain in their own right. The first of these was sugar, which in the first years of the 16th century brought huge wealth to much of the archipelago. In time the trade dropped off, damaged by the availability of cheaper sugar from Brazil and central America. Slavery, too, declined after its abolition in 1537, at least in theory, for Tenerife continued to be a marshalling point for African slaves before their forced shipment abroad.

Wine In place of slaves and sugar came wine, a monocultural crop which soon dominated many of the Canaries' eastern islands. Malvasía, malmsey or 'sack', as the distinctive, sherry-like wine was called, became one of the most fashionable drinks in both Europe and the New World. It was especially popular in Elizabethan and Jacobean England, where it was much sought after by the likes of Raleigh and Drake, and praised in the works of Shakespeare and others. By the end of the 17th century, some

The Casa del Vino wine museum – enjoy your visit!

10,000 'pipes' of the wine a year were being exported to London. Tenerife became the islands' largest single producer, with towns such as Garachico, La Orotava and La Laguna becoming rich as a result. Many of the historic buildings in these towns date from this period.

Decline Tenerife's burgeoning prosperity did not go unnoticed, and over the years it not only became a smugglers' haven, but also the subject of pirate and other attacks, of which the most famous was Nelson's doomed raid on Santa Cruz in 1797 (see page 44). These ultimately had little effect on trade, although wine, like sugar before it, was soon to decline in importance, as a result of trade disputes, diseases which ravaged the vineyards, pricing problems, wars in Europe, wars in Spain's American colonies and – not least – the rise of the rival wine of Madeira. Wine continued to play a part in the island's economy, but by 1822, when Santa Cruz achieved the status of a free port (thus further promoting trade), the Malvasia boom was over.

❏ 'That which doth most make my muse, and me, is a cup of Canary wine'. Ben Jonson ❏

Cochineal Tenerife's ability to adapt to changing circumstance is one of the common threads of its history, up to and including its present-day reliance on tourism. This flexibility was further underlined in 1825 by the arrival of a new commodity, cochineal. Originally from Mexico,

Bananas were introduced to Tenerife in 1855

cochineal is a red dye extracted from a small insect which lives as a parasite on cactus. Vast spreads of prickly pear cactus were planted across much of the Canaries to support the trade. Tenerife, wisely as it turned out, refrained from tearing down its native pines in favour of cactus, a move which would have jeopardised the island's water supply (pine needles absorb water and feed it back into the ground). None the less the trade flourished in parts of the island, only tailing off in the latter part of the 19th century with the development of new aniline chemical dyes. By this time, however, yet another commodity had appeared as the island's economic saviour – the banana.

■ **Waves of emigration followed the collapse of the cochineal and banana trades, Tenerife's economic mainstays during the middle and late 19th century. Greater strife was to follow, however, when General Franco used the island to launch the coup which precipitated the horrors of the Spanish Civil War and 36 years of fascist rule.** ■

Bananas Tenerife rarely rested on its laurels over questions of trade. In 1852, Queen Isabella II of Spain made the island a free trade zone, a move designed to stimulate its faltering economy. A few years earlier Santa Cruz, renowned for its excellent port, had been made the capital of the Canarian archipelago. Both measures, combined with the advent of the steamship, led to an upturn in trade, a trend reinforced by Europe's increasing commercial ties with its colonies in Africa. In 1855, an entirely new venture was pioneered, banana production, introduced by British entrepreneurs from Indo-China (see page 68). By the 1880s, after the death throes of the cochineal industry, banana plantations had been established across much of northern Tenerife, and by the end of the century they formed the island's economic bedrock.

Emigration Bust has invariably followed boom in Tenerife, which throughout its history has repeatedly committed itself to precarious monocultures. The banana was no exception, and during the upheavals of World War I trade in the fruit suffered badly. Competition from South American bananas, which were cheaper to produce, exacerbated the problem. In time, economic misery compelled thousands of *Tinerfeños* to emigrate to the New World. Such emigration was nothing new. Canarians accompanied Columbus on his

Isabella II of Spain, Tenerife's economic saviour

first voyage to the Americas in 1492. Others travelled abroad to fight alongside the Spanish *conquistadores*. In the 18th century, with the collapse of the wine trade, thousands emigrated to Cuba and Venezuela, where the burgeoning sugar plantations were crying out for labour. More followed a century later, when the cochineal trade went the way of wine.

35

A memorial of the Spanish Civil War in Santa Cruz

❏ As a result of emigration, it is believed that 300,000 people of Canarian descent live in Caracas (Venezuela). ❏

Division Tenerife stagnated during the first years of the 20th century, with political change producing little effect. In 1912, a measure of self-government was introduced with the creation of various *Cabildos Insulares*, or Island Councils, and in 1927 the Canary Islands as a whole were divided into two provinces (western and eastern). More radical change arrived in 1936, but of a threatening variety. In March of that year General Francisco Franco (1892–1975), a former commander-in-chief of the Spanish army, was posted to Tenerife as the island's *Comandante-Generale*. Already accused of complicity in several attempted coups, the Spanish Republican government had decided to neutralise his threat by posting him as far from mainland Spain as possible. Tenerife, in the event, proved not far enough.

Dictator Franco survived three assassination attempts during his four months on the island. He also used the time to plan a further coup, eventually securing the allegiance of the Tenerife garrison on 13 June 1936. At dawn on 18 July, he discovered that his planned coup had started a day early (in Spanish Morocco). Remaining just long enough to broadcast his manifesto on Tenerife radio, he flew to Tetuan in Morocco to assume control of the insurgents. Within just two days, Tenerife had succumbed to fascist control (La Palma would hold out for eight days).

Thus was unleashed the barbarity – torture, summary execution and family set against family – that over the next few years would characterise the Spanish Civil War. A million people lost their lives in the conflict before Franco and his Nationalists established the dictatorship which prevailed in Spain until 1975.

❏ During World War II, plans by both the Allies and Axis powers to invade the Canaries were dashed by Spain's neutrality. ❏

■ **Franco's repressive dictatorship continued until his death in 1975, a period which not only saw the creation of an independence movement on Tenerife, but also witnessed the island's gradual emergence from economic recession as a result of improved infrastructure and the development of a flourishing tourist industry.** ■

Change Franco might have launched his coup from Tenerife, but he clearly felt little sentimental attachment to the island, which he visited just once (in 1953) in the course of his long dictatorship. At the same time he improved the island's infrastructure, largely through the building of military roads, and maintained the Canaries' free trade status (in contrast to the isolated and protectionist tendencies pursued on mainland Spain). For the most part, however, Tenerife and the other islands of the archipelago remained hugely neglected under Franco. On the one hand this spared the islands the worst of the mainland's social, political and cultural repression. On the other it meant that education and other matters of social welfare were also ignored. On Franco's death the illiteracy rate in many villages exceeded 50 per cent: even today, some 20 years on, the average figure across Tenerife is between 8 and 12 per cent, higher than in most other parts of Spain.

Separatism Tenerife's backwater status under Franco exacerbated a long-standing feeling of separation on the part of *Tinerfeños* from the mainstream of Spanish life. Physical distance had always meant the island was out on a limb. In the grip of dictatorship, resentment at rule from afar only increased. Under the firm hand of fascism, discontent found

Political graffiti, often the work of Canarian separatists

little means of expression, but following Franco's death in 1975 many islanders soon gave voice to long-standing grievances. The protests were quick to erupt. In 1975 Juan Carlos became King of Spain. In 1978 a new democratic constitution was ratified. Between these two dates discontent had already turned to violence, with the explosion of several terrorist bombs by Canarian separatists fighting under the slogan *fuera godos* ('goths' – meaning mainland Spaniards – 'out').

Movements No one was killed in these attacks, whose cutting edge was slightly blunted by the granting of greater autonomous powers to the Canaries and Spain's other regions in 1982. Under the new directive, the islands received their own regional constitution and were able to elect their own representative bodies. Yet the separatist impulse is far from dead. Over the years there have been many independence movements, from the radical extremism of groups such as the AWANAK, whose graffiti adorns many a Tenerife tenement and roadside, to the more mainstream political parties such as the Coalición Canaria, the Canarian Nationalist Party, which under leader Manuel Hermoso recently formed a minority government after successes in the 1995 local and parliamentary elections.

❏ A 1995 survey revealed that 47 per cent of islanders regarded themselves as Canarians: only 18 per cent felt that they were Spanish. ❏

King Juan Carlos of Spain at General Franco's funeral

Europe Tenerife's separatist and increasingly autonomous approach to life takes place against a background of increasing wealth, the result largely of the tourist trade (see page 12), and a growing realisation that Canarian ways of life, not to mention Tenerife's environment, should not be sacrificed to the ugly, concrete gods of mass tourism. It also takes place, paradoxically, against a background of growing integration with Europe, the Canaries having become full-fledged members of the European Union in 1993 (seven years after membership was extended to the Spanish mainland). Tenerife is now looking to the future with a view to constructing more stylish tourist developments, but also with the dilemma shared by many smaller regions with distinct cultural identities: how to reconcile its regional and nationalist aspirations with integration into the larger mainstream.

37

SANTA CRUZ DE TENERIFE

SANTA CRUZ DE TENERIFE

Information

Tourist information is available from the Oficina di Turismo at the Cabildo, Palacio Insular Plaza de España (tel: 60 55 00). *Open* daily 9–1, 4–7.

Parking

If you are driving into Santa Cruz for a day trip or a morning's shopping, it is advisable to avoid trying to park in the busy streets of the city centre. The best place to leave your car is in the big car parks on the seafront which have *vigilantes* (attendants). Head for Avenida de José Antonio Primo de Rivera.

Shopping

Santa Cruz is sold by most tour operators primarily as a shopping trip. Yet, while the city certainly boasts a wide number of shops, quality, prices and the range of goods are not exceptional. The prime area is on and around Calle del Castillo, the street striking off west from Plaza de la Candelaria. A notable feature are the Asian-owned bazaars, which are some of the few places on the island where you can try your hand at price negotiating. The best shopping experience is the Mercado de Nuestra Señora de África (see page 48). Remember that most shops close in the afternoon from 1–5pm, and open again later. Credit cards and Eurocheques are accepted in most larger stores.

Previous pages: Plaza de España Opposite: detail of the Circulo de Amistad XII de Enero

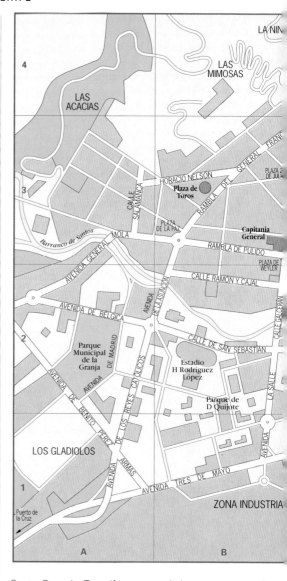

Santa Cruz de Tenerife – or, as it is more commonly known, Santa Cruz – is Tenerife's capital. It is also the capital of the Spanish province of Santa Cruz de Tenerife, an administrative region which embraces the western isles of the Canary archipelago – Tenerife, El Hierro, La Palma and La Gomera (the eastern Canaries – Gran Canaria, Lanzarote and Fuerteventura – make up the province of Las Palmas de Gran Canaria, which has its capital at Las Palmas on Gran Canaria). Its name – 'Holy Cross' – comes from the cross planted here in 1494 by the Spanish *conquistador* Alonso Fernández de Lugo (see pages 30 and 44). Its development and prosperity derive largely from its harbour, whose position at the crossroads of trans-Atlantic shipping lanes has turned it into one of

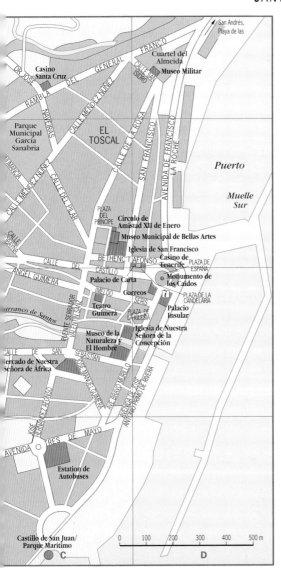

Day trips by bus

It is simple to make day trips to Santa Cruz from elsewhere on the island. If you are based in Playa de las Américas you can take the express (*directo*) service (journey time is 90 minutes), while from Puerto de la Cruz the bus makes the journey to the capital in an hour. Aim to arrive early or in mid-morning, as many shops, museums and churches close during the afternoon siesta (generally between 1 and 4.30pm).

Entertainment

The Teatro Guimerá on Plaza Isla de la Madera is Santa Cruz's principal venue for classical concerts, opera, theatre (Spanish-language only) and ballet performances. The Tenerife Symphony Orchestra (TSO) play here regularly during the winter. For information and tickets contact the Cabildo Insular; tel: 60 58 01. Next to the theatre is the Centro de Fotografía (Photography Centre) where temporary exhibitions are held (tel: 29 07 35 for information). Rock concerts are sometimes held in the Plaza de Toros. If you fancy playing black-jack or roulette visit the Casino Santa Cruz at the Hotel Mencey, Dr José Naveiras 38.

SANTA CRUZ DE TENERIFE

A musician in traditional dress at one of Santa Cruz's May festivals

Children
Santa Cruz is not really a city for children, though older children and teenagers may enjoy the somewhat gruesome mummified Guanches at the Museo de la Naturaleza y El Hombre (see page 49), while younger children are best taken to the Parque Municipal García Sanabria (see page 54), which has an attractive children's playground. A splash in the Parque Marítimo (see page 54) might also appeal, but a trip to Playa de las Teresitas (see page 84) is probably the best option of all.

Opposite: Santa Cruz's port is one of the largest in Spain

Spain's largest ports (handling some 14 million tonnes of cargo annually). Much of its trading success dates from 1852, when the Spanish Crown awarded the town the status of a 'free port', thus lowering duties and trade barriers, and offering a much-needed boost to the Canaries' flagging commercial fortunes.

Visitors Since that day, the city has hardly looked back. At the same time it has a strange status on an island renowned for tourism, for it is one of only two major centres (La Laguna is the other) which sees little by way of visitors. Traditionally tour operators use the city as a morning stopover, its main attraction being a shopping centre (see panel, page 40).

This rather peripheral appeal does have its advantages, however, for Santa Cruz has managed to preserve a distinct character of its own. Few would argue that it is a particularly attractive city, and particularly not in the suburbs, which are blighted by light industry and modern apartment blocks (the total population is around 230,000). At its heart, however, it has a pleasantly faded Spanish air, as well as several fine churches and grand old buildings. The island council, moreover, has recently begun to realise the capital's tourist potential, making concerted efforts to smarten up the centre and entice visitors away from Puerto de la Cruz and the southern resorts. Its tiny shops, jumble of narrow streets and vaguely chaotic air remain, but after many years the seafront promenade has been spruced up, making this a pleasant place to stroll amid the palms and oleanders.

Orientation This said, shopping remains the main lure (see panel, page 40). Possibly the only exception comes in February, when Santa Cruz hosts a carnival considered by many as second only to that of Rio de Janeiro (see panel, page 50).

Another major lure is the nearby presence of **Playa de las Teresitas**, one of Tenerife's best (artificial) beaches (see page 84). Whether partying, sunbathing or shopping, however, you should also take time out to visit one or two of the city's sights. Finding these is fairly straightforward, much of what you want to see lying within a 200–300m radius of the central area.

The main square is **Plaza de España**, a rather drab piazza close to the waterfront. Immediately to the west lies the more appealing **Plaza de la Candelaria**. West again is **Calle del Castillo**, the city's main shopping street.

Attractions Among the more far-flung sights is one of the city's best attractions, the **Mercado de Nuestra Señora de África**, the best food and general market in the Canaries (see page 48).

On your way here you could drop in on two other inviting sights, notably the **Iglesia de Nuestra Señora de la Concepción** (see page 46), among the city's most important historical buildings, and the **Museo de la Naturaleza y El Hombre** (see page 49), which is devoted to Tenerife's history, flora and fauna.

Slightly further afield, but well worth the walk or taxi ride, is the **Parque Municipal García Sanabria**, one of the most beautiful parks in the Canaries.

Nelson

■ **Santa Cruz's story begins with the uncharted history of the Guanches, Tenerife's shadowy first inhabitants, and continues with the arrival of Spanish invaders and adventurers during the 15th century. None of its historical episodes, however, is quite as gripping as the doomed attempt by Admiral Lord Nelson to seize the city in 1797.** ■

Defeat with honour
The defeated band of British sailors who succeeded in landing in Santa Cruz during Nelson's doomed attack on the city were led back to their ships by the victorious Spanish to the accompaniment of local brass bands. Around 250 of Nelson's men were killed or wounded in the assault, and many drowned in heavy seas before they could land. The defenders were magnanimous in victory, however, and some 25 wounded British sailors were treated by the Spanish in Santa Cruz's hospital. The various ensigns captured from the British were not returned, though, and hang to this day in the city's Museo Militar (see page 52).

Nelson is wounded during his doomed raid on Santa Cruz in 1795

Settlement Santa Cruz's many natural advantages, not least its superb deep-water harbour, must have long made it a favoured point of settlement for the Guanches, Tenerife's first inhabitants. Their first significant contact with the outside world came in the 1460s, when the Spanish adventurer Sancho de Herrera landed at a place then known as Añaza (or Anazo), Santa Cruz's future site. There he built a fortress and established a small community, probably with the compliance of the local inhabitants. Within time Guanche co-operation was withdrawn, however, and escalating disputes with the islanders forced the Spaniards' eventual withdrawal.

Conquest By 1498, and the arrival (for the second time) of Alonso Fernández de Lugo, the Spaniards were in more robust mood. De Lugo's army was promptly installed in a newly built castle, a defensive bastion which provided the launching pad for the conquest of Tenerife. Within two years the island had been subjugated. Soon after, the settlement of Santa Cruz took root, the town's name borrowed from the *Santa Cruz* (Holy Cross), brought to the island by de Lugo. The deep-water harbour and sheltered anchorage, not to mention Tenerife's position relative to the Americas, soon made the port a vital staging post for ships bound for the New World. Santa Cruz boomed on the back of trade with South America and the Caribbean, its burgeoning power recognised in 1723 when it replaced La Laguna as Tenerife's capital. Over the years, however, the port's wealth made it the target of pirates, adventurers and rival seafarers, not least of whom was Britain's Horatio Nelson.

Intrepid Nelson was 39 and enjoying the rank of Rear-Admiral when in 1797 he was ordered to weigh anchor in Cadiz and set sail for Tenerife to seize 'the Town of Santa Cruz by sudden and vigorous assault'. Nelson was more than happy to obey the order (issued as part of Britain's attempts to achieve naval supremacy over the French and Spanish), having long viewed the town as a valuable target and a means of bolstering his burgeoning reputation. As an added incentive, there was the chance of capturing *El Principe d'Asturias*, one of a pair of Spanish ships returning from Manila laden with silver bullion. Nelson's skill and bravery were not in question. He had already lost an eye in a raid on Corsica three years earlier and in the same year as his attack on Santa Cruz he defeated a superior French force at Cape St Vincent.

Nelson

Attack He was less fortunate at Santa Cruz, however, where the defending forces were forewarned of his supposedly surprise attack. Nelson personally commanded the flotilla of tiny boats used in the assault, launched at night on rough seas from the admiral's main fleet. He led the force of some 1,000 men crouched in a rowing boat with just two companions. Weather and circumstance, however, doomed the venture to failure. A heavy swell smashed many boats against rocks, or caused men to miss their landing points. Artillery fire rained down from the Castillo de San Cristóbal. A cannon shot destroyed Nelson's arm, forcing his retreat (the arm was eventually amputated). In the end just one small force landed and proceeded to capture a Dominican convent, only to find itself confronted in the early hours of the morning by a Spanish force of 8,000 men. The Spanish commander demanded – and received – an honourable retreat. The Santa Cruz debacle was to be the only significant failure in Nelson's illustrious career.

Exchanging pleasantries
Death and defeat in battle did not, however, mean the end to a civilised exchange of pleasantries between victors and vanquished. Defeated British sailors were returned to their ships with gifts of bread and wine from Santa Cruz's Spanish commander. Nelson reciprocated with gifts of cheese and ale, together with an ingratiating letter of thanks: 'I beg your excellency', he wrote, 'will honour me with your acceptance of a cask of English beer and cheese ...'

45

SANTA CRUZ DE TENERIFE

►► **Iglesia de Nuestra Señora** *41C2*
de la Concepción

Plaza de la Iglesia
Closed for restoration until 1999

Santa Cruz's oldest and most important church, trans-
lated as 'Church of Our Lady of the Conception', was
begun in 1502, damaged by fire in 1652 and heavily
restored during the 17th and 18th centuries. For years its
distinctive six-tiered belfry, a Moorish-looking tower built
in the mid-18th century, was one of the city's key landmarks. Inside, its imposing naves provided the home for
some of Tenerife's most sacred treasures, among them
part of the famous *Cruz de la Conquiste* (Cross of
Conquest) from which Santa Cruz took its name, an icon
originally carried by Alonso Fernández de Lugo when he
arrived on the island in 1494 (see pages 30 and 44). The
church also housed a banner captured from Rear-Admiral
Horatio Nelson following his abortive raid on the city in
1797 (see page 44), temporarily transferred to the Museo
Militar during restoration (see page 52). Despite these
illustrious artefacts, the church became badly dilapidated

*The Moorish-
influenced bell-tower
of Nuestra Señora de
la Concepción*

over the years, a situation only recently taken in hand by extensive restoration – work is expected to continue until 1999. Once renovation is complete, it is not known whether the church's treasures will be returned to their original home. Whatever their fate, the building's enchanting interior should once again be restored to its former baroque splendour. Pride of place should go to the glorious choir stalls, the marble and alabaster pulpit (1736), and Luján Pérez's sculpted figure of the Mater Dolorosa above the high altar.

The church of San Francisco has one of the city's loveliest interiors

► 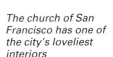 **Iglesia de San Francisco**   *41C3*
Plaza del Príncipe
Right next to the Museo Municipal de Bellas Artes (see page 53) stands the peaceful Church of San Francisco, reputedly founded as a chapel by Irish Catholics fleeing religious persecution during the reign of Elizabeth I of England. The present building dates from around 1680, when it served as the monastery church of San Pedro de Alcántara, a Franciscan friary now partly occupied by the Museo Municipal de Bellas Artes (see page 53). The square flanking the church, the **Plaza del Príncipe** – originally the friary garden – contains a wonderful jumble of plants and shady Indian laurel trees. Concealed within the foliage is a quaint bandstand.

A baroque portico leads into the church's cool and gloriously decorated interior, much of which was restored during the 18th century. Outstanding treasures underneath the beamed ceiling and amid the many age-darkened paintings include a painted arch, two 17th- and 18th-century *retablos* (altar-pieces) and an imposing organ, the last still used for occasional recitals. Also eye-catching is the chapel to the right of the high altar, which boasts a beautiful *mudéjar* (Moorish-style) ceiling.

Plaza de Iglesias
Whether the Iglesia de Nuestra Señora de la Concepción is open or not, it is still worth coming to the Plaza de Iglesias to catch a glimpse of the church's façade, not to mention the rather faded ensemble of 19th-century buildings that lie dotted around the square. Foremost among these is the façade of the Tinerfeña Fábrica de Tabacos (Tenerife Tobacco Company), an imposing edifice built in 1880 which dates from the 19th-century heyday of Tenerife's wealthy tobacco barons.

*A flower stall at the
Mercado de Nuestra
Señora de África*

Flea market
Stalls selling a
bewildering variety of
household and other goods
spill over into the streets
surrounding the Mercado
de Nuestra Señora de
África (Calle José Manuel
Guimerá is one of the
most vibrant). These are
great fun to browse in,
though few are as engag-
ing as Sunday's lively flea
market, or *rastro*, which
takes place alongside
the site of the *mercado*.
This Sunday jamboree
is a good place to wander
at leisure or hunt for junk,
knicknacks, *objets d'art*,
leatherware and other
craft items. Stamps
are also a speciality,
philately being something
of a Spanish obsession.
The market is a great place
to visit, but pickpockets
operate, so keep an eye
on your bags and
valuables.

Fiestas
Santa Cruz has more than
its fair share of festivals.
Over and above the famous
carnival celebrations (see
page 50), there are also the
following: New Year (*Año
Neuvo*) festivities, when
tradition demands you
swallow a grape and a sip
of *cava* (sparkling wine) as
each strike of midnight
tolls; the *Cabalgata de los
Reyes Magos* (Cavalcade
of the Three Kings – 6 Jan),
which celebrates the
coming of the Magi with a
lively procession; a fiesta
to celebrate the Virgin on
16 July; celebrations to
commemorate the city's
victory over Nelson (July);
and fiestas to celebrate
*Nuestra Señora de la
Candelaria*, the Canaries'
patron saint (15 Aug).

▶▶▶ **Mercado de Nuestra**   *41C2*
Señora de África
Calle de San Sebastián
*Open: General market, Mon–Sat 8–1; Flea market
(Rastro) Sun 10–2*
No visit to Santa Cruz is complete without a trip to
the Mercado de Nuestra Señora de África (Our Lady of
Africa market), perhaps the liveliest and most colourful of
any market in the Canary Islands. Bustling street-life and a
cornucopia of sights, smells and colour make this an
essential stop-off, whether or not you intend to embark
on a spending spree.

Located in one of the city's oldest quarters, close to the
traditional red-light district, the *casbah*-like market is
entered via a vast arch flanked by a small army of flower-
sellers. Beyond this lies an arcaded central courtyard, a
wonderfully bustling area festooned with stalls of fruit,
vegetables, flowers, meat and fish. Live animals are also
often on sale. Stalls sell exotic as well as everyday goods:
anything from local wine and honey to pungent spices
and obscure mountain cheeses. Look out in particular for
queso herreño from the island of El Hierro, made from a
mixture of goat's, cow's and sheep's milk: it's available
either *ahumada* (smoked) or *curada* (mature). If you've
taken a fancy to Canarian music, you can also pick up
cheap cassettes of local or Latin American *orquestas*. If
you like markets, be certain not to miss the equally enticing Sunday **flea market**, which is held alongside the
Mercado (see panel).

▶▶▶ Museo de la Naturaleza y El Hombre

41C2

Calle Fuentes Morales
Open: Tue–Sun 10–8. Admission charge: inexpensive

Santa Cruz's Museo de la Naturaleza y El Hombre (Museum of Nature and Mankind) replaces the city's tired Archaeological Museum. As a museum of the history and culture of the Canary Islands, it ranks second only to the Museo Canario in Las Palmas on Gran Canaria. Located immediately south of the Iglesia de Nuestra Señora de la Concepción (see page 46), it is housed in the former Antiguo Hospital Civil (Old City Hospital). The museum's main displays deal with the art, history and customs of the Guanches, the Canary Islands' first peoples (see pages 26 and 136). The most eye-catching exhibits are various mummified bodies (with information as to how the mummifying process was achieved), several gnarled skeletons and around 1,000 skulls, some displaying signs of the mysterious trepanning (drilled holes) for which the Guanches were famous.

Also displayed are tools, fragments of pottery, crude pieces of jewellery and a wide variety of simple everyday objects. There are also exhibits relating to pre-Hispanic burial sites and where various artefacts were discovered. The museum signs off with displays devoted to the Canaries' flora and fauna.

49

The Museo de la Naturaleza y El Hombre occupies part of the old city hospital

■ **Santa Cruz's annual carnival is one of the world's largest and most colourful, rivalling the famous Rio de Janeiro Carnival for size, splendour and sheer dazzling spectacle. Visitors and locals alike indulge themselves in days of eating, drinking and dancing, donning fabulous fancy-dress costumes to join in the huge variety of festivities and processions.** ■

World record
Santa Cruz's Carnival is probably the world's second largest after the famous Rio de Janeiro Carnival in Brazil. In 1987, it gained a place in the *Guinness Book of Records* when an estimated 240,000 revellers gathered in Santa Cruz's main Plaza de España to take part in what was officially the world's largest-ever carnival ball.

Tasty morsels
All sorts of special food and drink are consumed in vast quantities during Carnival. The favourite tipple is *cubata*, a cocktail of rum and coke, while the foods favoured to sustain the crowds through long nights of partying are *churros*, a type of Spanish doughnut, *pinchitos* (kebabs), *pepitos* (steak-filled rolls) and *manzana garrapunda* (toffee-apples).

Farewell *Carnaval* is the great annual celebration held before the privations of Lent, a festival which probably has its origins in pagan ceremonies to celebrate the departure of winter and imminent arrival of spring. Believed to take its name from *carne valle*, the Latin meaning 'farewell to meat', it takes place in the days preceding Lent (when meat or fat were traditionally taboo). It usually reaches its climax on Shrove Tuesday with a massive procession. In Spain, the Carnival was banned for years on the whim of General Franco. However, on Tenerife the wily *Santacruceros*, Santa Cruz's inhabitants, circumvented the injunction by organising what they described as Fiestas de Invierno (Festivals of Winter).

Preparation Carnival's fun and festivities are by no means for the benefit of tourists. To the people of Santa Cruz and Tenerife, the event is the highlight of the year, a time of hedonistic celebration when the worries of the rest of the year can be forgotten. Preparations for this event often begin a few days after the close of the previous Carnival. Each year a different theme is chosen for

Carnivals and other festivals provide interesting glimpses of traditional Tenerife life

the great *Coso*, or Grand Procession, embracing anything from Disneyland to Ancient Egypt. The choice of theme is the cue for work to begin on fantastic costumes and magnificent feathered head-dresses, the finest of which will be worn by entrants in the hotly contested competition to find the year's 'Carnival Queen'.

Festivities All *comparsas* (processions) involve decorated floats and troupes of men and women in fancy dress, or glittering swathes of near-naked participants dancing to the frenzied accompaniment of local Latin and American bands. Troupes are sometimes accompanied by *murgas*, groups of satirical singers. Outdoor dancing is *de rigueur*, and during the 12 days of Carnival, the infectious rhythms of rumba and samba reverberate around the streets day and night (a good night's sleep during this period in central Santa Cruz is highly unlikely). People come from across the world to join in, but especially from South America, a region whose citizens are linked to Spain and Tenerife by centuries of emigration.

Burial Of all the ceremonies and festivities associated with Santa Cruz's carnival, none is stranger than the 'Burial of the Sardine' on Shrove Tuesday. This involves a large cardboard and papier-maché sardine, a monster that can reach anything up to 10m in length. A symbol of Tenerife, it is carried in procession around the streets by eight bearers. Accompanying them is a band of musicians and a group of 'widows' – usually men in drag wearing black hats, veils and high heels – who wail and shriek as if in mourning. En route the 'sardine' and its entourage are cheered on by laughing crowds, moving slowly between the hordes towards a pre-ordained spot near the waterfront. There, a mock funeral oration takes place and the sardine is burned on a huge bonfire, or encouraged to explode with fire-crackers, its demise providing the signal for a large fireworks display.

Carnival processions feature masses of decorated floats

Entertainment
Carnival and other fiestas on Tenerife often provide an opportunity to watch traditional dancing and folk singing. If you are lucky, you may also see displays of Canarian wrestling (see page 19) and other age-old customs, notably *pulseo de piedra* (weightlifting and trials of strength involving vast pieces of rock), the *lucha de garrote*, *juego de palo* or *banot* (fast-moving duels fought with sticks dating from pre-conquest times) and – in more rural areas – the *salto del pastor*, in which shepherds compete by jumping across ravines and rocky clefts.

*Exterior decoration
at the Museo Militar*

Plaza de Weyler
This popular square stands
at the end of Calle de
Castillo, Santa Cruz's main
shopping street, its lawns
and trees a favourite
lunchtime retreat for the
city's office workers. The
large, white, marble fountain at its centre is of
Italian (Genoese) extrac-
tion, while the plaza's west
side is dominated by the
Capitanía General, built in
1880. For many years the
latter was the seat of the
island's military governors,
and in the years leading up
to the Spanish Civil War
served for a time as the
home of General Franco.

► **Museo Militar** 41D4

Calle San Isidro
Open: Tue–Sun 9.30–1.30. Admission charge: inexpensive
Tenerife's regional military museum found a permanent
home on its present site in 1988, occupying part of Santa
Cruz's **Cuartel del Almeida**, a semicircular fortified
barracks constructed between 1854 and 1884 (it remains
a military headquarters of some importance). The building
lies some 10 minutes' walk north from the main Plaza de
España. Note that you may have to offer some proof of
identity (a passport) to gain entry to the museum, and
may also be escorted during your visit, usually by young
men doing their national service.

A large part of the museum, inevitably, is given over to
Nelson's doomed attack on Santa Cruz in 1797 (see page
45), the most famous legacy of which is *El Tigre* (The
Tiger), the cannon said to have fired the shot which shattered the British admiral's right arm. Also on display are
paintings depicting the battle, a copy of the grovelling
letter of thanks addressed by Nelson to Santa Cruz's
Spanish commander, and the now threadbare banners
taken from Nelson and HMS *Emerald* in the aftermath of
defeat (currently transferred here from the church of
Nuestra Señora de la Concepción: see page 46).

Of equally poignant interest is the area of the museum
given over to General Franco, the Spanish dictator who
for four months served as *Comandante-Generale* de
Canarias (see page 35). On show are the despot's desk, a
photograph of his famous meeting with fellow insurgents
near Las Raíces (where all pledged allegiance to a
proposed coup) and a map depicting the route taken by
the infamous *Dragon Rapide* aeroplane which – having
flown from England – took him from the Canaries to

Morocco and the outbreak of the Spanish Civil War. Other exhibits in the museum include a range of ancient Canarian weapons, which compare badly with the more advanced armaments of their Spanish conquerors, also on display. Just north of the museum, incidentally, at the junction of Rambla del General Franco and Avenida de Anaga, stands a monolithic monument to the dictator.

►► Museo Municipal de Bellas Artes   41C3

Calle José Murphy 4-Plaza del Príncipe
Open: Mon–Fri 1–8, summer Mon–Fri 10–7.45. Closed Sat and Sun. Admission charge: free.

Santa Cruz's Municipal Museum of Fine Arts opened its doors in 1900, utilising part of the city's former Franciscan friary to display Tenerife's finest collection of sculptures and paintings. The municipal library shares part of the building, while alongside lies the friary's former monastery church, the **Iglesia de San Francisco** (see page 47). The slightly raised square in front of the museum, the Plaza del Príncipe, was originally the friary garden.

Busts of famous Canarian musicians, poets and philosophers adorn the museum's exterior, a prelude to two floors of exhibits which embrace the works of Spanish, Canarian, Italian and other foreign artists. Among the eminent painters represented are Madrazo, Brueghel, Van Loo, Jordaens, Ribera and Guido Reni. Look out for a variety of interesting historical scenes, among them a depiction of Alonso Fernández de Lugo's landing at Santa Cruz in 1494 (see page 30). Also displayed in the museum are various contemporary works, collections of ships' models, coins, arms and armour, as well as paintings and artefacts on loan from major galleries on the Spanish mainland.

Círculo de Amistad XII de Enero
To the left of the Museo Municipal de Bellas Artes, in the corner of Plaza del Príncipe, stands the Círculo de Amistad XII de Enero. This was once the former home of a recreational society, an élite organisation. Constructed in 1903 – the same year as the Círculo's foundation – the building is one of Santa Cruz's loveliest, showcasing a pastiche of numerous architectural styles which have benefited from recent restoration. It can be admired from the Plaza, but is sadly only open to the public on special occasions as it is a private club (contact the tourist information office for details).

A painting by Fernando Ferrani adorns part of the Museo Municipal de Bellas Artes

Part of the impressive lido at the Parque Marítimo

Palacio de Carta

Whether or not you need to change money in Santa Cruz, you should pay a visit to the Palacio de Carta, a superb old building (built in 1742) hidden behind a rather drab grey basalt façade at Plaza de la Candelaria 9. It is currently occupied by the Banco Español de Crédito, which has beautifully restored the building's interior. Newly revealed is a perfect array of carved dark-wood Canarian balconies and plant-filled patios. These are open to the public during business hours, which for banks are normally Monday to Friday 9–2 and Saturday 9–1, except June to October, when banks are closed on Saturday.

▶▶ **Parque Marítimo**　　41C1

Castillo de San Juan
Open: daily 10–5. Admission charge: inexpensive

The Parque Marítimo is an ambitious piece of urban redevelopment aimed at turning part of Santa Cruz's industrial dockyard into an area which will eventually boast a cultural centre, a maritime museum, a folk museum, an exhibition space and a variety of other leisure facilities. The complex is being built around the old Castillo de San Juan (Castle of St John), while its design will correspond to the specifications, landscaping ideals and strict Canarian environmental standards laid down by the late Lanzarote architect César Manrique (see panel, page 104). Already built is an impressive sea-water lido, constructed along the lines of Manrique's celebrated Lido San Telmo in Puerto de la Cruz (see page 104). To reach the development you can drive, walk or take a bus along Avenida de José Antonio Primo de Rivera, the coast road which leads south from the city centre.

▶▶ **Parque Municipal García Sanabria**　　41C3

Calle Méndez Núñez
Open: daily 9–dusk

The Parque Municipal García Sanabria, which takes its name from a former mayor of Santa Cruz, is among the largest and most beautiful of any city park in the Canaries. Designed and laid out in the 1920s – and thus now full of mature trees and shrubs – it is a lovely place to seek a few moment's peaceful solace amid the noise and bustle of downtown Santa Cruz. Its six hectares contain numerous tropical and sub-tropical plants and flowers, many exotic species of trees, tiled benches, refreshment kiosks and plenty of shady walkways and peaceful corners. Pieces of modern sculpture are dotted throughout the grounds (remnants of a sculpture competition held in 1973), along with fountains, water gardens, aviaries, animal enclosures, a children's playground and a famous **floral clock** (near the southern entrance). If you like this park you might also want to make the short walk necessary to reach the quaint little Plaza 25 de Julio near by.

▶▶ Plaza de la Candelaria 41D2

The pedestrianised Plaza de la Candelaria adjoins the Plaza de España, with which it shares the title of Santa Cruz's main square. Like its neighbour, it makes a convenient starting point for shopping and sightseeing tours of the city. At its heart stands *El Triunfo de la Candelaria* (Triumph of the Virgin of Candelaria), a neo-classical statue representing the Madonna de la Candelaria, patroness and protector of the Canaries (see page 60). As an icon she is usually depicted holding a child in one hand and a candle in the other. Carved around 1773 in white Carrara marble (and erected in 1778), the statue is often attributed to the celebrated Italian sculptor Antonio Canova, but is probably the work of another Italian, the Genoese sculptor Pasquale Bocciardo. At the foot of the sculpture's narrow supporting column stand four figures representing Guanche *menceys*, or chieftains, symbols of a 'heathen' people converted to Christianity following the arrival of the Spanish.

Shoppers and window shoppers leave the square bound for the Calle del Castillo, Santa Cruz's principal shopping street, which runs off the plaza to the west. Before joining the crowds, however, look briefly at two of the square's older buildings: the **Palacio de Carta** at No 9 (see panel, page 54) and the **Casino de Tenerife** at the junction with Plaza de España. The latter is a mid-18th-century palace which belonged to the island's oldest private club, though its murals, the work of leading Canarian painters, are only rarely open to the public.

▶ Plaza de España 41D2

Plaza de España is the hub of Santa Cruz, the place to start either your sightseeing or shopping adventures. Big, busy and flanked by concrete highrises, it is not the prettiest of squares, but contains the post office and tourist information offices. It also leads to the start of Calle del Castillo, the city's principal shopping street. The **correos** (post office) occupies one of two vast buildings from the Fascist era. The main tourist office occupies the other, the **Palacio Insular**, a sombre pile given over mostly to the offices of the island government. You might want to wander into its foyer to admire the scale model of Tenerife and some stained glass decorated with vignettes of Tenerife life. Yet more drab fascist masonry sits at the square's heart, the **Monumento de los Caídos**, a monument to the dead of the Spanish Civil War (1936–9). Its base houses a little memorial chapel and the entrance to a lift, though the top of the monument – which offers harbour views – is now only occasionally open to the public.

Cafés and bars
The cafés on Plaza de la Candelaria provide a pleasant spot from which to take time out from shopping or sightseeing. The best known are the Atlántico and the prominent Olympo opposite, which despite showing every sign of being a tourist trap has good food and views. Elsewhere, you might want to try the Café del Príncipe in Plaza del Príncipe, which has a garden and sells good cakes and snacks.

Statue of the Virgin of Candelaria, Plaza de la Candelaria

ANAGA AND NORTHEAST TENERIFE

Previous pages: the spectacular view across the Anaga Mountains from Mirador de Jardina Below: the church of San Pedro in El Sauzal

Northeast Tenerife is a highlight, yet despite its great beauty, the best beach on the island, two of the island's finest museums and one of its most handsome and historic towns, the region is still relatively unexplored. For independent travellers, this is in itself a major part of its appeal.

There are two principal highlights: **La Laguna** (see page 73), Tenerife's second most important town after Santa Cruz, and **Las Montañas de Anaga** (Anaga Mountains), a largely unspoilt region of spectacular landscapes tucked away in the region's easternmost corner. To make the most of the area you need a car, particularly in the mountains, though buses link Santa Cruz – a good base for exploration – to La Laguna and most larger towns on the coast to the north and south. Many people come here for one reason only, however – to swim and sunbathe on the **Playa de las Teresitas**, Tenerife's most pleasant beach (see page 84).

To come to the region and not visit La Laguna, however, would be to miss one of the Canaries' finest towns. Once the island's capital, it preserves some wonderful old architecture and maintains a distinctly Spanish atmosphere. At the other extreme is the tiny village of Chinamada (see pages 64 and 67), a virtually inaccessible settlement where many of the inhabitants

Beaches

It's a curious fact of Tenerife tourism that for all the island's reputation as a sun-and-sea destination, it actually possesses few outstanding beaches and swimming areas. The following list gives a summary of the best that the island has to offer:

Bajamar Small black-sand beach and good seawater pools (see page 60).

Playa de las Teresitas Superb artificial white-sand beach a few kilometres north of Santa Cruz. Just north towards Igueste is Las Gaviotas, a narrow black-sand beach popular with the young and with some nudists (see panel, page 84).

Puerto de la Cruz Excellent artificial lido, swimming pools and park at the Lido San Telmo/Lago Martiánez. Also new Punta Brava black-sand beach at the resort's western end.

Garachico Good artificial seawater swimming pools (see panel, page 118).

Icod de los Vinos Fine black-sand beach at nearby San Marcos (see panel, page 120).

Los Gigantes Good black-sand beach at Playa de la Arena (see page 124).

El Médano The biggest and best natural white-sand beaches on the island (some undeveloped). Safe bathing for children, but can be windy: popular with windsurfers (see page 146).

Los Cristianos Playa de Teno to the west of the resort is an artificial beach protected by breakwaters (see page 151–2).

Playa de las Américas This resort, along with neighbouring Los Cristianos, has a number of artificial or improved grey-sand beaches: there are two to the west of the marina (Marina and Torviscas) and two near the Veronicas development (del Bobo and de Troya). (See page 158.)

still live in caves carved from the living rock. Other towns and villages are less appealing, although those with a religious interest or curiosity might wish to visit **Candelaria**, site of the island's most important shrine (see page 60).

Otherwise the region's lure is primarily scenic, thanks to the dramatic landscapes of the Anaga Mountains. On the flightpath of moisture-laden winds from the north, the jagged peaks are covered with trees and vegetation, their verdant appearance at odds with the dry, desert-like scenery of the south. Reasonable roads wind through the uplands, regularly interrupted by specially built *miradores* (viewpoints). More adventurous drivers can find their own scenic spots by exploring the area's minor roads, many of which wind down to tempting little bays and secluded coastal hamlets.

Perhaps the single finest road in the region, however, at least from a scenic point of view, is the one that runs along the so-called Cumbre Dorsal, the volcanic ridge that forms the island's backbone (see page 70). It runs west from La Laguna, climbing through pretty woodlands before emerging onto the bare uplands on the fringes of Mount Teide. This is perhaps the least travelled, but arguably the most spectacular of the four routes you can take to reach the mountain and its national park (see page 126).

Currents and high surf confine Bajamar bathers to swimming pools

▶ **Bajamar** 58B3

Resorts such as Bajamar – which means 'Down by the Sea' – are fewer and farther between on Tenerife's northern coast than on the island's sunnier southern margins. This slightly tired resort is among Tenerife's oldest, and is looking a little dated these days alongside the south's newer resorts. At the same time it is more remote and relaxed than the south's more brash centres, and well suited to those looking for a longer stay. As a result it still attracts visitors who return here faithfully year after year. Like the more go-ahead Puerto de la Cruz (see page 100), its almost equally venerable northern neighbour, it has only a modest black beach. Coupled with strong currents and high surf, this means that most swimming and bathing is done in the comfort of hotel or municipal pools (*piscineas municipales*).

Although once a small fishing village, the resort lacks any real centre. Instead it has a long promenade and a network of streets to the rear, all lined with the usual medley of bars, restaurants and shops. These are rarely crowded – part of the resort's charm – though considerable amounts of money are being invested in Bajamar's future. The resulting refurbishment and new polish may well alter the town's traditional appeal.

Just 3km to the north of Bajamar, on the coast road, lies **Punta del Hidalgo**▶ (see panel, page 62), another former fishing village which has been transformed into Bajamar's sister resort (the two are gradually merging into one). A touch more modern than its neighbour – though just as relaxing – many of its hotels enjoy panoramic cliff-top positions, views of Canary sunsets from these and the eponymous *punta* (headland) are some of the best in Tenerife. There are also good views inland over the Anaga Mountains (see page 80). The coast is largely rocky, however, so swimming and sun-bathing, as in Bajamar, take place mostly in hotel pools. Be warned, too, that as one of Tenerife's most exposed northerly points, the coast can also be buffeted by powerful winds. This is bad news for bathers, but good news if you want to take walks by the sea, as the wind whips up the Atlantic breakers to create any number of impressive seascapes. Fishing, too, can be excellent.

A favourite place among locals for a stroll or picnic is the **Playa de los Troches**, though new developments (a marina and resort complex) may eventually make the spot less appealing.

▶ **Candelaria** 58B1

Candelaria is Tenerife's main point of pilgrimage, home to a highly revered statue of the Virgen de la Candelaria, patroness of the Canary Islands. Situated some 17km south of Santa Cruz, the town is dominated by a pilgrimage church, the **Basílica de Nuestra Señora de la Candelaria**, a point to which thousands of pilgrims journey on the days surrounding 14–15 August (the main festival in honour of the Virgin). Worshippers come from as far afield as South America, for the cult of this particular madonna has achieved worldwide renown.

How it came to achieve its extraordinary status is a curious mixture of pagan Guanche and Christian *conquistador* worship. In 1392, according to Canarian legend, two

Guanche kings
One side of the great square fronting the basilica at Candelaria is lined with nine vast statues, each representing an idealised image of the Guanche kings who ruled Tenerife before the arrival of the Spanish in the 15th century. For years the figures were made from rough-hewn red sandstone. These were replaced in 1993 by the present bronze statues.

Guanche fishermen discovered a Holy Image of the Virgin bearing a candle and naked Child in the rocks at Playa del Socorro (south of present-day Candelaria). Other versions of the story suggest the statue was washed into a nearby cave. Significantly, this was still almost a hundred years before the arrival of the Spanish *conquistadores*. What happened next varies according to who tells the story. Some say one of the Guanches accidentally cut his finger on his knife, only to find it miraculously healed when he touched the statue. Another story relates how the Guanches initially tried to throw stones at the figure, but were prevented from doing so by an unexplained paralysis of their arms.

For whatever reason, the Guanches informed their king, the Mencey of Güimar, of the discovery. He had the figure installed in a cave at Chinguaro, where it acquired the title of *Chaxiraxi* and became an object of pagan devotion. Worship continued until the arrival of the Spanish,

The statue of the Virgin of Candelaria is a major point of pilgrimage

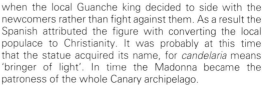

Viewpoint

For good views at Punta del Hidalgo follow the main road from the curious church at the centre of town to the headland, home to a lofty *mirador* (viewpoint) and a plaza with a statue erected in 1990 to commemorate Sebastián Ramos, a noted writer on the folklore of the Canaries. The view embraces rocky mountain slopes and the deep green of banana plantations mingling with the black of volcanic rock and white foam of the sea. A track drops from the mirador to the shore and cemetery at Playa de los Troches.

when the local Guanche king decided to side with the newcomers rather than fight against them. As a result the Spanish attributed the figure with converting the local populace to Christianity. It was probably at this time that the statue acquired its name, for *candelaria* means 'bringer of light'. In time the Madonna became the patroness of the whole Canary archipelago.

Over the years the statue underwent several trials. In 1789, it had to be rescued from a fire in a church, and worse followed in 1826, when a tidal wave swept through the rebuilt church and carried the statue out to sea. It was never seen again, and the figure revered today is a copy dating from 1830. This does little to dent the enthusiasm of pilgrims, or of the many thousands across the Catholic world who light candles for the Candelaria Madonna in mid-August. Much of the basilica is modern, and was completed in 1958. As a result it is of little interest for casual visitors, though the streets of the old town on the hill above the church – barely changed in centuries – are well worth a few minutes' exploration.

▶ ▶ ▶   Casa de Carta   58B3

Near Valle de Guerra, 25km from Puerto de la Cruz
Open: daily 10–8; shorter hours off season. Admission charge: moderate

The Casa de Carta is a beautifully preserved late 17th-century mansion in the heart of lovely countryside some 25km from Puerto de la Cruz (1km from Valle de Guerra on the C820 Tacoronte to Valle de Guerra road). In it is housed the **Museo Etnográfico de Tenerife**, the finest ethnographic museum in the Canary Islands. Normally one might have expected to find such a key museum in a town or city, but an inspired decision has placed this wonderful collection of folk artefacts in a delightful alternative setting. Lodged amid placid gardens full of tropical

The Casa de Carta, one of Tenerife's prettiest old buildings

plants, the **house** is an attraction in itself, and a first-rate example of typical Canarian architecture. Its rooms are a procession of wonderful patios, porticos and finely carved woodwork, creating an ensemble of a richness now rarely found under one roof. From the balconies and gardens you can look down over the lovely pastoral countryside around the village of Valle de Guerra, an area where the land rights were once administered by the Carta family, a dynasty whose members lived in the house for several generations.

The **exhibits** chronicle numerous aspects of Canarian rural and urban life over the centuries, bringing together all manner of agricultural, craft and other folk artefacts. Some of the most striking exhibits are the various Canarian costumes, beautifully woven and embroidered clothes which embrace the various outfits worn for fiestas, weddings and other occasions. Particularly interesting are the different styles and colours from the Canaries' different regions and islands, together with rooms given over to different crafts that allow you to see how the original clothes might once have been woven or decorated. Other displays include reconstructed period rooms, notably a bedroom and kitchen, as well as exhibits relating to ceramics and the typical peasant food of the islands (in particular *gofio*; see page 157).

Southern wine and cheese
The big resorts of southern Tenerife are not particularly known for their wine or culinary finesse. Some outstanding vintages you might look out for, however, are the Flor de Chasna wines made from the *lisan blanco* grape. Also look in food shops for cheese from the village of Arico, some of the island's best. For more information on wines from the north of the island look for the free brochure entitled *Tenerife: Wines, Gastronomy, Travel*, from tourist information offices.

63

You can taste and buy wine at the Casa del Vino shop and museum

▶▶ Casa del Vino la Baranda   58B2
18km east of Puerto de la Cruz, off the Autopista del Norte (El Sauzal exit)
Open: Tue–Sun 11–8; museum 10–6.
Admission charge: inexpensive
The 'Baranda House of Wine' lies on the coast road just to the south of El Sauzal and Tacoronte (see page 85). A relatively new tourist attraction, the 17th-century house has been arranged to offer an introduction to the wines of Tenerife (see page 98). For many people the main attraction here is the opportunity to sample a selection of wines, a small charge buying you the right to taste around 10 of the 150 or so wines available. If the idea of wine on an empty stomach is unappealing, a pleasant restaurant on site provides good food in panoramic surroundings. The house also offers a small museum and video introduction to the history of wine-making on Tenerife, with special reference to the renaissance it has enjoyed over the last few years.

ANAGA AND NORTHEAST TENERIFE

*Ancient cave
dwellings near the
Roque de Taborno*

The canary
Although best known to most people as a familiar cage bird, the canary lives wild on the Canary Islands, though it's unlikely the bird's presence resulted in the islands' name (see page 24). It is common and widespread on Tenerife, and is also found on Madeira and the Azores. Canaries can be found in all manner of different habitats from pine forest to agricultural land. They are primarily seed-eaters and spend much of their time foraging on the ground, though at other times they often perch on the tops of tall trees. The canary is particularly renowned for the quality of the male's song, which can be heard at almost any time of the year. Although they often sing from a perch, birds will sometimes perform fluttering, circular song-flights.

Piles or pyramids?
Güimar came to international attention in 1990 when the celebrated Norwegian explorer and anthropologist, Thor Heyerdahl claimed to have discovered 'pyramids' built by the Guanches, Tenerife's earliest inhabitants. These carefully formed piles of stone, he suggested, might have been ancient sites used during Guanche religious and cult ceremonies. Most other scholars are sceptical, claiming the mounds were simply piles of boulders made by the Spanish as they cleared the fields of stones.

 Chinamada   59C3

To look at the vast resorts of Tenerife's southern coast, it is hard to believe that the same island still contains villages such as Chinamada. Until 1993, this was a remote outpost without road access, and even today boasts only the most rudimentary access for locals and visitors. Secreted in the steeply terraced mountains above Punta del Hidalgo (see page 60), the village is famous for its troglodyte dwellings, ancient (but still inhabited) cave houses cut into the living rock. Approaches to the area take you through dramatic countryside, with views of the green-shrouded slopes of **Roque de Taborno** (707m), distinguished by its bullet-shaped basalt peak. Closer to the village, as the first houses come into view, you have still finer **views** over the emerald gorge of the Barranco del Tomadero. Sure-footed goats range over the harsh terrain, providing the meat and cheese that have traditionally supported Chinamada's inhabitants.

On arrival in the village you are able to walk past the remarkable stone-cut houses, which for all their modest size and prehistoric appearance are often remarkably well-appointed within. The area offers plenty of scope for short walks, and if you have the energy, or can arrange the necessary transport, you can begin a walk in Los Carboneras, visit Chinamada, and then continue to Punta del Hidalgo. The walk (see pages 66–7) takes about 3 hours, and is mostly downhill. Details of other walks can be obtained from local tourist information offices.

▶▶ **El Sauzal**   58B2

El Sauzal lies 16km northeast of Puerto de la Cruz, and has been much smartened up over the last few years. The most compelling sight is the **Mirador de la Garañona▶▶▶**, which offers a stupendous view over some of the north coast's most spectacular cliffs (which drop 130m to the sea). Pleasant landscaped gardens and a welcoming café provide places to sit and admire the view. Roads dropping down to the town and elsewhere are flanked by fish restaurants, while the hills are dotted with impressive villas. This stretch of coast is a favoured holiday home retreat for the business people of Puerto de la Cruz. Make a point of seeing the **Iglesia de**

San Pedro (Church of St Peter), distinguished by its Moorish-style dome. The adjacent town hall, built in classic Canarian style, is graced with a cascading waterfall and some lovely gardens spread over steeply ranked terraces. Note that in June the town holds one of the island's better local fiestas.

►   **Güimar**   *58B1*

Güimar, 25km southwest of Santa Cruz, is far from being Tenerife's prettiest town, nor is the nearby coast attractive, but it does have the busy and no-nonsense charm that is typical of Tenerife's less tourist-oriented towns. It has achieved a certain notoriety, thanks largely to several controversial 'pyramids' in the countryside near by (see panel, page 64). The village also has a local carnival fiesta in the first week of February, as well as a noted summer festival in June.

The Anaga Mountains tumble to the sea with spectacular cliffs: a view from the Mirador de la Garañona near El Sauzal

 **Chinamada**

A walk to the fascinating rock dwellings of Chinamada (4km; allow 1½–3 hrs)

This walk takes you to the heart of Las Montañas de Anaga (Anaga Mountains), reaching its climax in a village whose inhabitants still live in age-old caves carved into the mountainside. Until 1993 the village was cut off from all roads, the walk's route being the one followed by generations of villagers wishing to reach the outside world. An easy walk to follow, it is suitable for all ages, while much of the first half – while bumpy – could be undertaken in a car.

Las Carboneras

This small village comprises a church, and a handful of bars and houses.

Start by the main plaza and follow the wooden sign to Chinamada (where the road proper finishes and the new track begins).

The path from Chinamada leads – eventually – to the sea

Roque de Taborno

The first stretch of the walk is dominated by the green, velvety peak of Roque de Taborno, soaring away to the right. The summit exceeds 706m and has a distinctive, bullet-like peak. In winter the wonderful sweet smell of the retana plant fills the air along the route.

After about 15 minutes the track turns a corner away from Roque de Taborno, but without losing any of the superb views. Caves begin to appear, burrowed into the hillside. Take the next bend and the first cave houses of Chinamada lie to the right-hand side of the track. Ignore these and follow the track, which wiggles to the left through a tiny pass and continues straight ahead.

Barranco del Tomadero

There is a stunning view to the left of the track, across the deep ravine that separates Chinamada from the tiny white houses of Batán de Abajo. The ravine runs all the way to the sea at Punta del Hidalgo (see page 60). You

Map labels:

Punta de Tamadite
Punta Fajana
Punta del Frontón
Punta del Hidalgo
706m ▲ Roque de Taborno
Chinamada
810m ▲ Tenejías
Barranco del Río
Barranco del Tomadero
Taborno
Las Carboneras ★
Taganana
Batán de Abajo
Las Escaleras
Viñátigo
1024m ▲ Taborno
Ermita Cruz del Carmen
Pico del Ingles
La Laguna

0 ½ 1 km

67

will probably hear bells from the village. Goats graze on these seemingly impossibly steep terraced slopes, providing meat and cheese for the people of Chinamada.

Chinamada

Note the fine dragon tree to the right of the path (see page 122). Just beyond this point a newish chapel lies straight ahead. The houses of the 30 or so people who live here are small and cut back into the rocky ridge, but, as you will see, their interiors are a world away from the Stone Age. You can walk along the narrow path beside the houses. If you are feeling inspired by the scenery, it's an hour's walk all the way down to Punta del Hidalgo, from where buses run back to La Laguna.

Return the short distance to the small crossroads and climb the hill up the

steps to the right, which should be signposted Las Escaleras *(The Stairs).*

Las Escaleras

The steps don't last for long, quickly turning into a narrow path. This offers a pretty route, strewn with ferns and Canary bell flowers. The path initially skirts the hillside; to the right are more fine views across the *barranco*. There's only one route to follow, with a metal conduit running alongside the path to act as a guide.

After about 30 minutes you will see the main road down to the left. At this point you can descend and walk back to the village of Las Carboneras (0.5km) or continue along the path for another 10 or 15 minutes: the latter option offers more lovely views of these majestic hills. Follow the path back the way you have come and make the descent to the road.

■ **The green leaves of the banana tree, and the distinctive Canarian banana, are common sights in Tenerife's street markets and across the island's mild-weathered slopes. A successful commercial crop for over a century, the island's banana trade is now threatened by competition from the larger and more cheaply produced fruit of central and South America.** ■

Bananas and tourists
The banana, in a humble way, was responsible for introducing some of the first 'package' tourists to Tenerife and the Canary Islands. British and Irish companies involved in the trade, notably Fyffes and Yeowards, sailed regular banana- and mailboats between Liverpool and the Canaries. The trip usually took around two weeks and involved stops at Lisbon, Madeira, Las Palmas and Tenerife. In time the companies began to sell passenger berths on the boats, the influx of visitors eventually leading to the construction of the first large hotels in towns like Puerto de la Cruz.

More lethal than you think: banana liqueur

First Species Bananas were first introduced into Tenerife during the 1850s. They became a full-fledged commercial concern some 25 years later, replacing the island's economic dependence on cochineal, an industry devastated by the arrival of chemically produced aniline dyes in the 1870s. With the backing of largely British entrepreneurs, farmers imported a small, specialised variety of banana from Indo-China, *Musa cavendishii*, a species deemed likely to succeed in the Canaries less than perfect climate. Largely impervious to changes in weather, the hardy *Musa* was first planted in the Valle de la Orotava (where it still thrives) before being introduced across the rest of northern Tenerife. In time cultivation was also begun, though on a smaller scale, on the islands of La Gomera and Gran Canaria.

Trees There is little mistaking a banana tree, thanks to its large emerald leaves, and no confusing the strange upturned 'fingers' of its green unripe fruit. Nor will you forget in a hurry the huge lorries encountered on winding mountain roads burdened with vast loads of bananas: a full bunch of bananas weighs, on average, some 25–30kg, and on occasions reaches over 60kg. Plantations are usually planted at heights of around 300 to 400m, depending on the local microclimate. Trees produce fruit bi-annually, with a growing time of four to six months, depending on altitude and amount of sunshine. The tree, or plant, consists of a long stem made up of rigid sheaths. This culminates in large fleshy leaves, from which, when the plant is about a year old, a large knobbly flowering bud emerges. Female flowers cluster in the lower part of the bud, male flowers on the upper part. Once these have matured into fruit the plant dies back. Later the tree produces several new shoots, only the strongest of which are kept, the rest being removed by hand. After a year these then put forth a massive bud, and the growing cycle begins afresh.

Decline The first blow to the banana industry came with World War I, which for a while all but destroyed the trade, forcing countless thousands of peasant and plantation workers to emigrate to the New World. Today the industry is threatened by warfare of a different sort, namely that of the open market, a battlefield in which high production costs have seen the Canarian banana fall victim to the more cheaply produced bananas of central and South America. The choice of banana grown, the tiny

Bananas

Musa cavendishii, has also been a problem, for although tasty enough, it looks puny alongside its giant South American cousins. As a result it is now almost unsaleable in Europe, traditionally one of the crop's major markets. As a consequence, mainland Spain is forced to subsidise the industry by taking around 96 per cent of the Canaries' crop (around 400,000 tonnes annually).

Future Given European Union (EU) strictures on such matters, such support can only be a stop-gap measure, and in the near future the Spanish market will be compelled to admit bananas from other countries. At one point it seemed the EU might even fail to recognise the humble *Musa* as a banana at all. If Spaniards develop a taste for the larger banana, the modest Canarian fruit, not to mention its producers, are in trouble.

As a result, many have already anticipated the banana's bleak future, attempting to turn their land over to more exotic fruits and flowers. Orchids and tropical blooms are now grown as commercial ventures, while pineapples, avocados and papayas have also been successfully established.

Felled forests

The fate of the banana tree, which has been increasingly replaced by other crops, partly mirrors that of forests across Tenerife. For centuries ancient woodlands and mature forests were cleared to provide land for cultivation. More recently land has been cleared to make way for tourist development. Only over the last few years has a determined effort been made to preserve relic woodland. Its survival is not only vital for the preservation of threatened species of flora and fauna, but also for the role it plays in preserving the island's water supply (see page 123) and preventing flash-flood erosion on hillsides. National and other parks on the island have a vital role to play in environmental protection.

Bunches of bananas can weigh anything up to 60kg

ANAGA AND NORTHEAST TENERIFE

Travelling the hard way up the Cumbre Dorsal

70

Hot spot
Temperatures on Tenerife can be high at the best of times, but several times a year, usually in spring and autumn, they rise to extraordinary heights. These are caused by a hot sirocco wind from the Sahara known locally as *el tiempo de África*. On the whole the wind's effect is weakened in coastal and built-up areas, but in regions such as the Cumbre Dorsal and elsewhere, the effects can be dramatic. Humidity drops to almost zero, but temperatures can rise to 45°C. Often the wind brings with it clouds of red dust, particles of which infiltrate every nook and cranny, and winds can be powerful enough to ravage crops and plantations. Violent storms usually mark the end of the weather after about five days.

Woodland meeting
The Bosque de la Esperanza is a beautiful and densely packed forest of laurels and other trees. It is most famous for the fact that it was here that General Franco met fellow co-conspirators in 1936 in the build-up to the Spanish Civil War (see page 35). The site of the fateful meeting, known as *Las Raíces* (The Roots), is marked by an obelisk signposted left off the main road (about 4km south of La Esperanza).

Opposite: a panoramic view from the Cumbre Dorsal

▶▶▶ Cumbre Dorsal   58A1
There are four main routes by which you can approach Mount Teide, the vast peak which dominates Tenerife's mountain heartland (see page 126). Given that it sits at the centre of the island, no one region has a monopoly on the mountain or its park, and you could as easily approach it from the south and west. One of the least travelled, but arguably most spectacular routes, however, starts from La Laguna and travels southwest along the Cumbre Dorsal, the redoubtable volcanic ridge that forms the island's rocky backbone. The route is easily followed, for the TF824 road runs along the ridge for almost its entire length.

The highway, known as the **Carretera Dorsal**, was built by the military in the 1940s, and is one of the most scenic drives in Tenerife. You can access the road from the centre of La Laguna or pick it up at junction 6 of the main TF5 highway from Santa Cruz to Puerto de la Cruz.

Forest The major village south of La Laguna is **La Esperanza**, a straggling, drawn-out place of little interest, noted for marking the start of the **Bosque de la Esperanza▶▶**, a stunning laurel forest renowned for its Fascist connections (see panel). On a more cheerful note, the forest offers excellent walking country, and is crisscrossed by several marked trails: Franco's infamous obelisk (see panel), for example, makes a good starting point for a woodland stroll. Along or just off the road stand several good restaurants, this being a favourite area for locals to come for lunch and a walk in the woods. Two of the best and busiest restaurants are Las Rosas and El Gran Chaparral.

Viewpoints Beyond the Las Raíces turnoff, the road curves right and upwards, with wonderful views unfolding to the north. There is no official *mirador* (viewpoint) at **Montaña Grande** (1,120m), but it's well worth pulling over here to enjoy the panorama towards La Laguna and the Anaga Mountains. Soon afterwards comes the **Mirador Pico de las Flores** (1,310m), which provides similar views, and then, 7km beyond – with the road climbing ever higher – the **Mirador de Ortuño**, where

you have your first opportunity to see Mount Teide in something approaching its full glory. About 2km beyond, a little lane strikes off left to the **Mirador de los Cumbres►►►**, a worthwhile diversion, for the views here are probably the best of the trip. There are actually two *miradores*; one to the south embracing the Bosque de la Esperanza, and another to the north providing a magnificent view of Mount Teide.

Uplands Some 6km further on, in the lee of the Montaña de la Crucita (2,054m), a major marked trail, the Camino a Candelaria, crosses the road from east to west. It's a steep walk down from the Cumbre, but drivers can enjoy a taste of the landscape by taking the rough lane off the road to the left (a short diversion). About 4km beyond, shortly before a large curving hairpin to the left, you begin to emerge fully from the wooded slopes that have accompanied the road thus far.

Henceforth, proceed through the increasingly wild uplands of Mount Teide's lower slopes, though lower is something of a misnomer, for the road soon reaches the 2,000m mark (still 1,718m below Teide's summit). After a while you pass the space-age buildings of the Instituto de Astrofísica de Canarias (or Observatorio de Izaña) (no public access). Built in 1965, the observatory was designed to study the night sky, but has been forced by the light pollution of Tenerife's resorts and towns to turn its attention to solar research. The highway eventually meets the road up from La Orotava, where you find El Portillo's visitor centre, the Centro de Visitantes (see page 126).

The unearthly towers of the Instituto de Astrofísica de Canarias

The Calle San Agustín presents some of La Laguna's most charming buildings

▶▶▶ La Laguna   *59C2*

La Laguna, officially known as San Cristóbal de la Laguna, is Tenerife's second most important city after Santa Cruz. It is also one of the island's oldest settlements, founded in 1496 by Alonso Fernández de Lugo, Spanish conqueror of Tenerife (see page 30). He made it the Canaries' administrative capital after defeating the Guanches, borrowing its name from a small nearby lagoon (now dried up). The town remained the Canaries' political, social and intellectual hub until 1723, when it surrendered its leading role to Santa Cruz. Today, ironically, the two cities are growing at such a rate that their outer suburbs threaten to intermingle, creating one vast and rather unappealing metropolis. La Laguna's population, just 20,000 in 1930, now exceeds 120,000.

Charm It would be easy to be put off by the town's unedifying sprawl, but it's worth braving the traffic and restricted parking to visit the historic centre, a perfect Renaissance jewel. Here, in a little grid of streets, lies the town of de Lugo, a charming mixture of beautiful old townhouses and tiny squares little changed since La Laguna's 16th-century heyday. There are two good churches and a couple of excellent museums, but the main pleasure is in soaking up the streets' peaceful and cultured air, and enjoying the town's many incidental architectural details – redoubtable wooden doorways, creaking flower-filled balconies and crumbling stone coats of arms.

Itineraries All of La Laguna's principal sights lie in a reasonably small area within the grid of its historic centre. The best place to start a visit is in Plaza del Adelantado, the town's leafy main square, which is flanked by several

Shops and markets
La Laguna's main thoroughfare and shopping street is Calle Obispo Rey Redondo. Shops also fill the side streets near by, though the most colourful place to buy provisions or picnic supplies is the market held every morning from Monday to Saturday in Calle San Agustín near the central Plaza del Adelantado.

Information
At the time of writing there was no proper tourist office in La Laguna. The best alternative is the *oficina de turismo*, hidden in the depths of the *ayuntamiento* (town hall) in the northwest corner of the main Plaza del Adelantado. It should be able to provide a rudimentary map and basic tourist information.

La Laguna's old streets are full of architectural oddities

outstanding old buildings. From here you should head north on Calle Obispo Rey Redondo, the principal shopping street, stopping off at the catedral before continuing north to see the Iglesia de Nuestra Señora de la Concepción (see page 76). From here it's a short walk east to Plaza Junta Suprema, where you can pick up Calle San Agustín south, an evocative old street with the excellent Museo de Historia de Tenerife (see page 77) and several interesting historic buildings.

Calle Obispo Rey Redondo▶▶▶ Old La Laguna's historic main street contains many captivating buildings. Apart from the Santa Iglesia Catedral, Casa de los Capitanes and Iglesia de Nuestra Señora de la Concepción (see page 76), look out for the **Teatro Leal**, an overbearing pink and yellow confection with two bright-red cupolas dating from 1915. Near the street's top (north) end is the charming Plaza de la Concepción, where lovely old houses look out onto a square with two dragon trees (see page 122) and a bizarre art nouveau structure which hides an electricity substation.

Calle San Agustín▶▶ This is one of La Laguna's loveliest streets, and should form an integral part of any tour of the town (see page 73). Walking south down the street from Plaza Junta Suprema, the first significant building you come to is the **Instituto de Canarias Cabrera Pinto**, an imposing building on the corner of Calle Rodríguez Moure which once formed part of a 17th-century Augustinian convent. The convent's surviving church – the half-ruined **Iglesia de San Agustín** – lies a few steps away down the street (the convent was ravaged by fire earlier this century). Between 1742 and 1747 the convent housed part of the town's university, founded in 1701 (see panel, page 75), but today plays host to the Cabrera Pinto Institute of Canarian Studies. A distinctive bell-tower marks out the building, which is best known for its sublime inner **patio**, one of the island's loveliest. Beware, though, that long-term restoration may mean that it is temporarily closed.

If it is, walk on down the street to the **Palacio Episcopal**, the former Bishops' Palace, situated on the left between Calle Sol y Ortega and Calle Tabares de Cala. It, too, has a notable patio, tucked away behind its imposing baroque façade: it was laid out between 1664 and 1681 when the palace was originally built. Initially designed for a local noble family, the *palacio* later became a casino, passing to the Bishop of Tenerife in the 19th century. It then remained home to generations of Tenerife bishops, La Laguna's former importance having seen it made a bishopric whose jurisdiction extended across the island. The town is still a major religious centre, hence the large numbers of clerics you're likely to see amidst the townspeople.

Next to the palace lies the **Museo de Historia de Tenerife** (see page 77), while opposite is a building (currently an economics institute) which once formed part of the original university (see panel, page 75). At Calle San Agustín 16 stands the Consejo Consultivo de Canarias building, built in 1746, which features another perfect Canarian patio.

Cigars
The Canaries have many links with Cuba, Brazil and other areas of central and South America, bonds formed by centuries of emigration from the islands to the New World. One shared activity is the cultivation of tobacco, production of which in Tenerife is concentrated near Garachico and La Laguna. Both towns are renowned for their cigars, in particular the famous *palmero*, a hand-crafted cigar rolled inside a single leaf.

Catedral▶ (Plaza Fray Albino, off Calle Obispo Rey Redondo. *Open* Mon–Sat 8–1.30, 5–7.30. Sun, services only. *Admission charge* free). La Laguna's huge cathedral, the Santa Iglesia Catedral, stands in Plaza Fray Albino at the top of Calle Obispo Rey Redondo, a short walk north of the town's main Plaza del Adelantado. Although founded in 1515 as the church of Los Remedios (on the initiative of Alonso Fernández de Lugo), its façade dates from 1820, while the interior was extensively remodelled in neo-classical style between 1904 and 1905.

Outside, the little square of lofty palm trees and ornamental pond provides a lovely prelude to what turns out to be an initially forebidding interior. Gloomy and cavernous, the inside of the church is slow to yield its treasures, which lie dotted around the slender columns and rather plain walls. The most striking is the tabernacle on the high altar, the work of Luján Pérez, one of the most accomplished of Canarian sculptors.

To the altar's right stands a gilded baroque *retablo* in the Capilla de la Virgen de los Remedios (Chapel of the Virgin of Remedies). This contrasts with a tomb to the right and just behind the high altar, a surprisingly understated sepulchre given that it belongs to the infamous Alonso Fernández de Lugo, conqueror of Tenerife and La Laguna's founding father. He was buried here in 1525 under a memorial plaque which bears the inscription *Conquistador de la Tenerife y La Palma* (Conqueror of Tenerife and La Palma).

Also worthy of note are the pulpit (1767) and the altarpieces by the Flemish painter Hendrik van Balen (1575–1632), best known as the teacher of Van Dyck.

The university
La Laguna's old Universidad de San Fernando was founded in 1701, its original building lying opposite the history museum on Calle San Agustín. The new university, home to some 12,000 students, was built on the edge of town in the 1950s. To date it is the only university in the Canary Islands, which means there are never enough places to meet demand. This shortcoming has led to repeated calls for a second university to be built in Gran Canaria.

The imposing 19th-century façade of La Laguna's cathedral

Corpus Christi
The festival of Corpus Christi is celebrated across Tenerife, but few towns make as much of this important religious feast day as La Laguna. For much of the celebrations, which go on through parts of late May and early June, many of the old town's streets are smothered with vast and intricately arranged carpets of flower petals. Weeks of painstaking planning and arrangement go into the displays, whose spectacle is enhanced by the use of brightly coloured volcanic sands from Las Cañadas (see page 127). Once the petals fade, or are trampled in the religious processions, the displays are lost forever. Be prepared for big crowds if you visit during this time, for the festival is extremely popular.

Canarian churches
Tenerife boasts many outstanding churches which reflect the finer points of Spanish colonial-style architecture. Their most distinctive feature is the *mudéjar* (Moorish-influenced coffered ceiling panels). These ornamental concave panels are often beautifully crafted, full of otiose carving and also some-times colourfully painted. Other points of interest include the churches' *retablos*, the highly ornamental screen-like structures around the altars, of which there may be many in a single church.

A sumptuous altar-piece in the Iglesia de Nuestra Señora de la Concepción

Iglesia de Nuestra Señora de la Concepción▶▶▶ The Church of Our Lady of the Immaculate Conception was begun sometime between 1502 and 1505, making it among the earliest religious foundations in Tenerife.

Today it has the status of a National Historic Monument, though the earliest church on the site – while remarkably unscathed – has to some extent been submerged beneath the Gothic, Renaissance and baroque remodellings imposed on the building over subsequent centuries. The additions notwithstanding, it remains an important example of the type of sanctuary built across Tenerife following the Spanish Conquest. The building's most distinctive feature, its seven-tiered tower, dates from the 17th century, since when its Moorish-influenced profile has been one of La Laguna's most familiar landmarks.

Inside the church, you are immediately struck by the superb **wooden ceiling**, a familiar feature of Canarian churches, and by the variety of its multi-coloured coffered panels. Equally striking are the **pulpit**, a masterpiece of 18th-century cedarwood carving – many consider it the finest in Spain – and the dark-hued choir stalls, a decorative ensemble which contains some of the Canaries' greatest carving. Also noteworthy are the beaten silver decoration of the high altar, the figure of the *Mater Dolorosa* by Luján Pérez, Fernando Estévez's figure of *Nuestra Señora de la Concepción*, and an assortment of fine *retablos*, many dating from the 17th century.

To one side of the church, on Calle Obispo Rey Redondo, stands the **Baptisterio** (baptistery) (*Open* varying hours, but generally Mon–Fri 10–noon; Sat–Sun,

services only. More restricted hours are usually 5–6.30 and services), home to two large fonts, one of which (faced with glazed tiles) was reputedly used to baptise pagan Guanche leaders. The family trees picked out above show the lineage of some of those baptised.

Museo de la Cienca y el Cosmos▶▶ (Via Láctea, off the La Cuesta road to Santa Cruz. *Open* Tue–Sun 10–8; shorter hours in winter. *Admission charge* inexpensive). This is La Laguna's Museum of Science and the Cosmos, situated close to the university on the town's fringes. It is an entertaining museum which should appeal to both adults and children. Opened in 1993, it features 70 or more interactive modules, consisting of models, experiments and scientific tricks designed to explain the workings of the sun, the earth, the universe and the human body. Among the more popular exhibits are a lie detector test, a maze of mirrors, a special screen which enables you to see your own skeleton, a small planetarium, and an artificial uterus complete with sounds from the womb.

Saints' days
The end of the eight days, or *Octavo*, devoted to the Feast of Corpus Christi, leaves the way open for the beginning of the *romería* season. A *romería* is a fiesta designed to celebrate the feast day of a particular saint. Many are held in towns and villages across Spain, Portugal and the Canary Islands. Two of the largest and most popular in Tenerife are the Romería de San Isidro in La Orotava (usually in mid-June) and La Laguna's Romería de San Benito (usually late June or early July). Both involve dancing, singing, eating, fireworks and religious processions. In mid-September, La Laguna celebrates Santísimo Cristo, another holy day, in similar mode.

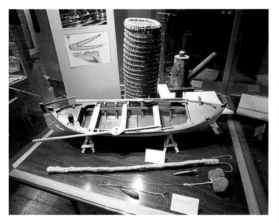

Exhibits in the Museo de Historia, which offers excellent coverage of the history of the island

Museo de Historia de Tenerife▶▶▶ (Calle San Agustín 22. *Open* Tue–Sat 10–5, Sun 10–2. *Admission charge* inexpensive) is by far the best historical museum in Tenerife, charting the history of the island through a series of well-displayed exhibits from the Spanish Conquest of the 15th century to the present day. Among the highlights is a room dedicated to a cartographic collection which includes some of the earliest maps of the Canaries.

Since 1993, the museum has been housed in the Casa Lercaro, a fine 16th-century townhouse (built in 1593) next to the old Episcopal Palace at the southern end of Calle San Agustín (see page 74). The house, as well as the street, is an attraction in itself, representing one of the Canaries' most impressive examples of a colonial-style nobleman's mansion.

Plaza del Adelantado▶▶▶ La Laguna's historic centre is small and compact, and best seen on the short tour which starts from the central Plaza del Adelantado. A lively little square, shaded with trees, it contains Tenerife's finest architectural ensemble of buildings, as well as a collection of cosy bars from where you can watch the world go by

The Plaza del Adelantado, a perfect spot to sit and watch the world go by

José de Anchieta

José de Anchieta was born in La Laguna in 1533 or 1534. At the age of 19 he emigrated to Brazil, where he became a Jesuit writer and historian. He also worked as a missionary (the first in Brazil), and is said to have converted over two million South American natives to the Christian faith. He was also instrumental in founding the Brazilian city of São Paolo. He died in 1597. An austere monument to him, a gift from the Brazilian government in 1959, stands just outside La Laguna in the middle of a roundabout on the Autopista del Norte.

before or after a tour of the town. Alternatively, drop into the town market, the **Mercado Municipal** (*Open* Mon–Sat 8–1), with its latticed gallery, to buy picnic provisions to eat on the square's leaf-shaded benches. The Plaza takes its name, incidentally, from *adelantado*, literally the 'advanced one', a reference to Alonso Fernández de Lugo (see page 30). The building alongside the market, the **Ermita de San Miguel**, was built on de Lugo's orders in 1507. It is now used as an exhibition hall.

Many of the square's larger houses are decorated with grand portals and coats of arms, or adorned with distinctive and beautiful balconies, a feature of many older Canarian townhouses. The first building to admire is the ayuntamiento► (town hall) in the northwest corner at the junction with Calle Obispo Rey Redondo. Founded in the 16th century, it was rebuilt with a typical Spanish-Canarian neo-classical façade in 1822. Inside are wall murals depicting scenes from the history of Tenerife, plus the flag reputedly planted by de Lugo on Tenerife when he claimed the island for Spain. Upstairs are some outstanding wooden panelling and a Moorish-style wooden-trellised oriel window. You should be able to get a glimpse of the interior during normal office hours (*Open* Mon–Fri 9–1, 4–7. *Admission charge* free). Alongside the town hall to the north (along Calle Obispo Rey Redondo) stands the **Casa de los Capitanes Generales** (House of the Captain Generals), built between 1624 and 1631 as the residence of the island's military marshals. It is currently used for temporary exhibitions and closed at other times.

Across the square's northern edge is the **Iglesia Convento Santa Catalina** (St Catalina Convent Church), noted for its unusual lattice-work gallery and an interior which contains a silver-plated altar and several first-rate baroque *retablos* (altar-pieces).

It is well worth wandering down Calle Dean Palahi, the street off the square to the right of Santa Catalina, to find the little courtyard by the church's side entrance. On one side of the courtyard note the door with the revolving cradle compartment, specifically built so that mothers abandoning their children to the care of the Church could do so anonymously.

Next to the church in the plaza's northeast corner stands the **Palacio de Nava**, a mansion built in imposing baroque colonial style. At the beginning of the 18th century it served as the town's leading social salon, playing host under its owner, the Marquis of Villanueva, to Tenerife's foremost writers, artists and thinkers. Opposite, in the plaza's southwest corner, stands the **Casa Padre Anchieta**, birthplace of the famous Jesuit missionary José de Anchieta (see panel, page 78).

From the square a tour of the town might continue with the Catedral (see page 75), reached via Calle Obispo Rey Redondo, or you could divert first to the church of **San Domingo**, situated on the street of the same name midway down the square's west side. Founded in the 16th century, it was originally the conventual church of a Dominican priory. Inside is a jarring mixture of old and modern paintings, the latter mostly the work of Mariano de Cossío (1890–1960). The adjoining garden contains a dragon tree (see page 122), less impressive now than in times past, having been struck and damaged by lightning.

Santuario del Cristo▶ Turn eastwards off Calle San Agustín on Calle Tabares de Cala (at the junction with the Museo de Historia de Tenerife) and a few minutes' walk brings you to the Plaza San Francisco, one of La Laguna's most imposing squares. In its southeast corner stands the Santuario del Cristo, a sanctuary church and important point of pilgrimage. The calm, narrow chapel within, an oasis of cool on hot summer days, contains the *Santísimo Cristo de la Laguna*, the Canaries' most highly venerated statue of Christ. Carved in the 15th century by a sculptor from Seville, the figure was brought to Tenerife by Alonso Fernández de Lugo in 1520.

79

La Laguna's cathedral dates from 1515, but has been altered many times over the years

Walking
Hiking has recently become easier in the Anaga Mountains, thanks to the designation of much of the area as the Parque Rural de Anaga. A new information centre with maps and pamphlets detailing set walks has opened at the Mirador Cruz del Carmen (see below), while marked trails have also been laid out by ICONA, a Spanish conservancy body, who also issue free maps.

English peak
Two theories account for the name given to the Pico del Inglés (English Peak) at the heart of the Anaga Mountains. One claims it was named in honour of an Englishman who managed to walk all the way here from La Laguna in a day. The other, more romantic notion, suggests its name dates from the era of Sir Walter Ralegh and Sir Francis Drake, when the English are supposed to have positioned spies on the peak to send signals to their treasure-seeking ships in the bays below.

Anaga birds
The roads from La Laguna to Las Mercedes wind their way through the most accessible areas of Tenerife's last remaining areas of native forest. The wooded slopes here are home to two of the Canaries' most threatened birds. Visitors should take advantage of viewpoints along the way and stop to look for rare and endangered Bolle's and laurel pigeons, both of which can be found here.

▶▶▶ **Las Montañas de Anaga**   59D3

The jagged and jumbled peaks of the Anaga Mountains fill Tenerife's northeastern corner, a beautiful and remote enclave still largely untouched by mass tourism. A wonderful area to explore on foot (see panel), with some of the island's most impressive landscapes, the region can also easily be seen by car (see Drive, pages 82–3), though the roads twist and turn and – despite constant up-grading – still leave much of the area inaccessible to drivers. Weather, too, can be a problem, for the mountains bear the brunt of the moisture-laden trade winds. As a result they are all too often shrouded in mist or (in winter) covered with a light dusting of snow. It's worth waiting for a good day, therefore, as mountain viewpoints are the region's main attraction. If you are travelling independently, it's possible to take a taxi tour or clamber aboard one of the TITSA buses from La Laguna which serve the area's outlying hamlets and villages.

Life and landscape The Anaga Mountains are some of the oldest on Tenerife, and as a result differ from the higher and more recent upland areas of Mount Teide. Peaks are steep and jagged, but relatively low – the highest point, Taborno, touches just 1,024m – though the fact that the slopes rise almost sheer from the sea lends them an added grandeur. Over millions of years the older, softer lava flows have been eroded, leaving only the harder basalt rocks, hence the mountains' rugged and contorted appearance. Close to, the slopes reveal themselves to be swathed in green, with vegetation running riot on the combination of fertile volcanic soils and the watery bounty of the wet northeasterly winds. Tucked away in the landscape's more tortured folds are ways of life that have remained unchanged for centuries: simple subsistence farming and ancient customs, as well as cave dwellings without power or running water.

Highlights La Laguna, and to a lesser extent Santa Cruz, are the best places from which to start a tour of the region. Any number of little villages such as Tacoronte (see page 85) and Bajamar (see page 60) can be incorporated into a road tour, together with more rewarding – if only because more remote – hamlets such as Taborno, Taganana, Almaciga and Chamorga. The region's real appeal, however, at least for non-walkers, are the quartet of *miradores* (viewpoints) that lie on key points on the road traversing the mountains' main ridges. If you are short of time, they can all easily be seen in reasonably rapid succession.

***Miradores* (Viewpoints)** Travelling east from La Laguna, the first of these is the **Mirador de Jardina**▶▶, which, as its name suggests, provides a belvedere for views over the Valle de Aguere and the garden-like hinterland of La Laguna. Close by, beyond the village of Las Mercedes, the mountain slopes are covered in the **Bosque de las Mercedes**▶▶, an important remnant of primeval laurel and evergreen forest. A little further east the road climbs to 920m and the **Mirador Cruz del Carmen**▶▶, which has a new visitors' centre, a restaurant and picnic area, and similar, if wider views over La Laguna and its surroundings. The little chapel here also boasts the much-venerated statue of Nuestra Señora de las Mercedes.

Next comes the highest (992m) and finest of the view-points, the **Mirador Pico del Inglés**▶▶▶, which offers one of the greatest views anywhere in the Canaries: on clear days you may even be able to see Gran Canaria. Its name, 'English Peak', has a variety of attributions (see panel, page 80).

Finally, much further east, the **Mirador Taganana**▶▶, or Mirador del Bailadero (759m), provides a bird's-eye view across both northern and southern flanks of the range. From here you can drive south to the superb beach at Playa de las Teresitas (see page 84).

Small hillside settlements dot the remote slopes of the Montañas de Anaga

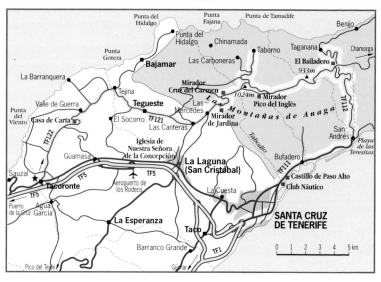

 **The Anaga Peninsula**

A drive through the Anaga Mountains, finishing at a superb beach and the city of Santa Cruz (72km; allow 4 hrs)

This excursion takes in the highlights of Tenerife's northeast peninsula, from the spectacular peaks and viewpoints of the Anaga Mountains to the golden sands and palm trees of the Playa de las Teresitas (see pages 83 and 84). Choose a clear day to get the best from the *miradores* (viewpoints) along the way, and aim to start in the morning to catch the Casa de Carta Museum. Note that this drive can be combined with the walk to the cave dwellings at Chinamada (see page 67).

Start from La Laguna or Tacoronte. To reach Tacoronte from La Laguna follow the main TF5 or the parallel, but more minor, TF820.

Tacoronte▶▶, a straggling town 20km east of Puerto de la Cruz, is famous for its wine and two fine churches (see page 85).

Take the TF122 north, noting the

ancient dragon tree as you are leaving town.

Just outside Valle de Guerra you come to the **Casa de Carta**▶▶▶, an excellent ethnographic museum housed in a wonderful late 17th-century mansion (see page 62).

Continue on the TF122 for 4km, turn right at Tejina onto the TF121 and continue for 12km through Tegueste, Las Canteras and Las Mercedes, stopping to admire the Mirador de Jardina and Mirador Cruz del Carmen (see page 80). After another 1.5km turn left (signposted toward Las Carboneras). Continue straight ahead, ignoring the second Las Carboneras sign, to Taborno (13km past the Mirador Cruz del Carmen).

Taborno▶ is a small village situated among the Anaga peaks at 1,024m, with marvellous views.

Retrace your route to where you turned left for Las Carboneras. Carry straight on, then rejoin the main TF121 road. This scenic road continues for 8km along the top of the main cumbre, *or ridge, with views to the north and south, offering a glimpse of the golden sands of Playa de las Teresitas. Turn off left towards El Bailadero.*

El Bailadero►► is another fine *mirador* (viewpoint), at which point you can either turn round and go south (left) to the beach at Playa de las Teresitas and Santa Cruz; drive further east to the hamlet of **Chamorga**►►, another good viewpoint; or head north to the village of **Taganana**► on an endlessly twisting road. Taganana is edged along a hillside which plunges to the coast, though the beaches here (2km) are not suitable for swimming because of their dangerous currents. The village was once a centre for sugar-cane production, but is known for its wine. The roads to Chamorga and Taganana end in dead-ends, so you will need to return to El Bailadero (these diversions will add 20km and 14km respectively to the drive).

From El Bailadero head south on the TF112 to San Andrés and the Playa de las Teresitas.

Playa de las Teresitas►►► (see page 84) is a superb beach, purposebuilt with millions of tonnes of sand imported from the Sahara. It is safe for swimming, rarely too busy (except at weekends when the locals come) and remains pleasantly unspoiled by any surrounding development.

Continue back along the coastal road for 8km to the waterfront of Santa Cruz.

Just before you reach the centre of **Santa Cruz**►►► (see page 40), look for the Club Náutico (Yacht Club), beside which are the remains of the Castillo de Paso Alto. From here in 1797, Santa Cruz enjoyed its finest military moment, repulsing an attack by Rear-Admiral Nelson (see page 44). It is comparatively easy to park close to the centre of Santa Cruz on the main road in the late afternoon. This time of day, as the city emerges from its siesta and the streets come alive, is also a good time to visit.

An idyllic retreat in mountainous countryside near Taborno

Artificial but still beautiful, Playa de las Teresitas was constructed with Sahara sand

A quieter beach
It would be hard to take exception to the Playa de las Teresitas, but if you want a slightly quieter beach, then head for the nearby Playa de las Gaviotas. To reach it continue on the road beyond San Andrés towards Igueste, where a *mirador* (viewpoint) and headland provide excellent views of the Teresitas beach below. Further on, beyond the headland, you can look down on the small black-sand Playa de las Gaviotas. The beach, which is reached via a steep road, has a few facilities and is especially popular with nudists.

▶ ▶ ▶   Playa de las Teresitas   59D2

One of the most remarkable things about Tenerife's tremendous success as a holiday destination is that it has been achieved with the almost complete absence of beaches. The island, contrary to popular opinion, has few good stretches of sand, and those that it does have are often pebbly or made up of rather disconcerting black, volcanic sand. Compounding these ironies is the fact that the best beach on the island, the Playa de las Teresitas, just 9km north-east of Santa Cruz, is an artificial affair, created in the early 1970s with over four million sackfuls of sand (98,000 cubic metres) brought by ship from the Sahara desert.

Curving around an azure bay in an elegant crescent moon, the beach is a vision of pure white-yellow sand and picture-perfect palm trees. An artificial breakwater off shore not only keeps the sand from being washed away, but also ensures a safe and gently shelving area for swimming and bathing. The locals are justifiably proud of their 'instant' beach, which remains clean and well-groomed despite its proximity to Santa Cruz. It's also surprisingly uncrowded, except for peak weekends in spring and summer, when local people make it a busy home from home. Parking is available off the road which curves behind the beach, and pedalos – and a few other watersports opportunities – are also available. There is also a popular windsurfing school.

At the far end of the beach lies the village of **San Andrés▶**, a fishing port which has managed to retain a fair amount of its intrinsic charm. It's particularly well known for bars and fish restaurants, most of which are spread out along the coast road below the old village centre.

85

Mesa del Mar

Mesa del Mar is a smallish resort just 3km north of Tacoronte, reached by steep and narrow flower-edged streets. Its hillsides are covered with the usual medley of small houses and large apartment blocks, together with one particular hotel complex noted for its architectural daring. If you just want a quick dip, there are several small coves suitable for swimming and sunbathing.

▶▶ Tacoronte   58B2

Tacoronte's principal fame is its **wine**, the fertile arable land around the little township being one of the few areas in Tenerife where agriculture is possible without extensive artificial irrigation. Large local vineyards produce some of the island's most prized wines, many of them light, sherry-like Malvasia varieties with a staggering 17 per cent strength.

If wine holds little appeal, the lively little town, located just 20km east of Puerto de la Cruz, has a handful of other attractions. Chief among these are two churches, both within a few hundred metres of each other close to the bustling town centre and its teeming side streets. The first, the **Iglesia del Cristo de los Dolores** (Church of the Sorrows of Christ), is part of a former Augustinian foundation, and is famous for a graphic and much-venerated 17th-century figure of Christ. It is also notable for a high altar gilded in Mexican silver and several beautifully coloured coffered ceiling panels.

Some way down the hill, a distinctive grey and white tower marks out the **Iglesia de Santa Catalina**, founded in 1664, which also boasts several outstanding ceiling panels, as well as fine altar panels, appealing decorated woodwork, and several of Tenerife's largest and most impressive *retablos* (altar-pieces).

In front of the church is a little plaza graced with Indian laurel trees, though the most famous tree locally is a giant **dragon tree** (see page 122) close by on the Bajamar road: ancient and weighty, it is carefully propped up with iron supports. More arboreal interest awaits 2km south, at **Agua García**, with primeval forest made up of heath and laurel woodland.

There's no mistaking the bell-tower of the Iglesia de Santa Catalina

VALLE DE LA OROTAVA

VALLE DE LA OROTAVA

Viewpoints
It is worth dragging yourself away from La Orotava
and Puerto de la Cruz to
explore the Valle de la
Orotava, particularly the
network of little roads
which threads through the
area's forested reaches
above Icod el Alto, Palo
Blanco and Aguamansa. If
you are short of time and
want to enjoy one of the
best views of the region,
the finest viewpoint is
probably the Mirador el
Lance, located about 6km
west of La Orotava on the
TF221 road just before
Icod el Alto.

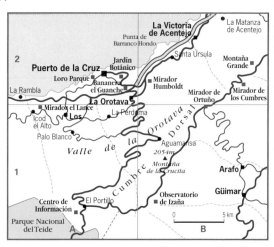

*Previous pages: the
magnificent inner
courtyard of Casas
de los Balcones, La
Orotava. Below: rock
formations in the
Valle de la Orotava*

The Valle de la Orotava (Orotava Valley) is not really a
valley at all, but a beautifully verdant plateau that slopes
gently from the mountains to the sea roughly midway
along Tenerife's northern coast. It measures just 10 by
11km, but contains two of the island's major towns – **La
Orotava** and **Puerto de la Cruz** – and a variety of landscapes that range from forest and barren mountains to
pockets of intensively cultivated land swathed with
bananas, fruit trees, vegetables and vines.

Not so long ago this was one of the most
beautiful areas on the islands, its chequerboard
of fields and woods framed by the sea on one
side and the looming slopes of Mount Teide on
the other. Today its green-swathed landscapes
are still memorable, especially when viewed on
a clear day from one of the region's many viewpoints (see panel). But at the same time the
modern sprawl of local towns and villages,
Puerto de la Cruz in particular, has dotted the
once pristine countryside with ever-increasing
amounts of newer development. Escape is still
possible, however, especially in the forests and
mountain reaches of the Caldera de las
Cañadas, an area dotted with mountain huts,
picnic areas, viewpoints and a series of well-
marked trails and footpaths.

Whether you venture into the hinterland or
not, the region contains two towns which
should not be missed: inland, La Orotava has a
wonderful old centre, full of narrow, cobbled
streets and historic buildings; and on the coast,
Puerto de la Cruz, atmospheric and blessed
with a life of its own, is the longest-established
and best of Tenerife's many coastal resorts.

It began life as La Orotava's port, a legacy of
the time when the area's fertile soils and
favourable climate made it one of the island's

*Opposite: part of the
Valle de la Orotava
as seen from the
Mirador Humboldt*

most prosperous little enclaves. Today La Orotava is
something of a backwater, albeit a prosperous one, while
its former port has become one of the Canaries' most
important towns.

VALLE DE LA OROTAVA

Arrival

Many people approach La Orotava from Puerto de la Cruz, a route which takes you along the C821 road and up through the modern part of the town to the northeast of the historic centre. Follow signs to the centre, attempting to park when you arrive on Avenida José Antonio. From here it's just a few minutes' walk to Plaza de la Constitución, the heart of the old town.

Sightseeing

Some of La Orotava's narrow streets are rather steep, but few places of note within the old centre are more than a few minutes' walk away from one another. The best place to start a tour is in the main Plaza de la Constitución. From here you could walk north on Calle Tomás Zerolo to see Santo Domingo, the Museo de Artesanía Iberoamericana and the Casa Torrehermosa. Then walk west on Calle Viera and south on Calle Cologán to visit the church of Nuestra Señora de la Concepción. From here the Colegio leads south into Calle San Francisco, one of the town's most rewarding streets. Here you'll find the town's best-known sight, the lovely balconied townhouse, the Casas de los Balcones.

Tourist information

The tourist office is at Plaza General Franco I (tel: 33 00 50).

▶▶ **La Orotava**   *88A2*

La Orotava is one of the most evocative townscapes in the Canaries. A superbly preserved historical fossil, its old centre is laced with steep, cobbled streets, fine old town-houses, lovely façades and handsome balconies, impressive public palaces, and a range of building styles and adornments that span some four centuries of colonial and indigenous architecture. It makes a lovely place to explore for an hour or so, providing an antidote to Tenerife's brash and more modern resorts, and fully living up to the claim emblazoned on its coat-of-arms to be a *villa muy noble y leal* – 'a most loyal and noble town'.

Situated close to the larger and more sprawling Puerto de la Cruz, the town lies at the heart of the Valle de la Orotava, its surroundings a mild-weathered oasis of prosperous agricultural land. Produce from this hinterland has long been the town's lifeblood, the settlement having grown rapidly almost from the moment of its 'official' foundation at the beginning of the 16th century. A town existed on the site before the arrival of the Spanish, however, when Araotava – as it was then known – formed the focal point of Taora, the richest of the Guanches' patchwork of kingdoms. After the conquest, its benign climate and strategic position attracted countless Spanish settlers, many of whom grew rich through the export of wine, bananas and cochineal. Eventually the inland town acquired a port, Puerto de la Orotava, a modest quay which in time would develop into the present-day Puerto de la Cruz. In 1648, it achieved the status of a township, courtesy of a decree by King Philip IV of Spain.

Today La Orotava still has a wealthy air, though its economic primacy has been surrendered to its former port, a town grown rich on the tourist boom of the last three decades.

Calle San Francisco▶▶ Historic La Orotava is a web of lovely old streets, but few of them capture the flavour of the town's 17th-century colonial heyday as nicely as Calle San Francisco. An occasionally steep thoroughfare on the west side of the old quarter, it contains the town's most famous sight – the **Casas de los Balcones** (see page 91) and – about 100m to the south – the **Hospital de la Santísima Trinidad** (Holy Trinity Hospital). Built in 1600 as a Franciscan monastery, the latter sight became a hospital in 1884, a function it still fulfils, now providing care for the mentally disabled. The courtyard cloister is only occasionally open to visitors (Mon–Sat 4–5.30, Sun 10.30–noon). Most people pause at the hospital, open or not, to enjoy the views of the Valle de la Orotava from its terrace and balcony. At the hospital entrance notice the small revolving cradle, a legacy of the days when foundling children and unwanted babies were anonymously left here to the care of the convent.

Across the road from the hospital, among the old houses and landscaped gardens, try to make out the strange-shaped building topped with an orb, one of several former flour mills for which the area was once famous. Power for grinding the wheat was provided by water cascading down the area's steep slopes. You'll come across more of these 17th- and 18th-century mills if

you continue south into Calle Dr González García. Some are still working concerns, though now they are driven by electricity rather than water. One or two, notably the mill at Calle Dr González García 3, have little shops and interiors which are occasionally open to the public.

Casas de los Balcones▶▶▶ (Calle San Francisco 3. *Open* Mon–Fri 9–1.30, 4–7.30; Sat 9–1.30. *Admission charge* (to museum) inexpensive.) La Orotava's most famous sight takes its name – 'Houses of the Balconies' – not from the lovely flower-hung balconies which look down over Calle San Francisco, but from the still lovelier wooden balconies which overlook this glorious building's beguiling interior courtyard. Begun in 1632, the present building – a superb example of traditional Canarian architecture – began life as two houses (now joined together) and was originally the home of a wealthy local family. Its early history is recalled in the interesting little museum on the upper floor. Approaching from the street, shadowed by the balconies overhead, you enter the building through some redoubtable doors, escaping from the bustle of the street into a verdant and stone-flagged courtyard festooned with ferns and other plants.

After admiring the beautifully worked wooden balconies you should wander the ground floor, which is

A townhouse on Calle San Francisco

Embroidery
Casas de los Balcones is an embroidery school of some repute. For over 50 years it has trained around two dozen pupils in the fast-vanishing traditional stitches and designs once practised across Tenerife. In the not so distant past the *calados* (open embroidery) of every town and village would have had its own distinctive pattern. Not so today, when only the work of bodies such as the school at the Casas de los Balcones helps preserve traditional designs.

VALLE DE LA OROTAVA

Historic flowers
Flowers have not always featured in La Orotava's famous Corpus Christi procession. They were introduced by a local aristocrat, the Señora del Castillo de Monteverde, when the traditional procession showed signs of dying out. She attempted to revive interest by laying a carpet of flowers in front of her house. The idea quickly caught on, with huge quantities of heather delicately singed to provide a range of colours from green to black. Flowers and petals were then overlaid to create the picture.

largely dedicated to an *artesanía*, or craft and souvenir shop, an over-busy commercial enterprise which at times is very busy with coachloads of visitors. This said, the quality of the crafts on display is high, and from time to time you can watch craftspeople demonstrating skills such as *bordados* (embroidery), basket-making and cigar-rolling. Local lace, superb embroidery (see panel, page 91), costumed dolls and miscellaneous table linen are the main wares, though various crafts from mainland Spain are also available. Prices are high, but if you're serious about buying, this is one of the better places to come. Napkins and tablecloths are some of the best buys, but if these are beyond your means, go for one of the cheaper, but still beautiful handkerchiefs.

When the buying and browsing begin to pale, head upstairs, where you walk along some of the balconies, all delicate pillars and intricately worked panels, to reach the upper floor and its museums. Here, amidst the smell of wood polish and creak of ancient floorboards, the sense of history is almost tangible, notwithstanding the fact that the rooms are now only half-heartedly decorated with antiques and paintings. In few other places, save the courtyard below with its pottery and old wine press, is the sense of La Orotava's former colonial splendour quite so strong. After leaving the house, be sure to pop into the Casa del Turista, a similar building across the street (see page 93).

Part of La Orotava's famous Casas de los Balcones

Casa del Turista►► (3 Calle San Francisco. *Open* Mon–Fri 8.30–6.30; Sat 8.30–5; Sun 8.30–11. *Admission charge* free.) The Casa del Turista, also known by the slightly more appealing name of the Casa de la Alfombra, lies virtually opposite the Casas de los Balcones (see page 91). Older than its neighbour – it was begun in 1590 – it originally formed part of the Convento Molina (the Mill Convent), part of whose former cemetery survives to the building's rear. Like the Casas de los Balcones, it is now largely given over to a craft and gift shop, offering similar goods to its competitor (though both shops are actually under the same management). Whether you want to spend money or not, it is well worth dropping into the building to admire the view over the Valle de la Orotava, and to watch demonstrations of the sand-painting techniques that are used during La Orotava's famous Corpus Christi celebrations (see panel, page 96).

Architectural details
Courtyards of the type used in the Casas de los Balcones were a direct lift from the Spanish preference for such features in large town- and country houses. Other borrowings included the use of complicated cast-iron balconies, a motif common in Portuguese colonial baroque architecture. Poorer houses on Tenerife tended to be single-storey white-washed dwellings, roofed with crude and irregular tiles. Decoration was usually restricted to occasional carving around doors and windows. On older houses windows were often arranged irregularly, a device which helps date such buildings to the 16th century. By the 17th century, windows were arranged more symmetrically around a central door.

Sand painting, on display at the Casa del Turista

Centro Cultural Canario►► (Calle Carrera 7, off Calle San Francisco. *Open* Mon–Fri 9–7.30; Sat 10–3: the restaurant and snack bar remain open later in the evenings Mon–Fri.) This enterprising and recently completed cultural centre just off Calle San Francisco consists of a museum, crafts shop, restaurant and *tasca* (snack bar). Most of its components have been skilfully incorporated into an old townhouse begun around 1610. The museum – known as El Pueblo Guanche – is the main draw, offering an enthusiastic and well-presented summary of the history of the local Guanche people. The key attraction, as ever in museums connected with the Guanches, is a wonderfully macabre mummy.

Hijuela del Botánico►► Immediately behind and to the southwest of the Palacio Municipal (see panel) lies the Hijuela del Botánico, La Oratava's lovely but little-known botanical garden. Its name means 'Little Daughter of the Botanical Garden', a reference to the fact that it is considered an off-shoot of the famous Jardín de Botánico in Puerto de la Cruz (see page 103). Begun in 1923, the garden now boasts some 3,000 tropical and sub-tropical plants and shrubs, many of them rare and exotic species, as well as a dragon tree (see page 122) and a collection of the Canary palms. These days its gates are all too often

Palacio Municipal
La Orotava's town hall stands in Calle Carrera del Escultor Estevéz. Built between 1871 and 1891, its austerity is relieved by the tympanum, which displays the town's coat-of-arms. This contains an image of what was once the largest and most venerable dragon tree in the Canaries (blown down during a tempest in 1868). Also depicted are allegorical figures representing History, Education, Justice and Agriculture. The square in front of the building provides the setting for the most ambitious coloured-sand and flower-petal displays during the town's Corpus Christi celebrations (see panel, page 92).

locked, though much of the interior can be seen from outside. If you are determined to get inside, special visits can sometimes be arranged through the tourist office or town hall. The entrance is on Calle Tomas Pérez, off Calle Hermano Apolinar.

Iglesia de Nuestra Señora de la Concepción►► Just off the pleasant little Plaza Casañas in La Orotava's north-western corner lies the Iglesia de Nuestra Señora de la Concepción, the town's most important church. A baroque masterpiece, the dusky-stoned building was constructed between 1768 and 1788 on the site of an earlier 16th-century church destroyed by an earthquake in 1705. With its high, honey-coloured dome and twin onion-topped towers, it forms one of the town's more distinctive landmarks. Its prominence and outstanding interior decoration made it a national monument in 1948. The interior, which is cool and restrained, may seem a little disappointing to the uninitiated (and is slightly in need of repair), though many of its fixtures and fittings are regarded as masterpieces of the sculptor's art. The chief treasures are the high altar and its stirring tabernacle, a work in marble and alabaster by the Italian sculptor Giuseppe Gagini, a survivor from the earlier church. Also outstanding are the screen, the gloriously carved choir stalls, the statues of the *Mater Dolorosa and St John* (by Luján Pérez) and the baroque *retablo* figure of the Virgen de la Concepción. If possible, also try to take a peek in the church's treasury, among whose collection of religious ornaments is a selection of artefacts which once belonged to St Paul's Cathedral in London.

Museo de Artesanía Iberoamericana►►► (Calle Tomás Zerolo 34. *Open* Mon–Sat 9.30–6.) La Orotava's most fascinating museum, the 'Spanish-American Handicraft Museum', occupies the superbly restored precincts of the former 17th-century Convento de Santo Domingo. It stands in the old town's northern corner, close to the church of Santo Domingo. Inside, arranged in rooms around the convent's cloisters, lies a first-rate collection of ceramics, textiles, basketwork, woodwork and musical instruments. Many are drawn from a variety of Latin American countries. Pride of place goes to displays on the museum's upper floor, which are devoted to pieces of folk art and a variety of interesting ritualistic artefacts used in ancient rites and ceremonies such as Mexico's Day of the Dead. Also here, a little out of context, are examples of modern furniture design as well as award-winning contemporary Canarian crafts. If you've not yet had your fill of island handicrafts, drop into the Casa Torrehermosa directly opposite the museum (see panel).

Opposite: Hijuela del Botánico, La Orotava's delightful oasis

Casa Torrehermosa
The Casa Torrehermosa is another in a long line of lovely old townhouses in La Orotava which have been converted to contemporary usage. In this case the building is run by an organisation which devotes itself to promoting the best of Tenerife's many high-quality handicrafts. (*Open* Mon–Fri 9.30–6.30, Sat 9.30–2)

Fun folk art from the Museo de Artesanía

Ceramic museum
About 2km west of La Orotava at Carretera de la Luz-Las Candias lies the Museo de Cerámica (Ceramic Museum), a 1,000-piece array of traditional Canarian pottery. The collection is housed in the Casa Tafuriaste, a fine 17th-century traditional house. Video displays describe how ceramics are made, and there are also occasional pottery-making demonstrations (*Open* Mon–Sat 10–6).

Corpus Christi
La Orotava's Corpus Christi day celebrations are some of the most famous on the island, thanks to the fact that many of the town's plazas are covered with designs worked in intricately painted and patterned sand and flower designs. Artists work on the pieces for weeks, producing a crop of vast floral and geometrical motifs (and the occasional Old Master). Time and effort notwithstanding, the designs are quickly trampled once the religious festivities and processions get underway. Aim to arrive in the days preceding the festival to admire the designs, or visit the Casa del Turista to see how they're achieved (see page 93).

Plaza de la Constitución▶▶▶ Plaza de la Constitución, La Orotava's main square, is not only the best place to start a tour of the old town, but also offers a sweeping overview of the town and the distant coastline from its loftily positioned parapet. Little can have changed in the panorama across the centuries, only the hazy modern suburbs of Puerto de la Cruz suggesting the passing of time. The square is the town's social heart, its bars and cafés making good vantage points from where to watch the world go by. Various historic buildings lie on or close to the plaza, most notably the monastery and monastery church of **San Agustín** (St Augustine). Begun in 1694, much of the former monastery is now given over to the Conservatoria de Música, a music school. The church, by contrast, distinguished by its dark-hued bell-tower, is still

consecrated, and boasts a handful of first-rate *retablos* (altar-pieces).

Slightly set back from the square on the hill to the south lies the **Liceo de Taoro**, a gentleman's club whose grand approach and surrounding park puts one in mind of an English country house.

Built in the 19th century, the house served as a school before becoming a club, though its present-day status doesn't stop you gaining a glimpse of the building. Its rooms are often opened to the public during art exhibitions, and there is a pleasantly smart café-bar with a balcony where you can eat and drink in style. Upstairs, try to see the club's permanent art exhibitions, among which figure the so-called *Romera Mayor*, portraits of the town's *romería* festival queens since 1956.

A dignified approach to the Liceo de Taoro

Wine and spirits

■ **Drinks are a major part of many people's holidays, whether it's wine with a meal or a leisurely coffee in a seafront bar. Tenerife's wines are of limited but ever-improving quality – though there are plenty of Spanish wines to choose from – but its spirits and liqueurs are of mind-boggling variety and strength.** ■

Coffee

Kick-start shots of coffee are essential parts of the Tenerife daily ritual. In a bar or after dinner ask for a *café solo*, similar to an espresso, or a *café con leche*, a milky coffee usually only drunk by foreigners. If you want a drop of milk with your *café solo* ask for a *cortado*. If you want it without sugar and condensed milk already added (as is common), ask for a *cortado natural*. For coffee with a shot of rum or brandy request a *carajillo*.

Beer

Tenerife's larger resorts sell all manner of British and foreign beers, often from the keg, but Spain and Tenerife's light, lager-like beers (*cerveza*) are the ones the locals drink. Tenerife's main brewery is known as C.C.C., but its beer is universally known as *Doradá* (ask for it by name). Larger towns have it *caña* (on draught), but in small village bars it may only be available in bottles. Note that it comes in two strengths: the normal 'Gold Top' is the most popular. San Miguel is the best-known mainland beer.

Heritage Wine in the Canary Islands has a long and proud history. Before the arrival of the Spanish, the primitive inhabitants of El Hierro, one of the Canaries' smallest islands, distilled a liqueur extracted from laurel berries (thought to be the only alcoholic drink on the archipelago before the conquest).

It's perhaps no coincidence that El Hierro's modern-day wine, *vino herreño*, is considered one of the Canaries' best. Around 400 years ago 'Canary Sack', or 'Malmsey' – made from the sweet malvasia grape – was one of Britain's most popular wines, celebrated in verse by Shakespeare and others. Its export made the Canaries rich, albeit for a short time, the fashion for it falling away almost as quickly as it had begun.

Production Today wine production across the islands is growing, with some ten per cent of all agricultural land given over to vines. Conditions for production are ideal on Tenerife, not least those offered by climate and soils, the latter a rich and fertile legacy of the island's volcanic origins. Since 1984 there has also been a shake-up in quality control, resulting in a renaissance in quality and sales. Which makes it a surprise that more wine – and better-quality wine – is not readily available to visitors. Most wine is made for local consumption – no rural home, it is said, is without its *salud* (wine cellar). As a result only a few bottles find their way onto supermarket shelves or restaurant tables. Small-scale production methods also make the wine expensive. This is why shop wines and restaurant house wines (*vino de casa*) tend to be imports from the Spanish mainland, where wine is produced almost as cheaply as water.

Varieties Good Spanish wines are easily found – try bottles from Rioja, Valdepenas and Jumilla. So, too, is Spanish *cava* (champagne) – Freixenet and Delapierre are names to look out for. Good local wines, however, are harder to come by. El Hierro's wine has a good reputation (see above), as does Tenerife's award-winning *Viña Norte* from El Sauzal, a village 16km northeast of Puerto de la Cruz (see page 64).

You can also still buy Malmsey or *Malvasía*, the wine which so excited Elizabethan England. It comes in two varieties: *dulce* (sweet) or *seco* (dry). The latter, incidentally, makes a good aperitif if drunk well chilled. *Sangria*, a well-known concoction, is a robust and potent mixture of red wine, orange juice, brandy, mineral water, ice and slices of fruit: it is usually reserved for foreigners. Normal

table wine is *vino del país*, a glass of wine in a bar *uno vaso de vino tinto* (red) or *blanco* (white).

Liqueurs If the selection of Canary wines is limited, the same cannot be said of its spirits. Tenerife's basic hootch is *ron*, a fiery white rum made from sugar cane (and often mixed with cola). It's available from just about every shop and supermarket on the island. Also common is *ron miel*, a dark, orange-tasting liqueur made from rum and 'honey', though the honey is distilled palm-tree sap (collected from La Gomera). Almost as ubiquitous are *cobana*, a yellow banana liqueur, and *Larios*, Tenerife's local brand of gin. You will also come across *coñac* (brandy), the two best-known brands being Soberano and Fundador. Other more exotic liqueurs are also made from oranges, almonds, cherries, coconuts and pineapples. At the other extreme, be sure to indulge in freshly squeezed *zumo* (fruit juice): *naranja* (orange) and *limon* (lemon) are the best.

Ice and water
Tap water in some parts of Tenerife may not always be reliable. To be safe stick to *agua mineral* (mineral water), either *agua con gas* (fizzy) or *agua sin gas* (still). Bear in mind that ice, unless made from mineral water, may be equally unreliable: to avoid it ask for a drink *sin hielo* (without ice).

Paying
Usually you pay more when sitting down in a bar or café indoors or at outside tables where there is waiter service: standing at the bar is the cheapest option. If you are spending the evening in a bar, then often you pay for the entire evening's drinks before leaving, not after each round of drinks.

Wine from the Canary Islands has been celebrated for over 400 years

VALLE DE LA OROTAVA

Information and transport

Puerto de la Cruz's tourist office is located at Plaza de la Iglesia 3 (tel: 38 60 00) at the heart of the old town close to the harbour. Maps and brochures of the town are available (most with English translations). You can also obtain bus timetables for links to other parts of the island. Buses depart from the Estación de Autobuses in the west of town. The main taxi rank is in Plaza del Charco (tel: 38 49 10 to call a taxi), while motorcycles and scooters can be hired from many outlets: check the total charge for rentals carefully and ensure that they include insurance.

Solidified lava forms part of Puerto's dramatic waterfront

►► Puerto de la Cruz   88A2

Puerto de la Cruz, more commonly known as Puerto, is one of the Canary Islands' major resorts. It is distinguished by a superb setting, with Mount Teide rising to the rear, and has managed to maintain an appealing life and character of its own. Its delightful old centre remains miraculously untainted by the presence of thousands of holidaymakers and the vast ranks of soulless hotels and modern suburbs that have mushroomed over the last two or three decades (Puerto has beds for over 30,000 visitors). Though a million people visit the town annually, local people still live here, lending Puerto a character and colour almost unknown in the big resorts.

There's also plenty to do and see, with countless bars, restaurants and clubs (plus a casino), while the old town is a charming array of little streets, open markets, a pretty harbour, flower-hung buildings and pleasant seafront promenades. Beaches are poor, and the weather occasionally cloudy, but you can swim and sunbathe in the superb **Lido San Telmo**, an artificial leisure complex of pools, cafés, sun terraces and green space. For entertainment, visitors from across the island flock to the **Loro Parque**, a wonderful zoo and wildlife park just out of town (connected to the town centre by free shuttle buses). Escape from the bustle of the town centre is also possible in the famous **Jardín Botánico** (Botanical Garden) and **Bananera el Guanche** (a banana 'theme park').

Puerto's history is simply told, for it began life at the beginning of the 17th century as a *puerto* (port) for La Orotava (see page 90), handling the sugar, wine, banana and other agricultural exports for which the Valle de la

There's more to see than just bananas at the Bananera el Guanche

Orotava was renowned. However, the town's rocky coastline and heavy swell also made loading and unloading ships difficult, and in time the bulk of Tenerife's sea trade passed to Santa Cruz de Tenerife. As trade declined, tourism took its place.

Bananera el Guanche►►► This fascinating and rewarding one-off attraction might easily be known as 'Banana World', for in essence it's a minor theme park devoted to all things banana, a commodity which for over a century has been one of Tenerife's staple exports (see page 68). Unmissable if you are at all curious about bananas and how they grow, the *bananera* (banana plantation) also offers a lovely pastoral garden in which you can relax and escape Puerto's frantic town centre bustle. Videos and display boards, seen on a self-guided tour, explain the various stages of a banana's development.

It is not all bananas, however, for the lovely garden area offers pleasant views of the Valle de la Orotava and contains a wealth of other exotic plants and trees, among them mangoes, passion fruit, papayas, pawpaws, pineapples, kiwi fruit and avocados (look out in particular for the avocado tree that produces some 1,500kg of fruit a year). Still more unusual trees and fruits you may not have encountered elsewhere include the *toronjas* (giant grapefruit), *zapote* (chewing-gum tree) and *chirimoyas* (custard apples). You can also see coffee trees, sugar-cane and cocoa plants, and enjoy a collection of some 400 cacti and the bright floral splashes of bougainvillaea, hibiscus and poinsettia.

Admission to the plantation usually includes a free banana, a taste of local cheese and figs, a shot of Tenerife's potent banana liqueur, and the chance to buy

Beaches
Puerto de la Cruz is built on a rocky and wave-battered coast, its seafront almost the last place you would normally choose to build a beach resort. To off-set the town's inhospitable natural coastline, the council have made sterling efforts to create a series of sheltered artificial beaches and bathing areas. The best and best-known is the Lido San Telmo complex (see page 104). Others include the Playa Jardín to the west of the town (see panel, page 106); the Playa Martiánez to the east; and the Proyecto Parque Marítimo Municipal, a new development west of the harbour that will include large areas of public open spaces.

VALLE DE LA OROTAVA

St Elmo

St Elmo, or San Telmo in Spanish, is the patron saint of sailors and fishermen, thanks largely to one of several unpleasant aspects of his death. An Italian bishop, he was martyred in the 4th century. In the course of his martyrdom he had his intestines wound around a ship's windlass. The intestinal angle means that he is also invoked against stomach disorders. 'St Elmo's Fire' is the name sometimes given to the blue stormlights on ships.

Tomás de Iriarte

Few of Tenerife's denizens have made a splash on the European stage. Tomás de Iriarte, born on the island in 1750, is an exception (though he left the Canaries at the age of 13 to live with his uncle in Madrid). In time he became an archivist and translator in the civil service, achieving fame at the same time as a writer, translator and playwright. As a writer he is best known for *La Música*, a didactic poem, and for *Fábulas Literarias*, a work which lampooned the literary failings of his day and attempted to improve the taste of the public at large. His plays were often satires on the lumpen idleness of the upper classes, which he contrasted with the honest toil and industry of the poor. He was also a member of the 'Fonda de San Sebastián', the leading Spanish literary circle of his day. He died in Madrid in 1791.

cheeses, local honeys and an assortment of tropical fruits and flowers ready packed to take home. Soil has been removed from the fruit and flowers and the produce sealed to meet UK customs entry requirements: packages can usually be delivered to your hotel on the eve of departure for easy transportation to the airport. The plantation lies some 2km from the town centre on Puerto's south-eastern margins, but can easily be reached by taxi or free shuttle buses from the waterfront near the Hotel San Felipe and Playa Martiánez. (On the La Orotava–Autopista del Norte road. *Open* daily 9–6. *Admission charge* moderate).

Capilla de San Telmo►► The Capilla de San Telmo, or Chapel of St Elmo (also known as the Ermita, or Hermitage of St Elmo), forms the focus of two or three sights on the popular and pretty waterfront promenade, the **Calle de San Telmo**, situated just to the east of the harbour and old town centre. The modest, brilliant-white chapel was founded in 1626 by local sailors in honour of St Elmo, their patron saint (see panel). Despite numerous fires and restorations over the centuries – not to mention the tourist bustle on all sides – it has managed ever since to retain the simple air of a fisherman's chapel. Its treasures are few, a once-revered statue of San Pedro González Telmo having been destroyed by fire in 1778 (the present statue is a 1783 copy). The various coats of arms behind the altar belong to seamen and Dominican clerics associated with the chapel across the years.

The Chapel of St Elmo, built by sailors in 1626

The square adjoining the chapel, the **Plaza de los Reyes Católicos** (Square of the Catholic Kings), takes its name from Ferdinand of Aragon (1452–1516) and his wife, Isabella of Castile (1451–1504), Spanish rulers at the time Tenerife was conquered on behalf of Spain. The bust at its heart represents Francisco de Miranda (1750–1816), a leading protagonist in the struggle for Venezuelan independence (his parents were born in Puerto de la Cruz before emigrating to Venezuela). Note the sentry boxes and old teak fences close by, remnants of the old defensive Battery of St Elmo. From here the promenade leads eventually to a little square known as the **Punta del Viento** (Windy Point), its black-rocked shore pounded by crashing breakers and overlooked by a modern sculpture of a wind-blown girl.

Casa Iriarte▶ This historic 18th-century house once belonged to the Iriarte family, and was the birthplace of the family's best-known scion, the writer and translator Tomás de Iriarte (see panel, page 102). Quite what he would make of his birthplace today is hard to imagine. Once regarded as one of Puerto's foremost pieces of old-style architecture, the house is currently a souvenir shop (one of many in this street), a function which has stripped it of much its of former charm and beauty. This said, the building retains a superb carved wood balcony, as well as a lovely interior courtyard and patio. Upstairs there is a rather half-hearted maritime museum, its collection of model ships and maritime ephemera only worth seeing on the rainiest of days (Calle San Juan, off Calle Iriarte. *Open* Mon–Sat 9.30–6 *Admission charge* moderate).

Jardín Botánico▶▶▶ Puerto's magnificent botanical gardens were founded in 1788 on the orders of King Carlos III of Spain (1716–88), making it the oldest of the town's major attractions. Whether you are a gardening fan or not, this a wonderful place to come for an hour or more's peace and quiet. It is more correctly known as El Jardín de Aclimatación de La Orotava (La Orotava's Acclimatisation Garden). The name hints at the garden's

Part of the Casa Iriarte, once an architectural treasure

Festivals
After Santa Cruz, Puerto is the best place on Tenerife to join in the island's famous Carnival festivities (see page 50). Puerto's second major festival is the Fiestas del Gran Poder de Dios on 15 July, when the town comes alive with processions, regattas, street parties and fireworks displays.

VALLE DE LA OROTAVA

César Manrique
Wherever you find a superb work of modern architecture in the Canaries, the chances are that the great Lanzarote architect, painter and sculptor, César Manrique (1920–92) will have had a hand in it. Included are Puerto's magnificent Lido and the Playa Jardín, the Parque Marítimo in Santa Cruz and the Mirador del Palmarejo on La Gomera. Much of Manrique's life was a personal crusade to save the Canaries from the worst architectural excesses associated with mass tourism. He established a world-wide reputation as an abstract painter and established the Museum of Contemporary Art on Lanzarote. He also took an interest in architecture, and was guided by the principle that wherever possible, buildings should remain in harmony with the natural landscape.

Safe and scenic: swimming in the Lido San Telmo

original function, which was to provide a halfway house to allow plants removed from the world's tropical climes (but especially Spain's colonies) to acclimatise before they were moved to more temperate areas of the Spanish mainland. As such the garden was a success, for the vast majority of imported exotics readily took to Tenerife's benign climate and rich soils. For many species, however, the garden proved to be as far as they travelled, for the next stage – propagation in Spain – was singularly unsuccessful (the Iberian peninsula proved too chilly for most of the warm-weathered species). Similar halfway houses were attempted with little success in the royal gardens of Madrid and Aranjuez.

Today the plants' fondness for their Tenerife home is manifest in the profusion of greenery spreading across the gardens' two-and-a-half hectares. Some 200 species of trees and shrubs prosper here, though the number of spectacular flowers is relatively small. Many have grown to magnificent proportions, none more so than the gardens' centrepiece, the 200-year-old South American rubber tree, *Coussapa dealbata*. Cinnamon trees, pepper plants and tulip trees are just three of the exotic species which can be admired, while various varieties of orchids and other delicate plants are grown in the gardens' hothouses. (Calle Retama 2, off Carretera del Botánico. *Open* Apr–Sep, daily 9–6. *Admission charge* inexpensive).

Lido San Telmo ►►► It is rather strange, given Puerto de la Cruz's long-standing reputation as one of Tenerife's premier resorts, that for decades the town had virtually no decent beaches or bathing spots. This was put right in 1977, when the celebrated Lanzarote architect, César Manrique (see panel), the man responsible for many excellent and restrained developments across the Canaries, was commissioned to produce a seafront

complex of pools and open spaces for swimming, sunbathing and relaxation. The result was the widely and justifiably acclaimed Lido San Telmo, also known as the Costa de Martiánez or Lido/Lago de Martiánez, an artificial creation that occupies the bulging spit of land just to the east of the old town centre.

Now one of Puerto's leading tourist attractions, the Lido consists of eight small swimming pools, a large artificial lake, and an array of lava islands, one of which periodically 'erupts' – to general delight – as a vast fountain. The whole complex is superbly laid out, managing to give the impression of space and tranquillity even when crowded with people. Large green lawns and well-planned open spaces stretch out between the pools, offset by numerous exotic flowers and shrubs, sculptures, palm-shaded sunbathing areas, and an extensive black and white lava rockery. On top of the admission charge you can also hire sunbeds and beach umbrellas, while a wide range of cafés and restaurants allows you to enjoy anything from sandwiches and snacks to a five-course lunch. And if a day here isn't long enough, there is also a subterranean nightclub to while away the evening (Playa Martiánez, Avenida de Colón. *Open* daily 10–5. *Admission charge* moderate).

Loro Parque▶▶▶ Puerto's premier attraction, the widely advertised Loro Parque (Parrot Park), would be the envy of any town. Created in 1972 – but expanded many times since – this highly popular complex has attracted over 11 million visitors since its foundation. Its chief attractions, as the name suggests, are parrots – some 300 different species in all – a tally that makes this the world's largest collection of the bird in captivity. An important breeding programme is underway to preserve many species endangered in the wild, but plenty of the birds can be seen in free flight and in the various parrot 'shows' held throughout the day. You can also enjoy films in the complex's cinema, whose special 180-degree screen displays, among other things, an aerial view of various human activities seen from a bird's point of view.

These days the park is devoted to far more than parrots, however, having recently expanded to become an extremely well-run zoo and wildlife park. A dolphinarium was opened in 1987, its dolphin and sea-lion shows now some of the park's most popular attractions. There is also an aquarium, fitted with one of the world's longest aquarium tunnels (18.5m), a novelty which allows you to 'walk through water' with sharks twisting and turning just centimetres from your face. Still in aquatic mode, there are flamingo pools, a crocodile house, cranes, water-fowl, duck ponds and Galapagos turtles. Other highlights include the gorilla colony, the nocturnal bat cave and monkey house, together with a dragon-tree site, a Thai village, jaguars

105

One of the stars at Puerto's Loro Parque

Puerto's Loro Parque: popular and well planned

Playa Jardin
The Playa Jardin is one of Puerto's newest seafront developments and, like the Lido San Telmo, bears the stamp of the great Lanzarote architect César Manrique (see panel, page 104). Opened in 1992, the black sand beach is fringed with beautifully landscaped gardens, while the region's notorious breakers have been tamed by an offshore barrier of 20-tonne concrete blocks. Alongside the development is the Castillo de San Felipe, a fine Spanish colonial-style fortress built early in the 17th century. It is named after Philip IV of Spain (1621–65), the ruler responsible for the creation of La Orotava and its port (now Puerto de la Cruz). Today it operates as a cultural centre, playing host to temporary art exhibitions and small-scale classical concerts.

and – one of the newest ventures – Natura Vision, a breathtaking film laden with special effects which 'flies' visitors through several Spanish national parks, over Mount Teide, on to Florida's Key West, and finally to Venezuela and the South American rainforest.

As if all this were not enough, the park has a beautiful natural setting, included in which are some 12.5ha of tropical and sub-tropical gardens, around 2,000 palm trees, an orchid house with over 1,000 blooms, and numerous well-designed public spaces, viewing galleries and picnic areas. The park is situated in Calle San Felipe, 3km from the town centre in the Punta Brava district. Numerous free shuttle buses run out here from Puerto's Playa Martiánez and the resort of Playa de las Américas on the island's southern coast (*Open* daily 8.30–6.45, last admission 5. *Admission charge* expensive).

Parque-Casino Taoro▶▶ You do not need to walk around Puerto long before catching a glimpse of the noted Casino Taoro, a distinctive building perched on the garden-swathed hillside above the town. The Canaries' most famous casino, it began life in 1892 as the Grand Hotel Taoro, in its day the largest hotel anywhere on Spanish territory. Until a disastrous fire in 1929, it was the most prestigious place to stay in the Canary Islands. In 1975, several of its rooms were given over to a casino, an establishment which has evolved into a gamblers' paradise, with French and American roulette, blackjack (pontoon) tables, craps and ranks of slot machines where a 100 pesetas stake might win you a five million pesetas jackpot. If you want to enter the casino, remember you need to be over 18 years of age, present your passport (essential), and adhere to the smart dress code (jacket and tie are recommended – but not obligatory – for men). Doors open daily between 7 and 8pm, but the action is liveliest around midnight. Closing time is between 3 and 4am. Whether or not you want to gamble, it is still worth coming to the casino – by day or night. In the evening you could slip into the bar simply for a cocktail: the 'Cocktail Taoro' – champagne, lemon, caviar, calvados and banana liqueur – won the 1988 Spanish Cocktail Competition.

By day you should visit the **Parque Taoro** (entrance close to the casino), which comprises a series of lovely ornamental gardens, a beautiful café and garden, lakes full of waterfowl and water lilies, and the **Risco Bello Jardín Acuático**, a series of pretty aquatic gardens.

Plaza del Charco►► There's no better introduction to Puerto than a drink in a bar on this fine, raised square, the old town's physical and social heart, coupled with a relaxing half hour watching the streetlife (the Paraiso de Tenerife is one of its more popular bars). Always full of life, the plaza is invariably busy with buskers, visitors in cafés, old men playing cards or chess, and locals parading and chatting during the daily *paseo*. Its bustling environs are shaded by ancient Indian laurel trees brought from Cuba in 1852 (from whence they spread across Tenerife). On the square's west side stands the **Rincón del Puerto**, a beautifully restored old-style Canarian building, complete

The 17th-century Casa de la Real Aduana (Royal Customs House) overlooks Puerto's old harbour

107

VALLE DE LA OROTAVA

108

Shrimp square
Plaza del Charco's full name is the Plaza del Charco de los Camarones (Shrimp-Pod Square), a reference to the days when the surrounding area used to fill with water at high tide and locals would come here to fish for shrimp.

Plaza statue
A statue in Plaza de la Iglesia commemorates Augustín de Béthencourt, a colourful character born in Puerto de la Cruz in 1798 (a nearby street is also named after him). Trained as an engineer, he eventually found his way to Russia, where he achieved the rank of general in the Russian army. Much of his career was absorbed in building roads, bridges and canals for Tsar Alexander I.

The church takes pride of place in the aptly named Plaza de la Iglesia

with balconies and a plant-filled inner courtyard. Built in 1739, it is occupied today by a number of pleasant bars and restaurants.

A stone's throw from the square's northwest corner (reached on Calle de María) lies the colourful old fishing port, the **Puerto Pesquero►►►**, a small but still working harbour with a couple of piers, a black-pebble beach and a handful of brightly painted boats (Puerto has plans for a new marina and harbour here). On the waterfront stands the **Casa de la Real Aduana** (Royal Custom House), built in 1620 and one of Puerto's oldest surviving buildings. It served as the customs post until 1833. Today, inevitably, is sells souvenirs. To the rear are the remnants of Santa Bárbara, an artillery fortification built in the 18th century. From here the cobbled Calle las Lonjas passes the modern *ayuntamiento* (town hall), almost opposite which stands the **Casa Miranda** (built in 1730), family home of Francisco de Miranda, a leading light in the battle for Venezuelan independence (you may have seen his statue in the Plaza de los Reyes Católicos at the end of Calle de San Telmo, see page 103). Today it is a smart restaurant, bar and coffee shop.

Walk a little further and you will come to the **Plaza de l'Europa,** a modern square opened in 1992 which took its inspiration from architectural styles of old military fortifications (hence the half dozen old cannons dotted around its margins). The plaza offers some invigorating sea views.

Plaza de la Iglesia►►► With its ring of flowers and lofty palms, Plaza de la Iglesia is Puerto's prettiest square, as well as the site of its most important church, the **Iglesia de Nuestra Señora de la Peña de Francia** (Church of Our Lady of the Rock of France). Built between 1681 and 1697, the church is a lovely building, with baroque lines uncompromised by the more recent bell-tower, added in 1898. Inside, the appealing side chapels are adorned with, among other things, a fine baroque *retablo* (altar-piece) by Luis de la Cruz, figures of Santo Domingo and the Virgen de los Dolores by Luján Pérez, as well as an impressive statue of Cristo del Gran Poder by an unknown 18th-century sculptor. Also look for the pulpit, a wooden creation cleverly painted to resemble marble, and for the organ, which was built in London and installed here in 1814 by Bernardo de Cologán, a Puerto resident with Irish ancestors.

The square is also home to the **tourist office**, while close by, in the adjacent Calle Quintana (part of the centre's pedestrianised zone), lie two of Puerto's oldest hotels, the **Hotel Marquesa** (built in 1712) and **Hotel Monopol** (1742). Despite extensive renovations, both are elegant remnants from a gentler age of tourism, with old-world Canarian patios and balconies that hint at the splendour of late 19th-century holidaymaking. You can wallow in a little of this atmosphere by taking a drink on the Marquesa's terrace (open to non-residents) and by watching Puerto's citizens parade around the plaza during the early evening *paeso*. Note, however, that this can be a slightly noisy part of town in which to stay, and that parking opportunities, as so often in Tenerife's larger towns, are few and far between.

VALLE DE LA OROTAVA

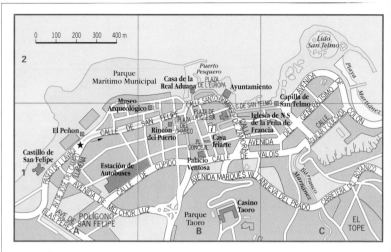

Walk Puerto de la Cruz

A walk through the older streets of Puerto de la Cruz (1km; allow 1½hrs – excluding time spent in the museum).

Puerto de la Cruz remains a Spanish colonial town, with many tangible reminders of its past. This walk provides you with a taste of the

town's history and architectural highlights. Avoid Monday if you wish to visit the Museo Arqueológico (Archaeological Museum), which is shut on Mondays.

Calle de San Felipe and its fine buildings are typical of Puerto's old quarter

Start from the El Peñon ('The Rock') religious monument, which is located next to the football stadium, and walk along Calle de San Felipe.

Calle de San Felipe
This is a charming, old street of one-storey fishermen's houses and some good local restaurants. Look out for the unusual green decorated oriel window at No. 16.

Take a right turn, Calle de Lomo, if you wish to visit the Archaeological Museum. Then retrace your steps to Calle de San Felipe and turn left to Plaza del Charco.

Museo Arqueológico (Archaeo-
logical Museum) is housed in a fine 19th-century mansion on Plaza del Charco (effectively marking the centre of town). It hosts a variety of temporary exhibitions. Be sure to look into the Rincón del Puerto, a fine typical Canarian balconied courtyard, built in 1739.

Continue on Calle de San Felipe towards the fishing port.

Casa de la Real Aduana
(Royal Custom House)
To the right-hand side of the port is this beautiful black-and-white stone house, the oldest building in the town, dating from 1620. Note the fortifications to the seaward side. On the opposite side of the street is the Casa Miranda, which dates from around 1730.

Turn left onto Calle de San Telmo.

Calle de San Telmo
The start of Calle de San Telmo, a promenade, is known as the Punta del Viento (Windy Point), marked by a modern sculpture of a windswept girl. Below, the waves break spectacularly into black-lava rockpools. The tiny, snow-white Capilla de San Telmo (Church of St Elmo) dates from the 18th century.

Go back to the start of the prome-nade, continue for a few metres, then turn right into Calle La Hoya, which leads to Plaza de la Iglesia.

Take time out from walking at a pavement bar or café

Plaza de la Iglesia
Note the old-fashioned *bodega* (wine shop) on the left before entering the plaza. This is Puerto's loveliest plaza, with an elegant swan fountain in the centre, dating from 1900. The Iglesia de Nuestra Señora de la Peña de Francia (Church of Our Lady of the Rock of France) is a beautiful 16th-century building (its tower was added in 1898) with excellent baroque altar-pieces and side-chapels.

Leave the Plaza de la Iglesia by Calle Cólogan and take the second street on the right, Calle Iriarte.

Casa Iriarte
Calle Iriarte contains the Casa Iriarte, an 18th-century house with a balcony that overlooks the street and a lovely interior courtyard. It houses craft-sellers (mostly embroidery) and a small naval museum. On the square opposite is the Colegio San Agustín. This occupies the 18th-century Palacio Ventosa, of which the most notable feature is the tall tower.

Turn right into Calle Blanco. This leads back to the Plaza del Charco.

THE NORTHWEST

THE NORTHWEST

Trade winds
Do not be surprised in western Tenerife if you find a bank of cloud developing during the morning. The clouds, which disperse by early evening and rarely bring rain, are caused by the trade winds, which blow almost constantly year-round from the northeast (though their effects are less marked during the winter). The winds begin as warm air rising at the Equator to the south. The air cools as it rises and flows northwards towards the North Pole. As it cools further, it begins to sink, falling earthwards more or less at 30°N, close to the location of the Canaries. It then flows back towards the Equator closer to the earth's surface. Clouds form when the winds encounter Tenerife's high ground and are forced to rise.

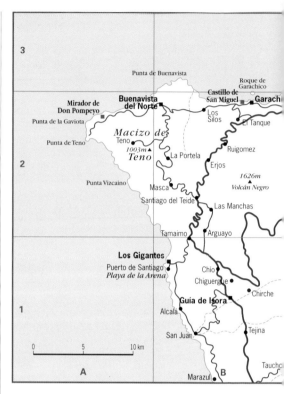

*Previous pages: Garachico, once Tenerife's most important port
Below: Castillo de San Miguel at Garachico*

The northwest corner of Tenerife is one of the most attractive parts of the island. Not only does it contain several interesting small towns, but it also boasts two or three unmissable sights and some of the Canaries' finest landscapes. Major resorts are few and far between – there is nothing here, for example, to compare with Puerto de la Cruz or Playa de las Américas. At the same time, the adjacent little resorts of **Los Gigantes** and **Puerto de Santiago** are two of the island's nicest, their relatively low-key and rather up-market image appealing to a slightly older and more easy-going clientele than the resorts to the south.

This is not to say that the area is without its crowds. Coach tours from across the island flock to **Icod de los Vinos**, a pretty little village renowned for its magnificent dragon tree, an astonishing centuries-old tree that has become something of a symbol of Tenerife.

Many tours then progress to **Masca**, once a village all but cut off from the outside world. Today it retains its picturesque appearance and evocative setting, but has been made more accessible by the improvement of the area's roads. Fewer people make it to peaceful **Garachico**, arguably Tenerife's most charming and least spoilt small town.

Equally worthy of exploration are the Teno Mountains, a knuckle of rugged upland landscapes tucked into Tenerife's northwestern tip. Much of their best scenery can be seen by car, and in particular from the adventurous road linking Masca with the modest town of Buenavista

Water

Northwest Tenerife – Mount Teide excepted – is greener than much of the island, where a shortage of water has always been a problem. Rainfall everywhere is relatively low, and much falls onto the porous rock of the interior. Reserves of water therefore tend to be deep underground. As a result, around 1,000 vast bore-holes and *galerías* (galleries) have had to be drilled: some are over a kilometre long. Water is then extracted and pumped to consumers, or stored in large *presas* (open reservoirs). Sources of water are often in the hands of private extractors and landowners, many of whom can date their claims back for generations. Shares are owned by large consumers such as farmers or hotels. The increase of tourism has put further strain on an already precious resource, and water on Tenerife, not surprisingly, is a correspondingly expensive commodity.

del Norte. Little you will see here, however, compares with the scenery of the **Parque Nacional del Teide**, a national park which protects the majestic landscapes of Mount Teide, the vast volcanic peak that broods over central Tenerife. Note that access to the park is possible not only from the northwest of the island, but also from La Orotava, La Laguna and the south.

Gentle pastoral countryside in northwest Tenerife

116

▶ **Buenavista del Norte** *114B2*

Buenavista del Norte – more commonly known as Buenavista – is a sleepy agricultural town in Tenerife's secluded northwest corner. Located some 22km west of Puerto de la Cruz, it lies at the foot of the Macizo de Teno (Teno Massif), and is best seen as part of a small circular tour that takes in Masca, Garachico and Icod de los Vinos (the last lies just 6km to the east). If you have time, also make a point of driving out to Punta de Teno, a lonely headland at the end of a scenic road a few kilometres west of Buenavista (see below).

The town's tidy old centre is crammed with narrow streets, and makes a pleasant spot to sit down briefly to enjoy a leisurely coffee as the streetlife unfolds before you. The best place to take time out is the main plaza, a square dotted with a handful of fine 18th- and 19th-century mansions. It is also home to the town's main church, **Nuestra Señora de los Remedios** (Our Lady of Remedies), whose highlights include a superb *mudéjar* ceiling, several *retablos* (altar-pieces) and Alonso Cano's 17th-century painting of St Francis.

Punta de Teno▶▶ Buenavista del Norte means 'Beautiful View of the North', but while the views in and around the town are nice enough, none are as striking as the panoramas which unfold as you drive out of town to Punta de Teno (11km to the west on the TF1429 road). En route to the promontory, Tenerife's most northwesterly point, you pass through groves of coffee and banana trees, skirting imposing cliffs before reaching the **Mirador de Don Pompeyo** (after 6km), from where you can enjoy views back along the coast to Buenavista. The promontory itself is a lonely, rocky place, the road ending in a flat expanse strewn with the multi-hued debris of past volcanic explosions. There's a tiny sand-and-shingle beach here, though your best chance of a swim is from the rocks or small fisherman's jetty near by.

Life is quiet in Buenavista del Norte

▶▶▶ Garachico

Garachico is a quiet but fascinating little town still largely untouched by the flood-tide of tourism. Located on the coast some 31km west of Puerto de la Cruz, it has a friendly and welcoming air, its narrow cobbled streets the very picture of a typical Canarian town.

Had history been different, it might now be the island's capital. Founded in 1496 by a Genoese banker, Cristóbal de Ponte, it served – thanks to a magnificent natural harbour – as the island's most important port for almost 200 years. Exports of wine and sugar flooded through its docks, producing immense wealth, and attracting prosperous inhabitants to its flourishing streets in the process. Its heyday was cut dramatically short on 5 May 1706, when the nearby Volcán Negra volcano erupted, sending a sea of molten lava cascading towards the town. Almost overnight the harbour was blocked and vast areas of the town engulfed. Many buildings were destroyed, and though the town was rebuilt on the newly formed lava peninsula (today's elegant cobbled streets follow the lava's curving course), neither the harbour nor Garachico ever really recovered.

Castillo de San Miguel▶▶▶ You can make out the lava flow that so altered the course of Garachico's history from several points around town. One of these is the Castillo de San Miguel (St Michael's Castle), from whose roof there is a lovely panorama of the sea on one side and a view of the route taken by the lava down the cliffs on the other. The castle itself, built in the 16th century, is one of the few buildings in town to have survived the disaster, its colossal walls having proved almost impervious to the molten rock swilling around its base. The lava's solidified legacy has now been landscaped into an appealing area of gardens and swimming pools (see panel, page 118). The castle was once owned by the Counts of Gomera, nobles who seem to have houses and fortresses in most parts of

Coats of arms of the Counts of Gomera on the Castillo de San Miguel

Local tour
Garachico makes a perfect stop-off on any tour of Tenerife, as well as the starting point of a pleasant little circular tour that takes in Icod de los Vinos, Santiago del Teide, Buenavista del Norte and the lonely Teno peninsula beyond Buenavista.

Tourist office
Garachico's tourist office is situated in the Centro de Artesanía el Limonero (Handicrafts Centre) at Calle Esteban de Ponte 5 (tel: 13 34 61) on the seafront opposite the Castillo de San Miguel. It is an excellent source of information on most points of local interest.

Rocks formed by cooling lava make an ideal place for sunbathing

Swimming
Garachico is not only a town where you can spend a happy hour or so exploring, but it also offers the chance for a dip in the sea, notably in the series of rock pools formed by cooling lava on the seafront. Steps have been cut down to the pools, the haunt of local children, who dive off the rocks. You should avoid swimming when the wind is up, for the breakers and huge swell pushed into the pools makes bathing dangerous.

Arab attractions
Children are likely to enjoy the Camello Center, located in the El Tanque just outside Garachico. Camel caravans depart regularly, there are *burro* (donkey) safaris, and you can take mint tea in an authentic Arab tent. It can be wise to book ahead (tel: 83 11 91). (*Open* daily 10–6).

the island. Miscellaneous inscriptions, combined with some of the counts' coats of arms, crown the castle's redoubtable main portal. Inside is a small museum of fossils, minerals and shells, together with the inevitable craft stalls selling embroidery and metalwork. For further information, tel: 83 00 00 (*Open* daily 9–6. *Admission charge* inexpensive).

Plaza Glorieta de San Francisco►► Garachico's castle was not the only building to withstand the 1706 eruption. The **Convento de San Francisco**, a former Franciscan convent, was another. Situated on Plaza Glorieta de San Francisco, one of the town's main squares, the building now serves as the **Casa de Cultura** (Cultural Centre), hosting a variety of events and temporary exhibitions (*Open* Mon–Fri 9–7; Sat 9–6; Sun 9–1. *Admission charge* moderate). These are worth seeing whether they interest you or not, for they allow you to see inside the old convent buildings, and in particular its two former courtyards, one of which is beautifully planted with palms and rose bushes. Inside is the **Museo de las Ciencias Naturales**, a disjointed but rewarding collection of natural history and folk exhibits, including old pictures of Garachico that underline how little in the town has changed. Look out in particular for the aerial picture of the town which graphically illustrates the course of the lava flows three centuries ago. Also look into the convent's beautiful 16th-century church, **Iglesia de San Francisco**.

On the square's southern side stands the **Casa-Palacio de los Condes de la Gomera**, a former residence – like the Castillo de San Miguel – of the Counts of Gomera. Built in the 17th century, its condition deteriorated over the years, but has recently been saved by a timely restoration.

Plaza de Arriba▶▶ Adjacent to the Plaza Glorieta de San Francisco lies the Plaza de Arriba, a modern but pleasant raised square dominated by the **Iglesia de Santa Ana**, Garachico's most notable church. Much of the original building, founded in 1509, was buried in the eruption of 1706, and much of the rest destroyed by the fire which blazed in the lava's aftermath. Rebuilding on the original foundations took place between 1714 and 1721, resulting in a triple-aisled church topped by a pleasing little bell-tower. The interior, as ever, has some outstanding *retablos*, together with two figures by Luján Pérez of St James and Santa Ana (St Anne). Also in the square stands a statue (1970) of Simón Bolívar (1783–1830), leading light in the movement for South American independence from the Spanish. Bolívar's mother was born in Garachico.

Walk on beyond the Iglesia and you come to the Plaza de Juan González de la Torre, on one side of which are some lovely sunken gardens known as the **Parque Puerto de Tierra**. This was once part of the old port (*puerto*), part of which still functions on a much-reduced scale. Before the 1706 catastrophe, a massive 16th-century gateway arch marked the entrance to the harbour area. The arch has subsequently been excavated from the lava and re-erected in the square on its original site. Near by stands another fossil from the town's past, a gargantuan 17th-century wine press, or *lagar*, graphic testimony to the former importance of the town's wine trade.

Museo de Arte Contemporáneo▶ Garachico's Museum of Contemporary Art lies on the edge of town in the rather gloomy interior of the Convento de Santo Domingo, a former Dominican monastery. Most of the works of art on display are by Spanish artists, and though few are of more than passing interest, some are startling in their modernity (*Open* Mon–Sat 9.30–6. *Admission charge* inexpensive).

Viewpoint
The best place to get a view of Garachico and the lava field which engulfed it in 1706 is from the Mirador de Garachico. This is located on the C820 road to Icod de los Vinos above the town. To reach it requires a drive along 9km of winding road via the village of El Tanque (en route you pass the grassy cone of an old volcano). The effort is worth it, for the belvedere offers a superb and much-photographed bird's-eye view of the town and its famous offshore Roque de Garachico. Note the cross on top of the rock, erected by the townspeople to ward off another volcanic catastrophe.

The sunken gardens of the Parque Puerto de Tierra

THE NORTHWEST

San Marcos
Icod de los Vinos lies just inland of San Marcos (3km), formerly a little fishing village, but now developing into a small-scale resort. Park short of the harbour if you are in a car and walk down to the sea, which is backed by cliffs and fringed by an excellent black-sand beach. As yet only a handful of high-rise buildings intrude. Fishing boats still bring in their catch, which can be eaten in the restaurants and bars which line the village's seafront promenades.

The famous Drago Milenario, a symbol of the island

▶ ▶ ▶ Icod de los Vinos   115C2

Icod de los Vinos, a quaint little town some 22km west of Puerto de la Cruz, contains one of Tenerife' most famous sights. The Drago Milenario (Thousand-Year-Old Dragon Tree) is the largest and oldest variety of a tree (*Dracaena draco*) associated for centuries with magic and mystery (see page 122). The town is also a delightful place to visit in its own right, and with a trip to Garachico and an after-noon on the black-sand beach at San Marcos near by (see panel), makes for a perfect day's excursion from Puerto de la Cruz. The Guanches had a town here, a settlement which went by the name of Benicod (Beautiful Place). The Spanish colony which replaced it was founded in 1501, making it one of Tenerife's oldest towns. The area has also long been famous for its wines, as its name suggests (*vinos* means wines). Two of the best are *Icod* and *La Guancha*, samples of which can be tasted (usually free) and bought from various outlets around town (see panel, page 121).

Drago Milenario▶ ▶ ▶ There's no missing Icod's famous tree, which is well signposted and invariably surrounded by visitors disgorged from the tourist buses which descend on the town. Crowds notwithstanding, it's a magnificent sight, a tight-knit web of densely packed branches spouting upwards into a huge mushroomed canopy of green. Guanche chieftains, it is said, held court beneath its branches. Around 16m high and 6m across the trunk, it's the largest tree of its type on the island, for which it is also a virtual symbol. It's also probably the island's oldest tree, though its precise age is difficult to know. For years it was assumed to be two or even three thousand years old, though current estimates put its age at no more than a few hundred years. But whatever its

age, time has taken its toll, and though the tree is still very much alive, concrete, sadly, has had to be poured into some of its lower reaches to help support it and the tangle of branches.

The most obvious place to view the monster is from the **Plaza de la Iglesia**, whose surroundings have been landscaped to give the tree the natural surroundings its grandeur deserves. The classic picture-postcard shot is taken from here, a view which embraces an almost equally impressive palm on the left and a whitewashed house with a typical wooden Canarian balcony to the right. The square is smothered in exotic vegetation of its own, including a superb array of *Pandanus utilis* trees from Madagascar. Also here are several shops selling every type of Tenerife souvenir imaginable. The best of them is probably the **Casa del Drago**, which in addition to cigars and embroidery also offers the chance to taste and buy bottles of the town's renowned wine. Bars and shops here also sell dragon tree seeds and seedlings, which make novel if frustratingly slow-growing gifts.

The town▶▶▶ To the tree's rear, slightly raised, stands the whitewashed **Iglesia de San Marco** (St Mark's Church), whose orange-tiled roof and trim little tower set the seal on a picturesque little square. Building began in the 15th century, and the exterior is graced with a fine Renaissance portal, while the interior is renowned for its coffered ceiling, carved from Canary pine, and its treasury, home to a magnificent silver filigree crucifix.

An almost equally good place to admire the dragon tree is from the balustrades of the nearby **Plaza de Andrés de Cáceres**, which is also shaded by some wonderful old trees, in particular a huge *Ficus macrophylla*. To see the rest of the town, visit the adjacent **Plaza del Pilar**, a peaceful oasis away from the tourist bustle. Then walk up the cobbled lane from the dragon tree (Calle Arcipreste Ossuna) to **Plaza de la Constitución**, an old square fringed with palms, laurels, oleanders and a rare eight-branched *Washingtonia*.

Souvenir shops are occasionally attractive: Icod de los Vinos' La Casa del Drago

Shopping
Souvenir shops come and go, but in Icod de los Vinos, the Casa del Drago, Sálon Canario del Vino and Casa del Vino (all within a few steps of each other in Plaza de la Iglesia) offer a good range of Tenerife and Canarian wines and a selection of interesting Canarian comestibles. Plaza de la Constitución also has a variety of souvenir shops selling pottery, lace, shawls and basketwork.

■ **No one can come to Tenerife and fail to notice the island's immensely lush vegetation and magnificent variety of exotic trees, from the mysterious dragon trees and verdant banana plantations of the north to the panoply of pines and date-palms that lend a distinctive appearance to landscapes across the island.** ■

Dragons Of all the Canaries' many rare and magnificent trees, none is quite as majestic or distinguished as the dragon tree (*Dracaena draco*). A member of the Liliaceae family (closely related to the yucca), it is found only in the so-called Macaronesian islands, namely the Canaries, the Azores and the islands of the Madeiran archipelago. Naturalists have called it a living fossil, for it dates back to the Tertiary era, an age when dinosaurs still roamed the earth. Even without its great age it would be a remarkable tree, not least for its name, which it takes from its resin, a strange substance that turns a deep blood-red on exposure to the air (hence 'dragon's blood'). Small wonder, then, given its dramatic appearance, that the Guanches attributed it with magical powers, using it to treat wounds, ward off evil spirits and embalm their dead. Today the tree is still seen as a symbol of fertility, while the sap is believed to be a cure for leprosy. In time the resin was exported to Italy, where it was used as a dye to

Pine forests are a common feature of Tenerife's interior uplands

stain marble. It was also used to varnish musical instruments and as an ingredient in cosmetics.

Augury It is not only the dragon's resin, however, that accounts for the tree's air of mystery and sorcery. Its appearance is equally striking, its branches growing together in a tight web to create a trunk before splitting off into a dense web. Branch ends are tipped with dark green and deadly looking sword-shaped leaves. The Guanches used the tree's bark to make shields, and believed that the tree's blossoming augured well for the year's harvest (dragon trees only put forth branches after they have blossomed, so the young tree bears little resemblance to the age-old monsters such as the tree at Icod de los Vinos).

No one is in any doubt that dragon trees grow to a great age. Unfortunately the tree has the peculiarity of not producing growth rings, so the precise dating of any tree is extremely difficult. One rough and ready way of determining age is to count the number of branches, or the number of forks in individual branches. This, too, though, is a slightly haphazard device, as branches fork at irregular intervals and there is much debate as to where one branch starts and another ends.

Pines While dragon trees are few and far between, the Canary pine (*Pinus canariensis*) is a familiar feature of the Tenerife landscape. It frequently grows at high altitudes (from about 1,500m in the north, and 1,000m in the warmer south), often forming a dense forest band just below the island's sparsely vegetated upland slopes. This position means trees thrive on and capture the moisture-laden trade winds, with rain falling or mist condensing on the pine's needles and dripping to the ground. This subtle condensation not only nourishes the tree, but also contributes greatly to replenishing the island's water supply. Pines also appear across Tenerife in another guise, namely as the hard, reddish-coloured timber used to craft the island's beautiful old balconies and wooden ceilings (though only the pine's old heartwood, known as 'Spanish tea' is used).

At lower altitudes than the pine, in the same climatic zone as the dragon tree, grow the banana (see page 68) and the Canary date-palm (see panel, page 170), the latter having spread from the Canaries to many parts of the Mediterranean. The palm is endemic to the Canaries' drier, more easterly islands, but despite its name, sadly, does not produce an edible fruit.

Canary laurel
The Canary laurel (*Larus canariensis*) is one of Tenerife's more special and threatened trees. Centuries ago vast areas of the island would have been blanketed with laurel woodlands. Over the years the woods – which are rare at the best of times – have been severely depleted by felling and clearance. Some beautiful woodlands survive, however – dank, slightly eerie places – notably the Mercedes woods near La Laguna, and in several parts of the interior of La Gomera. The tree's distinctive leaf, elliptical and pointed, is occasionally used as a herb.

Tenerife timber put to good use in Garachico

THE NORTHWEST

Pottery

If you are interested in ceramics, you might want to make the short trip from Puerto de Santiago to the small village of Arguayo. To get here take the road north to Tamaimo (6km); turn south on the main road to just short of Chío (4.5km) and then take the minor road north to Arguayo. Here, at the Centro Alfarero, you can see pottery made much as it was by the ancient Guanches, entirely by hand and without the aid of a wheel. (*Open* Mon–Sat 10–1, 4–7.)

Beaches and coves

Trying to find that fabled 'deserted beach' on an island as geared to holidaymakers as Tenerife is rather like looking for the Holy Grail. Most of the best beaches have long been developed. There are exceptions, however, notably on the island's western coast below Puerto de Santiago. A relatively minor road runs along the coast (linking to the main road at Adeje), from which a succession of dirt roads or footpaths lead – often by way of a scramble through tomato or banana plantations – to a quiet little cove or beach.

Vast cliffs rear up above Los Gigantes' black-sand beach

▶▶ **Los Gigantes–Puerto de Santiago** 114B1

Puerto de Santiago▶▶ Had you come to Puerto de Santiago a decade ago you would have found a small fishing village miraculously untouched by the advent of mass tourism. The fact that the village had an excellent black-sand beach, however – the Playa de la Arena – meant that its pristine appeal was unlikely to survive for long. Development has indeed taken hold, a string of relatively restrained hotels, villas and apartments having sprung up along the craggy coastline and beachfront promenade. Little of the charm of the old fishing village remains, though it is still possible to sit yourself at one of the harbour bars and watch fishermen tending their nets or landing their catch. The village is also well kept and quiet, at least by Tenerife standards. The beach, however, while attractive, is only about 200m long. Bathing here is also dangerous in certain conditions (red flags fly when the undertow is strong), though most of the time the gently shelving sand is perfectly safe. Plans are in hand to create 'Lago Santiago', an ambitious project designed to create a beachfront lido along the lines of the award-winning Lido San Telmo in Puerto de la Cruz (see page 104). As this progresses, Puerto de Santiago's popularity is likely to increase accordingly.

Los Gigantes▶▶▶ Los Gigantes (The Giants) is the name given to a magnificent array of cliffs and a small nearby resort midway along Tenerife's western coast. Though just 1km from the larger resort of Puerto de Santiago, Los Gigantes is unlikely to grow, its site being constrained by the cliffs to the north and the small bay on which it is built. The resort is one of Tenerife's nicest, and has an up-market reputation, something reflected in the slightly higher prices in many local shops and restaurants. It's also relatively quiet, and – given its size and distance from other major resorts – likely to remain so. There are also no outstanding beaches locally, nor any great diversity of nightlife and other entertainment. Development is mainly low-rise, with buildings in whitewashed local style and plenty of flourishing gardens. At the same time, it is full of the usual bars, restaurants and English 'pubs', so much of the old, local atmosphere has now largely disappeared.

Most activities revolve around boat trips to view the cliffs, or excursions to fish offshore or watch dolphins. You can also fish from the seafront promenade. One of the nicest excursion boats is the *Katrin*, built in 1940 as a working fishing boat, a pleasant change from the modern tourist boats that tie up at the resort's marina. Crystal clear seas also make this a good scuba-diving area, with plenty of charter boats and equipment rental outlets available to enthusiasts. For swimming and bathing there is a small and gently sloping beach with low surf.

Most people who simply pass through the resort are here to see the **cliffs**, whose full name is the 'Acantilado de los Gigantes'. Excursion boats flock here from several points around the island, notably Los Cristianos, appearing as tiny bobbing specks against the cliffs' towering rock walls (over 600m high in places). Some boats continue north, taking visitors along the cliff-edged coast as far as Punto de Teno on Tenerife's northwestern tip.

THE NORTHWEST

Large park
The Parque Nacional del Teide covers 13,500ha. The entire area lies above 2,000m, and all is protected from development. There are plans to extend the protected area to 18,500ha, which would make it Spain's fourth largest national park.

Birds
Birdwatchers in the Teide National Park should scan the skies above for plain swifts, and study the open slopes in the hope of seeing birds such as Berthelot's pipits and trumpeter finches. If you are exploring by car, try stopping off on your way down through the park's forested borders. There, amidst the Canary pines, you may find blue chaffinches, canaries and great-spotted woodpeckers.

Moon-like desolation on Mount Teide

▶▶▶ **Parque Nacional del Teide** 115C1

No one can come to Tenerife and miss Mount Teide, not only the highest point in the Canaries (3,718m), but also the highest point in all Spanish territory. And no one should come to Tenerife without visiting Mount Teide, whose vast volcanic peak and superb surrounding countryside – including some of the world's greatest volcanic landscapes – are protected by the 1954 Parque Nacional del Teide (Teide National Park). Weather permitting, the mountain's classic pyramid profile can be seen from most parts of the island.

A visit here is essential, whether you reach the summit, accessible by foot or cable car, or just drive through the park's magnificent scenery. Good roads converge on the park from all points of the island, each providing wonderful views and points of incidental interest. Which you take will depend largely on where you are based, but one of the most interesting approaches is via the Cumbre Dorsal, the long mountain ridge that falls away from the central massif to the east (see page 70).

Information It is worth planning a route so you begin your tour in the east (meaning an approach on the road from La Orotava and Puerto de la Cruz or along the Cumbre Dorsal from La Laguna). This has the advantage of taking you to the park's Centro de Visitantes (Information Centre) at **El Portillo** (meaning 'the gateway') (*Open* Mon–Fri 9–1.30, 2.30–4; occasionally daily 9–4). Unfortunately the centre has a rather poor reputation. Staff have been known to be unhelpful and most of the information is in Spanish only. This said, it does offer a short introductory film covering all the national parks in the Canaries with an English commentary. There are also displays and models relating to the park's geology and natural history, together with rock specimens, a bookstall

*Flowers bloom
miraculously from
dusty volcanic soil*

and information about of the park's fascinating flora (see panel) and fauna .

The centre is also an essential port of call for anyone intending to **walk** in the park, for it provides a variety of maps and pamphlets on various marked trails and recommended hikes (see page 132). It also offers advice on path closures and weather conditions, for the park can be a dangerous place, especially in winter. If you don't wish to walk independently, you can join one of the professionally led **walking tours** which depart from the centre. The hikes are generally free, but you must reserve your place (tel: 29 01 29 or 29 01 83). Given the slightly disorganised nature of the office, it is worth trying to find a Spanish-speaking person (perhaps at your hotel) to make the call for you and confirm whether or not the guide is English-speaking. If not it is probably still worth making the trip as the scenery is the main attraction.

History Mount Teide's classic pyramidal profile suggests a fairly straightforward geological history, its size and shape hinting at a single massive eruption. In fact the mountain is part of a larger volcanic area covering much of the island's heart, and its history part of the longer and larger story of the Canaries' formation (see page 130). Some three million years ago, a vast volcano – far larger than Teide – is thought to have occupied central Tenerife (estimates put its height at a staggering 4,880m). At some point this volcano collapsed in on itself, either as a result of an earthquake or an eruption. All that now remains of this original cone is a vast ring of volcanic walls, a feature known as a *caldera*. Today these walls, or what remains of them after erosion, enclose Mount Teide and a series of other smaller and more recent volcanic cones. The *caldera*, known as the **Caldera de las Cañadas**, has a diameter of 16km, measures some 45km in circumference, and in places still touches heights of 500m.

Landscapes The area of the Caldera de las Cañadas corresponds almost exactly to the area of the national park, and it is the Caldera's superlative volcanic landscapes, together with the mountain summit of Teide itself, that make up the park's chief appeal. Many of the surreal and almost lunar landscapes can be enjoyed by car

Flora
On an island already renowned for its flora (see page 14), the flowers and vegetation of the Teide National Park are still more outstanding. Flora should be sparse given the park's altitude and poor soils, but in fact there are some 45 species, many rare and endemic to the region. The most famous is the extraordinary endemic giant bugloss (*Echium wildpretii*), whose huge red flower spikes – anything up to two metres long – dot the landscape. If you are very lucky, on the highest slopes, you may find the rare Teide violet (*Viola cheiranthifolia*), discovered by Alexander von Humboldt, the 19th-century scientist and geographer. Other endemic plants include a Teide daisy and the white- and yellow-flowered Teide broom.

Weather
While the rest of Tenerife basks under a north African sun, the slopes of Mount Teide can experience very different weather. The summit is snow-capped for much of the year – annual precipitation is around 40cm, most of which falls as winter snow. Summer temperatures can reach a staggering 40°C (104°F), but as in the desert, can fall sharply at night. Humidity here is often very low – usually below 50 per cent and sometimes under 25 per cent.

THE NORTHWEST

Walking

Over and above the main route to the summit of Mount Teide, the national park features a handful of other reasonably well-defined walks suitable for those with moderate hiking experience. One involves a walk which begins from a point just south of the Parador Nacional de las Cañadas. It then contours northeastwards below the road to the visitors' centre at El Portillo (12km). Another walk starts from the centre and ambles westwards over Teide's slopes to meet the main track to the summit that begins from the road. For full details of these and other walks pick up pamphlets from the El Portillo visitor centre.

Rocks

Even non-geologists will find it hard to remain unimpressed by the sheer variety and beauty of Mount Teide's rocks and rock formations. Many display a wide range of colouring, from the green of rocks containing copper sulphate, to the deep reds and blacks caused by the oxidation of manganese (as a general rule, the newer the lava, the blacker the rock). Light-coloured pumice is also common, as is jet-black obsidian, a glassy rock used by the Guanches to make sharp-edged tools and weapons known as *tabonas*.

on the C821, which traverses the park from west to east. By far the most famous and spectacular of the park's many volcanic features are **Los Roques de García** (Rocks of García), located just off the park road close to the **Parador Nacional de las Cañadas**, a state-owned hotel and an excellent place to stay if you wish to base yourself in the park (see page 201).

The rocks form part of the old crater walls, and feature on most coach tour itineraries. As a result they are often swarming with people. Crowds notwithstanding, they remain an impressive sight, with majestic views of Teide to one side and the vast lunar emptiness of the **Llano de Ucanca** to the other. The rocks' most eye-catching feature is the Roque Chinchado, a 30m pinnacle known locally as the 'Tree of Stone', a formation recognised across Spain, for it features on the country's 1,000-peseta banknote. Close by, a few hundred metres to the south-west, stand the rocks known as **Los Azulejos**, coloured an almost luminous jade-green by the presence of iron hydrates and copper sulphate.

The Llano de Ucanca, by contrast, is a vast expanse of virtual nothingness, one of several yellow-coloured sedimentary plains in the park created by the accumulation of

Dramatic rock outcrops have formed at Los Roques de García

fine rock debris, possibly in the bed of a former lake. Look out for the distinctive rock formation rising from its surface, a feature whose shoe-like shape has seen it christened the Zapato de la Reina (Queen's Shoe).

Cable car The most painless way to ascend Teide is by *el teleférico* (cable car), which climbs close to the summit from a point on the main park road midway between the El Portillo information centre and the junction at Boca del Tauce. The *teleférico* takes just 8 minutes to climb from the cable-car station at 2,356m to a point 170m below the summit. Unfortunately the cars themselves are small and the numbers of people wishing to make the ascent large. At busy times, it's not unusual to have to queue for over 2 hours. If possible arrive first thing in the morning or last thing in the afternoon to avoid the crowds (see *opening times*, page 132). It's also vital to ensure the cable car is running, as services are suspended when it's icy or too windy, or when the annual winter maintenance comes around. Never assume the car is in service just because you see it running; it may well just be carrying maintenance staff. For information tel: 38 37 11.
Continued on page 132.

Film locations
The extraordinary scenery of the Parque Nacional del Teide has seen it used as a backdrop to several well-known Hollywood films, among them *The Ten Commandments*, *Planet of the Apes* and *One Million Years BC*.

The creation of Tenerife

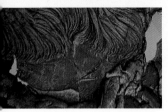

■ **Tenerife and the Canary Islands contain some of the world's most majestic and beautiful volcanic landscapes. Many parts of the archipelago are still active, or merely temporarily dormant, continuing a fascinating geological process which has been proceeding in spectacular fashion for some 20 million years.** ■

Lava

Volcanic landscapes are an open-air geological 'museum'. On Tenerife you will find rocks such as basalt, the island's most common volcanic rock; the light-coloured and coarse-surfaced trachyte; the glassy-green obsidian; the grey-green phonolite; and many others. You will also find great seas and flows of solidified lava, usually either 'pillow' lava, formed by slower moving molten rock which cools into slab-like folds, or 'pahoe-pahoe' lava, named after the Hawaiian term for rope-lava, formed by faster-flowing magma which cools into rope-like coils.

Volcanic boon

Farmers first surveying the volcanic ash and other debris from eruptions that lay over their crops must have despaired at the damage. Imagine, then, their surprise and delight when the crops not only began to grow through the cinders, but were also healthier than before. Farmers soon discovered that the porous black *lapilli* or *picon* (pumice particles) helped to soak up what little moisture was in the air. This extra moisture helped nourish the plants. The knowledge was first acquired, it seems, on Lanzarote following an eruption in the 1730s, and soon the spreading of *lapilli* became a common agricultural method, applied in particular to the growing of tomatoes, onions, vines and potatoes.

Volcanoes Tenerife and the other Canary Islands are all volcanic islands, created when molten lava forced its way from the earth's core through vents in the seabed to create distinctive cone-shaped islands. Tenerife and Lanzarote in particular contain some of the world's most dramatic volcanic landscapes (only those of Hawaii and Iceland are comparable). These include not only the classic cone-shaped volcanic mountains such as Mount Teide, but also the vast barren *malpais* (badlands), comprised of lava and other volcanic debris, which characterise the islands' central moonscapes. The exact nature of the terrain depends on the size of the eruptions on different islands, and the degree to which nature and the forces of erosion have reworked the blasted landscape. These factors in turn depend on how long ago eruptions on the various islands occurred.

Age Tenerife and the Canaries are young in geological terms, one of the reasons their evocative landscapes hold so much appeal to the geologist and casual visitor alike. The oldest islands are those in the east of the archipelago: Fuerteventura (formed around 20 million years ago) and Lanzarote (16 million years ago). Then came Gran Canaria (13 million years ago) and the larger western isles, Tenerife and La Gomera (between 8 and 12 million years ago). The newest islands, La Palma and El Hierro, are just two or three million years old. This difference in age is seen in the islands' hills and mountains: more rounded in Lanzarote, where nature and the elements have had more time to work; higher and more rugged in Tenerife and La Gomera, where the violence of the islands' birth has yet to be disguised.

Hot spots A persuasive, but not yet universally accepted theory has been devised to account for the creation of the Canaries. Magma (molten rock), it is believed, collects at certain key areas in the earth's crust, the point it accumulates, it seems, remaining more-or-less constant across the millennia.

When a pool of magma reaches a critical mass and pressure it bursts through the earth's crust to create vast volcanic eruptions. If this occurs at sea, islands are formed, namely Lanzarote and Fuerteventura in the case of the Canaries. Over the years, however, these new islands 'move' as a result of continental drift (the movement of large 'plates' on the earth's crust). In the Canaries this movement is between 2–3cm a year in an easterly direction. At the same time, magma collects again at the

original point in the earth's mantle, eventually breaking through to create a new island – Gran Canaria – the earlier islands having moved eastwards over the course of the intervening millennia. And so the process continues, ending with El Hierro.

Ongoing This theory is far from accepted, though its basic premise seems to be correct. It has, in any event, put paid to a long-held notion that the Canaries, or at least Lanzarote and Fuerteventura, were once part of mainland Africa. It also seems to explain the creation of the larger island grouping of which the Canaries are a part, namely the Macaronesia (Blessed Isles), which includes the other volcanic archipelagos of the Azores, Madeira and Cape Verde Islands.

In the Canaries, Lanzarote and Gran Canaria are still smouldering. The most recent eruptions have been on La Palma in 1949 and 1971. In Tenerife, Mount Teide, the islands' finest volcanic legacy, was smoking when Columbus sailed past in 1492. It erupted again in 1604, 1704 and 1798. The last significant eruption was in 1909. Given the Canaries' geological history, however, further eruptions are surely only a matter of time…

Multi-coloured volcanic debris near Los Roques

Different debris
Volcanic debris on the flanks of Mount Teide can be divided into three main types. The first are *picon*, or *lapilli*, tiny, feather-weight cinder particles useful to Tenerife farmers (see panel, page 130). The second is *escoria* (pumice), another light rock that floats on water and is produced by the formation of gas bubbles in slow-cooling or slow-flowing lava. The third type are volcanic 'bombs', heavy and often large rocks which have a fragile outer shell.

THE NORTHWEST

The easy way up: a cable car approaches the upper slopes of Mount Teide

Once you've boarded a car, there is a 25-minute walk to reach the summit from the upper cable-car station. However, be warned that the air is already thin up here, and that you should not attempt even this moderately short walk if you are pregnant or suffer from heart or respiratory complaints. The sun is also likely to be strong, so it goes without saying that you should take a sun-hat, sunglasses and sun-cream. You should also take a sweater or light jacket, for the wind is invariably chilly despite the sunshine (*Open* daily 9–5 in summer; 9–4 in winter. *Admission charge* expensive).

By foot One of the first recorded ascents of Mount Teide on foot was in June 1799 by Alexander von Humboldt, the noted German scientist and geographer. These days an estimated 300,000 people a year puff their way to the summit. For all but the most experienced hikers and climbers there is one main, well-defined **trail** up the mountain. This starts from a point south of the station on the El Portillo–Boca del Tauce road about 2km east of the cable-car station. The path begins at a marked car park and it takes about 3 to 4 hours to reach the summit. The total ascent involved is around 1,500m.

Most people walk up and take the cable car down, but if this is your plan, check the cable car is running and note its popularity (see page 129). The round trip can be accomplished in a day (at least in summer, when there are more hours of daylight), but you may wish to make the trip a 2-day excursion by staying overnight in the Refugio de Altavista, a mountain refuge a few hundred metres below the summit (check opening times and the availability of beds at the El Portillo information centre).

Climbing the mountain is an exhausting and exhilarating experience, but is not a trip that should be undertaken lightly. You should be fit, wear good boots, and take plenty of water, spare food and warm clothing (even in summer). Note, too, that the air is thin at this altitude, making the trip more strenuous than it might otherwise be. Also be sure to call in at the El Portillo information centre (see page 126) to check on the current viability of paths: while the basic route remains the same, various stretches of the trail open and close regularly, seemingly at random. Don't attempt the climb in poor weather, and don't tackle the mountain in winter if you are at all inexperienced.

The **route** from the car park proceeds first to the **Montaña Blanca** (White Mountain), so-called because of its mantle of light-coloured *lapilli* rocks, which consist of pumice and phonolites. You should reach this point after an hour or 75 minutes, by which point you should know if you have the legs and lungs to manage the full ascent.

Even if you turn back, the effort will not have been wasted, for this peak is a worthwhile climb in its own right. If you press on, the route from here takes you past the huge black volcanic boulders known as **Los Huevos del Teide** (Eggs of Teide). Later you pass the so-called **Cueva del Hielo** (Ice Cave) and a series of smouldering sulphurous blowholes where you can warm your hands. Disappointingly, the actual **summit** can sometimes be closed for 'repairs', leaving you to languish some 170m short of the top at the upper cable-car station.

Opposite: the summit of Mount Teide from Los Roques

▶▶▶ Masca 114B2

The idyllic little village of Masca sits at the heart of the **Teno Massif** (Macizo de Teno), a remote group of hills and mountains in Tenerife's northwestern corner. A wonderfully peaceful area, the region is cut by craggy gorges and smothered in palms, pines and vegetation which has grown lush from the mountains' plentiful spring rains. Until recently much of the area was all but cut off from the outside world. Today the odd road has been improved, but access is still slow and laborious, and a good map is essential if you are to make sense of the often badly surfaced or badly signposted roads. Car drivers will find few of the purpose-built *miradores* (viewpoints) common on the rest of the island, but this is still a rewarding area to explore. The road leading south from Buenavista del Norte, in particular, is picturesque, cutting through much of the region's best scenery.

Masca After 14km of twists, tight turns and precipitous climbs, the recently revamped (but still narrow) Buenavista road eventually brings you to Masca, a picture-perfect village that is now – despite its perilously narrow approaches – on the itinerary of most of the island's coach tour operators (a few years ago the only access here was by mule track). For all its new-found popularity – the streets are sometimes overrun by visitors – the village's superb but isolated setting means its appearance is likely to remain unspoiled. Only a handful of bars, shops and restaurants have opened to take advantage of its popularity: previously much of the village was abandoned, many of its inhabitants having emigrated in search of a better life. Some of the houses occupy narrow ridges, tiny

Masca, peaceful but increasingly well known

platforms of rock which plunge down into a lush valley of dramatic rock formations. Others lie at the foot of sheer cliff walls, edged around by terraced fields and flanked by little side valleys. Many houses are built into the hills, with flights of wooden steps to their doorways. Try to come here early in the morning or late in the afternoon to avoid the crowds, and to see the village at its peaceful best. Note, too, that Masca can also be reached slightly more easily from Santiago del Teide, 4km to the east, though this is a scenically less rewarding approach.

Barranco de Masca►►► The Barranco de Masca is the most important of the deep ravines that drop away from the village towards the sea. As the popularity of the village has increased, so, too, has the popularity of the walk through the gorge, a trail which wends its way through tremendous scenery and areas of great botanical interest. The trail is about 8km long and takes around two hours to walk, but is not an excursion to be undertaken lightly. Good boots and plenty of water are needed. The return uphill to the village from the sea takes far longer – allow three to four hours – for which reason many people make the trip downhill and organise a boat from Los Gigantes or Puerto de Santiago to pick them up on the coast (see page 124). The path is waymarked in places, and is becoming increasingly well-defined as more people walk it. This said, if you're an inexperienced walker it can still be worth hiring a guide. Other walks are possible in the area, notably an easier hike through the Barranco del Natero, which begins at Santiago del Teide and enters the Natero gorge by way of Casas de Araza (a hamlet) and the **Degollada de Cherfe**, the pass separating Masca and Santiago del Teide. This same pass is also traversed by road, and makes an excellent belvedere for drivers, with fine views of Mount Teide to the east.

Masca museum
At the time of writing, a small museum in Masca is being restored to present a brief account of the history of the village and the inaccessible back country of the Teno Massif. It is located down the hill at the bottom of a steep path through Masca's huddle of white cottages (the best bit of the village). From here a level walk takes you to the other half of the village.

■ **Before the Spanish Conquest, Tenerife was inhabited by a primitive people known as the Guanches. Lacking the resources and know-how of their fellow Europeans, their way of life resembled that of Stone Age tribes, complete with ancient rites and rituals, among which was the custom of mummifying their dead.** ■

Guanche art
Few Guanche artefacts have survived to the present day, and certainly none that suggest an artistically advanced culture. A few crude pots, all made without the use of a potter's wheel, have been found, as have a variety of seals known as *pintaderas*. The latter, made of pottery (more rarely of wood), are patterned, and were probably used to mark objects with the owner's personal insignia. The only other remains, and then merely fragments, are various stone and clay idols used in religious ceremonies.

Survival The Guanches were a primitive agricultural people, whose lives were devoted to growing basic crops and tending pigs, goats and sheep. Home for most was a cave – cool in summer, warm in winter. Clothing consisted of plaited palm leaves and *tamarcos* (rough goatskin cloaks). The plough was unknown, as was the art of weaving (despite the presence of wool), which meant that garments were bound together using thorns. Body-painting was probably also common. Food consisted largely of *gofio*, a combination of ground barley, honey and water rolled into balls and then roasted (it is still produced to this day – see page 157). Goats provided meat, milk and butter, while Tenerife's teeming woods and mountains yielded nuts, berries, wild fruits and mushrooms. The natural bounty of the sea, however, was largely beyond reach, for the Guanches, remarkably, appear never to have discovered boats.

Society For all their simplicity, the Guanches possessed a well-structured society. People were divided into three main groups: the king and his family; the nobles; and the common herd. Little separated the last two groups, however, nor was nobility inherited, but rather attained through personal achievement and then confirmed by priests. Wealth and other inheritance passed through the female line, though society was not matriarchal. Women could not rule, for example, but could take part in religious ceremonies, apparently enjoying an elevated and important status within society. Religious beliefs were confined to a single all-powerful deity, Abora, who was opposed by Guayote, an embodiment of evil. Guayote was believed to dwell in Mount Teide, and punished humans by creating volcanic eruptions.

Crude techniques were used to mummify the Guanche nobility

Guanche culture

Death One of the most fascinating aspects of the Guanches was their attitude to death, and in particular their habit of mummifying corpses in the manner of ancient Peruvian and Egyptian cultures. Only members of higher castes were mummified, however, and the crude techniques used meant that bodies decayed quickly, despite Tenerife's dry climate. Bodies were first soaked in goat's-milk butter and wrapped in animal skins. Attempts were then made to preserve corpses using smoke or by drying in the sun. Brains, intestines and other internal organs, however, were not removed, causing bodies to decay quickly. Mummified corpses have turned up in remote caves to this day, and many museums across the island have wonderfully macabre examples of the mummifier's art (or lack of it). Few corpses, though, are believed to be more than a few centuries old. Elderly people considered unworthy of mummification, incidentally, bade farewell to their families and were left in a cave to die alone.

Extinction Death arrived on a grand scale with the advent of the Spanish in the 15th century. The Guanches, lacking metal tools or weapons of any kind, were left to defend themselves using stones, wooden clubs and crude spears. They also lacked bows and arrows, and in close contact fighting were restricted to *tabonas*, or cutting stones, made from the razor-sharp volcanic rock, obsidian. It seems they even lacked the stone axes perfected by earlier neolithic cultures. Not surprisingly, few Guanches survived the invasion – estimates put the number of survivors at around a thousand – and those that did either died from diseases introduced by the Spanish or were assimilated into the invaders' way of life.

Today only hints of Tenerife's ancient people survive. Their language is all but lost (see panel), as are their mostly basic attempts at art (see panel, page 136). Only the odd facial characteristic, it is said – fair skin, blue eyes and blond hair – occasionally emerges as an eerie reminder of the island's mysterious early inhabitants.

A romantic portrayal of a Guanche ruler at Candelaria

Language
Among the many things the Guanches appear to have lacked was a written language, although fragments of hieroglyphics, pictographs and wall paintings have been found at sites around the Canaries (it may be that these were left by visitors to the island). None, in any case, have ever been deciphered, and none have been found on Tenerife or La Gomera. As for traces of Guanche language, which was probably similar across the Canaries, the only memorials appear to be contained in a handful of modern-day place names.

Holes in the head
Among the stranger customs practised by the Guanches was trepanning, or the boring and cutting of holes into the skull. This may have been a ritualistic procedure, or a form of surgery for genuine medical complaints. Guanche skulls in several Tenerife museums show signs of the practice.

THE SOUTH

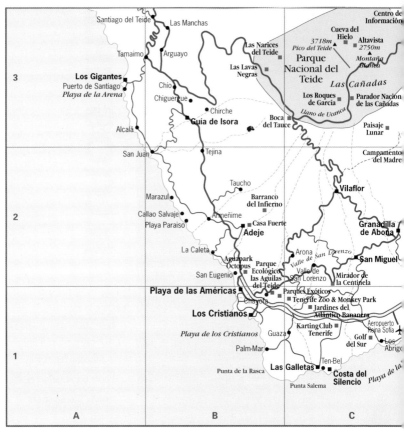

Large parts of southern Tenerife are what many people imagine when they think of the island, for this is the domain of vast seaside resorts, and the ranks of hotels, bars, restaurants and neon-advertised nightlife that draw many package-holidaymakers here annually in search of sun, sea and non-stop partying.

If you're young, young at heart or looking for a cheap and cheerful holiday with the family, you could do worse than come to one or other of the biggest resorts: **Playa**

Previous pages: El Médano, a wind-surfers' paradise Below: keeping busy on the beach at Los Cristianos

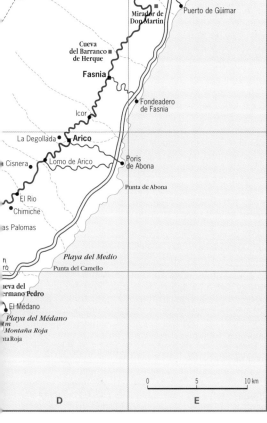

Tourism is not the only money-spinner in the south: fishing boats at Las Galletas

de las Américas and **Los Cristianos** make up a resort conurbation that looks destined to become the largest anywhere on Spanish territory. Of these two monsters, Los Cristianos is marginally the quieter, retaining the faintest vestiges of its fishing village origins. Playa de las Américas, which was built from scratch, has no such heritage, and displays all that is best and worst of the prefabricated package-tour resort.

If you want scenic beauty and old-world charm, you will avoid these good-time towns. You will also do well to consider avoiding this part of the island altogether, for the virtually year-round sun which first attracted developers here has resulted in a mostly dry, arid and unprepossessing array of landscapes. Only one scenic jewel demands attention, the **Barranco del Infierno**, a superb gorge that offers a simple but satisfying walk to those prepared to leave the car behind (it lies just 6km from Playa de las Américas). Some of the resorts' peripheral sights are also worth visiting (perhaps from elsewhere on the island), notably the quartet of environmental and wildlife attractions around **Los Cristianos**. And if you head north to Santa Cruz, taking the old inland road (*carretera*) instead of the motorway, you'll pass through a string of modest, unspoilt little villages where tourism has yet to establish a foothold.

Volcanic view
For the finest view of the whole south coast of Tenerife, visit the Mirador de la Centinela on the C822 road between San Miguel and the village of Valle de San Lorenzo (due north of the Costa del Silencio). Spread out below the viewpoint are the cones of dozens of extinct volcanoes.

THE SOUTH

Refreshment
On returning down the gorge to Adeje, take time out for a meal or cold drink in the bar-restaurant Otelo (tel: 78 03 74), ideally situated at the gorge entrance. Despite its fine position, and the number of visitors who pass through, it remains a friendly and unassuming place with reasonable prices and excellent Canarian food. It's particularly famed for its chicken (basted in chilli and garlic before cooking) and rabbit, both of which come in generous portions.

Old buildings still adorn Adeje's largely unspoilt streets

Opposite: the Barranco del Infierno, a scenic highlight of the south

▶ **Adeje**   *140B2*

Adeje is a small and largely unspoilt market town in Tenerife's southwest corner. Located just 6km north of Playa de las Américas, its proximity to some of the island's bigger resorts has altered its character over the last few years. Most people come here not so much for the town, however, as for the nearby Barranco del Infierno, a deep-cut ravine that ranks among the island's most impressive landscapes. If you come to walk the gorge, however, you will also see the town, which is well worth exploring.

Historically the area was one of the first to be settled after the Spanish Conquest, thanks largely to the abundance of fresh water, the stream running through the Barranco being one of the few on Tenerife's parched southern margins to flow year round. Before the arrival of the Spanish, the presence of water also accounted for an important Guanche town on the site which probably served as the capital of a far-reaching tribal kingdom. It may also have been the seat of the Guanche kings, the *Menceys*. A Guanche shrine, furthermore, was located at the nearby Roque del Conde. In 1497 the area became the feudal domain of Cristóbal de Ponte (Adeje's lords would control the town until 1840), and in the 16th century Cristóbal's son, Pedro de Ponte, built a *casa fuerte* (fortified house) in the town, which survives to this day (see below). For years the town prospered from the production of sugar cane: today tomatoes, bananas and tourism are the principal money-makers.

The main street, lined with laurel trees, retains something of its charm, with traditional older houses mingling with newer bars, restaurants and gift shops. The street contains the town's parish church, the **Iglesia de Santa Ursula** (see panel, page 144), a two-aisled building which dates from the 17th century. Inside, note the superb coffered ceiling and the two little balconies above the apse, the latter once reserved for the local nobility, who were sheltered from the prying glances of the congregation by wrought-iron screens. Also here is a statue of the Virgen del Rosario, the work of Fernando Estévez (1788–1854), one of Tenerife's leading nineteenth-century artists.

Elsewhere in the town, pay a visit to Pedro del Ponte's **Casa Fuerte** (1556), built to protect the region from attacks by pirates. In the event it was sacked by English pirates 30 years later, and then all but destroyed by fire in the 19th century. Once owned by the Counts of La Gomera, it later served as the focus of a vast sugar plantation worked by some 1,000 slaves. Over the years it accumulated workhouses, warehouses and a complex of residential quarters. It became a tomato-packing plant, and later still a banana-packaging warehouse. Now restored, plans are well advanced to open a history museum on the site.

▶▶▶ **Barranco del Infierno**   *140B2*

The traverse of the Barranco del Infierno (Gorge of Hell), is one of Tenerife's best-known walks, hiked by thousands of people annually from Adeje and the nearby resorts of Los Cristianos and Playa de las Américas. The spectacular canyon is one of only a handful of verdant

St Ursula
St Ursula was the daughter of the Breton King Maurus, who was pledged to marry Hereus, the son of the English king, Conon. The marriage was to take place on two conditions: first, that Conon had to wait three years, and second, that he convert to Christianity and accompany Ursula on a pilgrimage to Rome. Neither demand seemed too onerous (though Ursula seems reluctant to have entered into the marriage at all), except for the fact that the pilgrimage, according to legend, was to be made in the company of 11,000 virgins, and that the whole party was to be massacred by the Huns at Cologne on its return from Rome.

Cooling off in the Barranco del Infierno's waterfalls

Place of execution
For all its beauty, the Barranco del Infierno served a tragic purpose in the past which gave new meaning to its name (Gorge of Hell). In 1936 General Franco's forces used it as a place of execution, dispensing summary justice to Republican prisoners during the Spanish Civil War.

beauty spots on Tenerife's southern margins, owing its lush cover of vegetation – at least in parts – to the virtually year-round stream.

If you wish to walk up the gorge, aim to arrive in Adeje early: firstly so you can walk in the cool of morning, secondly so you can find a parking space in town; and thirdly so the gorge won't be too busy with walkers. The ravine entrance is easily found, reached by a steep road from the town (steeper than anything in the gorge itself). The gorge-bottom path is immensely well worn and easy to follow, and it's almost impossible to get lost, particularly with the large number of people around you. Boots are advisable, but not essential, and in all but the wettest weather you should be able to make the trip in a good pair of trainers. Be sure to take a sun-hat and something to drink. Walking the gorge one-way should take people of average fitness around 1 to 1¼hrs. The distance is around 8km both ways (you return the way you came), with a height gain of around 300m (more pertinent than the distance covered). There are few steep sections, and for most of the way the path is smooth.

Early signs on the path are not encouraging, for on entering the canyon you find yourself in a dry, rather desolate looking landscape of rocks and prickly pears. Above you on the rocky heights you can make out the dark holes of Guanche caves, seemingly inaccessible eyries in which numerous mummies have been discovered and removed over the years (see page 137). In time you reach the so-called *Bailadero de las Brujas* (Place Where the Witches Dance), a belvedere which provides lovely views.

Further up the gorge, the vegetation becomes more luxuriant, watered by a stream which is crossed and recrossed several times as you approach the head of the ravine (the pathways and stepping stones usually remain clear in all but the heaviest rain). Shaded by willows and other cooling trees, and refreshed by the sound of running water, you reach the head of the valley, where the reward – in winter and spring at least – is a modest waterfall tumbling part way down the gorge's cliff walls. On returning down the gorge to Adeje (allow two to three hours, with breaks, for the round trip) you should spend a few moments looking around the town and – more to the point – relax over a cooling drink, perhaps in the bar-restaurant Otelo (see panel, page 142).

▶ **Costa del Silencio**   *140C1*

Doubtless there was a time when the Costa del Silencio (Silent Coast) lived up to its name, but that must have been before 1978, when the opening of the Reina Sofía Airport a few kilometres to the east shattered what had once been a peaceful stretch of coastline on Tenerife's southernmost tip.

The airport proved the catalyst for the development of Los Cristianos (11km away to the northwest) and Playa de las Américas, resorts which rather leave the Costa del Silencio's more modest centres in the shade. This is also a rocky coastline, with no major beaches, merely the odd strip of shingle and a handful of coves with steps cut down to the sea.

The coast centres on **Las Galletas**, a former fishing village which lies just to the west of two purpose-built resorts: **Ten-Bel** and the **Costa del Silencio** itself. The former was built with Belgian investment, hence 'Bel' (the 'Ten' stands for Tenerife). Both resorts offer a predictable assortment of hotels, holiday apartments and bungalows, together with the usual roster of entertainment and recreational possibilities. Tropical gardens break up the modern developments, while several seawater swimming pools make up for the Costa's lack of proper beaches.

The two resorts have had a knock-on effect on Las Galletas, which has turned into a modest but friendly little resort of typical bars, hotels, restaurants and small shops. It also boasts two small sand-and-shingle beaches, together with a modest seafront promenade.

Like El Médano a few kilometres to the east, this is a good windsurfing area, and boards are available to hire from several points around town.

The Costa also provides golfing opportunities, offering two good local courses: the Golf del Sur (tel: 73 81 70) and the Amarilla Golf and Country Club (tel: 73 03 19). Note that the former, the island's best course, is only open to those with a recognised handicap.

Las Galletas, once a fishing village, is now a modest and amiable resort

Yellow submarine
The Costa del Silencio's most famous attraction is a novelty yellow submarine, the Finnish-built *Subtrek*. This will take you out to look at the often less than spectacular marine life of the Atlantic seabed. Free buses to the sub run hourly from Los Cristianos and Playa de las Américas. Telephone 71 50 80 for more information and to make reservations (space is limited).

THE SOUTH

*Most visitors come
to Los Abrigos to eat
in its noted fish
restaurants*

Los Abrigos

El Médano lies to one side
of the Reina Sofía Airport,
the small fishing village
of Los Abrigos to the
other. Aircraft noise
notwithstanding, the latter
is well known for its
remarkable fish and
seafood restaurants.
Locals, business people
and holidaymakers are
drawn here from far away
by the restaurants' superb
reputation. Most people
make for the arc of establishments which line the
village's small harbour,
offering similarly good food
at similar prices. Simply
choose the one you like
the look of the most and
follow a waiter to the cold
display to pick the fish or
seafood of your choice.
Many people also come
here for one last feast
before lurching towards
the airport to fly home.

►   **El Médano**   *141D1*

El Médano, like the nearby resorts of the Costa del
Silencio, hardly benefits from the presence of the Reina
Sofía Airport, barely 3km away to the west. In its favour,
however, the small resort has the advantage of southern
Tenerife's finest and longest **beach►►**, a strip of white
sand which stretches for some 3km southwest of the
village (it is Tenerife's only naturally light-coloured sandy
beach). The beach runs either side of a local landmark, the
Montaña Roja (Red Mountain), a 171m remnant of an old
volcanic cone. The sand shelves gently to the sea, making
the beach ideal for children. It has the disadvantage,
however, of strong winds – the *alisios*, or northeast trade
winds – so think about bringing a sunshade and wind-
break. The wind, and the sand dunes it produces, lend the
village its name (*médano* means dune).

But if the wind is anathema to bathers, it's a positive
boon to **windsurfers**, making the resort one of the sport's
major centres in Europe – it's often used as the venue for
international windsurfing championships. Surfers tend to
favour the beach east of the Montaña Roja (Playa de
Leocadie Machado), attracted by almost constant on-
shore breezes (this beach is also a favourite with the
camper-van crowd): bathers, by contrast, make for the
marginally more sheltered sand to the west (Playa de la
Tejita). Note that both these beaches become wilder and
more deserted as you head away from the resort. Part of
the beach nearer the village (Playa del Médano), sheltered
by local hotels, is also safe and popular with families and
bathers. Windsurfers will find plenty of places to hire
boards, and if you fancy taking up the sport, there are a
number of local windsurfing schools.

The **village** itself, at which Magellan is said to have
moored in 1519, is quiet and relatively undeveloped, at
least by Tenerife standards. Although lacking any great
charm, it retains a dash of its original local colour, with

a pretty village square, a few narrow streets and alleys, and a handful of fishing boats still drawn up on the beach. In the evening, visitors make for the bars, restaurants and small clubs gathered close to the square, pleasant places without the intensity and night-time fervour found in the larger resorts.

This said, development continues apace, and the number of hotels and apartment blocks on and around the beach is likely to increase. Given the ever-present wind, however, this resort is unlikely ever to join the ranks of Los Cristianos and Playa de las Américas.

Whether you come here for the calm or the beach or both, one excursion worth making is the short walk to the **Cueva del Hermano Pedro►►►**, a cave that lies virtually under the eastern end of the airport runway. It was once inhabited by Hermano Pedro (Brother Pedro), a missionary and monk born in 1619 in nearby Vilaflor. Pedro eventually emigrated to Guatemala, where he founded the Bethlehemite order of monks, a movement which later spread throughout Brazil and the rest of South America. His attempts to spread the word in Tenerife had met with less success: he was reputedly harried out of Vilaflor and forced to take refuge in the cave near El Médano which now bears his name. There he followed an ascetic and hermit-like existence before his emigration. He was canonised in 1980, and is one of Guatemala's patron saints, one reason the cave has become a point of pilgrimage.

A Mass is celebrated here twice a year in Brother Pedro's honour, though the leaving of votive offerings and photographs of nearest and dearest – poignant mementoes which once adorned the cave – now appears to have been discouraged. To reach the grotto walk beyond the Playa Sur Tenerife hotel and follow the sign-posted track. Fork right after some 200m and the cave lies 500m beyond.

Local flora
The arid countryside around El Médano may look lifeless, but it supports all manner of drought-loving plant and flower species that you might normally expect to find on the fringes of the Sahara. The most notable include *Euphorbia balsam-ifera, Tamarix canariensis* and *Launaea arborescens*.

El Médano is one of Europe's finest wind-surfing centres

■ Handicrafts are a way of life for many in Tenerife, forming part of an island tradition that stretches back over many centuries. Popular with visitors as souvenirs, they provide a valuable source of income for many islanders. Many of the old craft skills are disappearing, however, compromised by a flood of cheap imported imitations from overseas. ■

Old skills are kept alive: weaving at Hermigua's craft centre

Specialities
Towns particularly noted for their woodworkers include La Laguna, La Orotava and Buenavista. Musical instruments are made at Taganana and San Andrés. Wine presses and balconies are found in La Orotava and Los Realejos. Pottery, like embroidery, is ubiquitous, but is especially renowned at Los Cristianos, La Orotava, Güimar, La Gomera (Chipude) and Icod de los Vinos. For straw hats and baskets head for La Guancha, Masca and Buenavista. For the best open threadwork make for Granadilla, La Guancha, Los Realejos, La Orotava and San Juan de la Rambla.

Tradition To walk through almost any Tenerife resort would seem to suggest the island's handicrafts were invented solely for the benefit of tourists. Embroidery, straw hats, basketwork, clothes and a hundred other novelty items festoon the island's souvenir shops. Many of these trinkets are mass-produced (many in the Far East), and have little to do with local traditions that in reality stretch back over hundreds of years. Local woodturning and carving techniques, for example, are rooted in agriculture, stemming from the need to produce yokes, ploughs and other implements. Others were prompted by the demands of rural daily life, which required looms, furniture, pipes and even musical instruments. Similar demands led to the creation of pottery and basketwork, while embellishment for its own sake produced the embroidery and 'open' threadwork distinctive to Tenerife.

Genuine examples of all these crafts can still be found, often in their places of origin, in state-run shops (*centros artesanías*), at craft fairs (*ferias artesanías*), or – in more remote rural areas – from small roadside stalls.

Textiles By far the most common and readily available Tenerife handicrafts are *bordados* (embroidery) and *calcados* (open threadwork). The latter is a form of lacy needlework in which the cloth is stretched on a frame and partially unravelled. The threads are then drawn together with a special hemstitching technique that produces complicated patterns and motifs. Cloth is usually worked

Handicrafts

by more than one person. Different islands in the Canaries (and regions within islands) have developed different approaches, many of which have evolved into complicated and accomplished art forms. Embroidered or worked cloth often appears on traditional costumes worn at local festivals. More than with other crafts, this is an area where you have to beware of mass-produced foreign imports. Try to buy at the various schools of embroidery across the island, many of which have shops attached, notably that at Puerto de la Cruz, or the Casa de los Balcones at La Orotava (see page 91). Tablecloths and napkins are the most common items, but the work is also applied to collars, handkerchiefs and lacy tops.

Basketwork Artefacts in wood, cane and straw are also common, embracing everything from the humble straw hat to beautifully made musical instruments such as the *timple* (four-stringed Canarian guitar). Palm leaves are used to make hats, bags and other items, while the palm's sturdy central stem (*pirgano*) is used to make fans and brooms. At the other extreme, you can buy large carved wine-presses, and even miniature wooden balconies of the type encountered in buildings across northern Tenerife. Basketwork is executed in *vara* (twig), using wide strips of young wood (often chestnut), or in *cana* (cane), which is used for more delicate items. Sometimes a mixture of cane and twig is used to produce a combination of strength and delicacy. Rather less common is *palanqueta*, in which strips from the stalks of date bunches are used to create intricate decorative patterns. Straw is used to make hats, hampers and containers, while wood can be turned to produced anything from plates and cutlery to pestles and mortars.

Pottery Of all Tenerife's crafts, traditional pottery probably has the most venerable lineage. The oldest island pottery is that of the Guanches, copies of which are still made as they were in pre-Spanish days – without a wheel. Hands alone shape and raise the pot, which is kept from sticking to the surface on which it is being worked by a sprinkling of sand. Villages on La Gomera, notably Chipude, are particularly renowned for this type of ware, but you'll find similar pots and other ceramics in shops across the island.

Variety
Tenerife has countless handicrafts over and above textiles, pottery and work in wood, straw and cane. Other articles include straw and rag dolls in traditional costume, ornately handled knives, lace-work produced by the island's nuns, woollen shawls and cloaks, clay figurines, and *traperas*, which are rugs made from wool or woven from rags. Polished volcanic stones and engraved jewellery are also available: look out in particular for articles made from peridot, a green-hued semi-precious stone.

Needlework, a traditional Tenerife craft

Free buses
Los Cristianos' four major 'wildlife' attractions all lie within a few minutes' drive of the town centre. Lack of your own transport is no problem, however, for numerous free shuttle buses run to all four sites from a variety of pick-up and drop-off points around the town. If the buses are not convenient, all the attractions can reached easily and cheaply by taxi.

Room for more at Los Cristianos beach

► **Los Cristianos**   *140B1*

Los Cristianos is probably not somewhere to visit for its own sake, but as one of the largest resorts on Tenerife, may well be somewhere you are based as part of a package holiday. Little more than a fishing village until the 1970s, it has mushroomed over the last two or three decades into a fully-fledged resort, complete with ranks of huge hotels, new roads and the full gamut of bars, restaurants and nightclubs. As development continues, its borders are rapidly merging with those of neighbouring Playa de las Américas (see page 158), creating what may well become a 'super resort' to end all super resorts. This said, Los Cristianos has traditionally been the quieter, relatively speaking, of the two resorts, and tends to attract a slightly older cross-section of visitors. Unlike its neighbour, which spreads out in a disjointed sprawl of modern *urbanizaciónes*, or blocks, Los Cristianos has managed to retain a semblance of town life, its newer development still bearing social and geographical ties to the old town centre.

First impressions, therefore, are likely to be slightly misleading. From afar, all you see are the modern hotels, starkly pitched against barren and dust-dry mountain slopes (Los Cristianos' almost perfect climate, with virtually year-round sunshine, is one of the reasons for its success). Closer acquaintance reveals the usual panoply of British pubs and 'Full English Breakfast' signs. Around the tight little huddle of the old harbour, however, a different picture emerges. The port was once used to export vast quantities of locally grown tomatoes, and today remains the focus of what still passes for a proper Canarian town. Shops sell basic food and goods to Spanish-speaking locals, while in the evening the streets and church square resound to the sights and sounds of the daily *paseo*.

This is the place, therefore, to come for a touch of 'real life' when you tire of the hotel swimming pool and tennis

A typically bustling street in Los Cristianos

151

courts. It is a lively little spot from where to watch the town's various comings and goings, principally the arrival and departure several times a day of ferries and hydrofoils for nearby La Gomera (highlights of the Los Cristianos day). A spectacle is also provided by returning fishing boats, the buzzing of pleasure craft, and the elegant ranks of ocean-going yachts. The port and neighbouring promenades are therefore the place to settle yourself with a drink to watch the streetlife. It's also the place to come if you want to join one of the many fishing charters or other organised boat trips that regularly depart from Los Cristianos (see below).

The town► Los Cristianos offers little by way of sightseeing or entertainment outside the usual bar, café and nightclub scene. Most of the local 'attractions' are a little way out of town. However, the resort does offer the chance to book various watersports activities (ask for details from your hotel, which may organise similar activities of its own). More to the point, it is also the place to book places on the many **boat excursions** available locally. Some people simply make a day-trip to La Gomera (see page 162), others take charters to enjoy the area's superb offshore fishing. Many are tempted by trips to go shark-hunting, or to watch whales and dolphins, or by excursions advertising themselves as 'pirate' voyages or 'sangria-sailings' (trips where the emphasis is very much on enjoying yourself). Most trips are half- or full-day excursions, and are usually available for an all-inclusive price which includes food and drink.

Los Cristianos' sightseeing attractions may be limited, but the town does score over Tenerife's other big resorts – Puerto de la Cruz and Playa de las Américas – in claiming a **beach** of distinction. The town's sandy *playa* stretches for some 400m, reaching a width of 100m in places. It has recently been joined by the new Playa de

Getting out
There is no need to be confined to your hotel in Los Cristianos. There are numerous boat excursions and free shuttle buses to the outlying natural sights. It is also easy to rent cars, mopeds or bicycles from some of the many outlets around the town. Several companies also organise coach trips to other attractions around the island. Don't forget, either, that free bus trips are available to the popular Loro Parque (Parrot Park) just outside Puerto de la Cruz on the north of the island (see page 105).

THE SOUTH

San Telmo, another pale-sand crescent across the
harbour road, a development which has relieved some of
the pressure on the old beach. Both beaches are clean
and well kept. Imported white sand from the Sahara has
recently been introduced to spruce up the native sand.
Promenades full of bars and cafés, together with the
occasional colourful garden, line both beaches.

The back country►► One of the revelations of Los
Cristianos and its neighbouring resorts is the speed with
which you can escape the neon, nightlife and high-rise
hotels. Several country roads push north from the coast
beyond the Autopista del Sur, passing quiet villages and
traversing a near-desert landscape as they climb towards
the slopes of Mount Teide.

This other-worldly landscape, produced by southern
Tenerife's distinct lack of rain, is an attraction in itself,
offering the chance to view flora and fauna markedly
different to those elsewhere on the island. The vegetation
is dominated by cactus-like species of endemic spurges
and other drought-loving euphorbias. There are also rare
endemics, such as the Canary tamarisk, *Tamarix
canariensis*. Among the birds you might see are dry-
country species such as Barbary partridge, Berthelot's
pipit and trumpeter finch. If you decide to explore the
region, especially if you're likely to be on foot for any
length of time, be sure to take plenty of water and wear a
hat to keep off the sun.

*Cacti come in all
shapes and sizes*

*The Parques Exóticus
offer a life-like
'Amazon rainforest'*

Parque Ecológico las Aguilas del Teide►►► This beautifully landscaped zoo and wildlife park (The Eagles of Teide Ecological Park) is one of Tenerife's newest attractions, and since its opening in 1994 has drawn thousands of visitors tempted by the chance to see impressive displays of free-flying eagles, condors and other large raptors. Purists initially argued about its designation as an 'ecological park', saying that many of the plants and animals on display were foreign to Tenerife. This argument is likely to cut little ice with most visitors, who in addition to the birds of prey will find some 7.5ha of flora-covered parkland, together with displays of free-flying tropical birds, elephants, penguins, crocodile, flamingos, pelicans and pygmy hippos. One of the most popular events is feeding time for the crocodiles and penguins. Children are also likely to be attracted to the 'bumping' boats and bobsled rides. Free buses from the centre of Los Cristianos are available to the site, which lies some 3km from town on the road from Chayofa to Arona. (For further information, tel: 75 30 01 or 75 31 61. *Open* daily 10–6. *Admission charge* moderate.)

Parques Exóticos►► The so-called 'Exotic Parks' consist of 'Amazonia' and a combined 'Cactus and Animal Park', both more interesting than they might sound, and both easily accessible by free shuttle buses from Los Cristianos. Southern Tenerife is renowned for its barren and almost semi-desert landscapes, terrain which has

Ocean-going
Come to Los Cristianos in the winter months and the chances are you'll find its harbour filled with big ocean-going yachts. Many put up here as they wait for the favourable trade winds that blow at this time of year. When the winds are right the boats and their crews set sail for the Caribbean.

153

been put to good use in the cactus park, an area filled with cacti of virtually every shape and size imaginable. Information leaflets guide you around the many varieties, most of which are laid out according to the country of origin. Opened in 1985, the park and gardens have since grown to cover a wide area. They have also acquired a roster of other attractions, most notably a number of large walk-in cages, home to a variety of child-pleasing furry mammals including marmosets and squirrel monkeys. A series of aviaries also contains an impressive variety of free-flying parrots.

The same site is also home to 'Amazonia', a vast dome which encloses its own small slice of Amazonian 'rainforest'. Artificially controlled levels of heat and humidity have created a lush jungle-like foliage, together with a range of exotic plants and flowers. Around this forest microcosm flit more free-flying parrots and a 100 or so darting hummingbirds. Iguanas slither amidst the undergrowth, while over 5,000 butterflies flutter from flower to flower. (For further information, tel: 79 54 24 *Open* daily 10–7. *Admission charge* moderate.)

Jardines del Atlántico Bananera▶ Bananas are a recurring motif in Tenerife, and this working banana plantation (Atlantic Banana Garden) makes a good place to unravel their various mysteries, particularly if you haven't visited the excellent (and similar) Bananera el Guanche at Puerto de la Cruz (see page 101). Guided tours take you around the plantation and farm, offering the inside track not only on bananas, but also on a wide range of Tenerife's flora, fauna and natural phenomena. The guide, with the aid of video displays, explains the growth cycles and production methods involved in producing coffee, avocados, papayas and other fruits, together with information about the way water percolates down from Mount Teide and how it is used by farmers to irrigate the parched fields of southern Tenerife.

As with other sights, free shuttle buses run to the plantation. To get here under your own steam take the Santa Cruz–Los Cristianos motorway (Autopista del Sur) and exit at Valle de San Lorenzo (exit 26). Thereafter the attraction is signed. Note that it can be worth checking the precise times of tours: generally there around five a day in peak season. (For information, tel: 72 04 03. *Open* daily 10–6. *Admission charge* moderate.)

Tenerife Zoo and Monkey Park▶ Zoos can often be dispiriting places, and though Tenerife's is not as gloomy as some, its surroundings are still somewhat uninspired. Located close to the Parques Exóticos (see page 153), its main attractions are monkeys, orang-utans and other primates, some of which reach massive sizes. There is also a reptilarium, a handful of large cats and a variety of other animals including llamas, ponies and parrots, all designed to appeal primarily to children. A separate site, with separate or combined admission available, also offers the novelty of camel rides. As with other sites, free shuttle buses run here from a variety of locations. (The zoo is located close to exit 26 of the Autopista del Sur. For further information, tel: 75 13 68. *Open* daily 9.30–6. *Admission charge* moderate.)

An Indian langur and its baby in Tenerife Zoo

■ **Such is Tenerife's influx of visitors that many restaurants cater almost exclusively to foreign tastes. You could come to the island and never eat local food, though to do so would mean missing out on better and cheaper cuisine. For authentic local restaurants look in a resort's quieter corners and backstreets.** ■

Soups and stews *Sopa* (soup) and stew are some of the most typical Tenerife dishes. *Potaje* is a vegetable soup or stew: when meat is added it is known as *rancho canario*. *Sopa de verdura* is a plain vegetable soup, *sopa de ajo* a robust garlic soup, and *sopa de pescado* a rich mixture of fish and seafood (*zarzuela* is another name for fish soup). *Escaldón* is a soup which has been thickened with *gofio* (see page 157). *Puchero* – a pork and vegetable stew – is more substantial, and usually eaten as a main course. Another common stew is *garbanzo compuesto* (chickpeas with meat), also often available as a *tapas* (see panel, page 156). Heartier still is *conejo con salmorejo*, a favourite Tenerife casserole based around rabbit. Most of these dishes are flavoured differently with herbs such as thyme, saffron, marjoram, parsley and particularly cumin and coriander. For the most part, though, the basic ingredients are similar.

Meat On the whole only foreigners go for the island's big grilled steak (*solomillo*), beef for which is usually imported from Spain or South America. Meat is usually more likely to appear only as an ingredient in stews. This said, rabbit is common, though not as readily available as *pollo*

Etiquette
Eating out in Tenerife is invariably casual and informal. Reservations are required only at a handful of the very top restaurants. Children are welcome, indeed encouraged, virtually everywhere. Half-portions are usually available in tourist areas. Mealtimes are later than most foreigners are used to: lunch is around 2–3.30pm, dinner from 8–10pm (or later) – though hotels and resort restaurants often cater to their foreign guests by observing earlier hours.

155

Eating al fresco is one of Tenerife's pleasures

Eating out in Playa de las Américas

Tapas

Tapas are a light snack between or before main meals. Often, though, they amount to a meal in themselves, and usually include olives, fried fish, herring fillets, smoked ham (*jamón*), squid, octopus, tuna, meatballs, spicy sausage and potato salad with herbs. Also common are *tortilla* (omelette) or *tortilla española* (omelette with potatoes, onions and vegetables). *Tapas* are available in bars and cafés as well as in restaurants.

Areperas

An *arepera* is an ordinary café or bar-restaurant which serves *arepas*. Look for the word incorporated (often inconspicuously) in the restaurant sign. *Arepas* are small Venezuelan sandwiches made from semolina flour and deep fried. Fillings include *pollo* (chicken), *cerdo* (cold roast pork), *carne* (beef) and *atún salpicón* (tuna in a spicy sauce). A red pepper sauce and a cool green *aguacate* (avocado) sauce are usually offered separately.

(chicken), which is often simply fried or roasted: look out in particular for *pollo a la brassa* (charcoal-grilled chicken). On the north of the island you will come across *parillas*, (grills), often little more (literally) than a converted garage where the family mucks in to produce chicken and other meats grilled over wood-burning stoves and charcoal embers. Sometimes chicken is smothered in garlic and chilli sauce and then roasted or deep fried to acquire a delicious crispy coating. Another speciality is chicken which has been braised in a rich, spicy sauce. Lamb is sometimes available (cooked in oil and garlic it is known as *cordero al ajillo*), while at certain times of the year you may be lucky enough to find roast kid (*cabrito asado* or *cabrito al horno*).

Fish Tenerife's teeming seas make *pescado* (fish) and seafood the island's culinary staples. Both usually appear in some shape or form on most menus, often in a bewildering variety (though often not everything on the menu is always available). Cooking is usually simple – fish are generally boiled, fried or grilled, with straightforward presentation and accompaniments to match. Often you choose your fish simply by walking to the restaurant's cold cabinet or kitchen and looking over what's available that day. Your choice is then weighed and you pay by weight (note that it's perfectly acceptable to ask for a large fish to be divided between two people). You may be asked how you wish the fish to be cooked: the best bet is *a la plancha* – grilled.

The most popular fish are all members of the sea bass family – *cherne*, *abade*, *mero* and *cabrilla* – closely followed by *merluza* (hake) and *vieja* (the carp-like parrotfish). *Mero* and *abade*, both white fish, are especially common; *cherne* is larger and firmer, and is often eaten as 'steaks' like tuna and swordfish. Other common fish include *sardinas* (sardines), *bacalao* (cod), *espada* (swordfish), *caballa* (mackerel), *lenguado* (sole), *atún* (tuna) and *bonito* (better-quality skip-jack tuna). Sole is especially popular, but in all but the best restaurants may be frozen

Food

and imported from elsewhere. You may also come across *sama* (a large and thick-bodied fish) and *sargo* and *chopa*, both similar to seabream.

Seafood is plentiful, popular and invariably excellent. Look out for *calamares* (squid), *gambas* (prawns), *cangrejos* (crabs), *pulpo* (octopus), *mejillones* (mussels), *lapas* (limpets), *camarones* (shrimps) and *langostinos* (king prawns). Octopus and squid are also often chopped small and served as *tapas*, while prawns with a garlic dip are another popular starter.

On the side The traditional accompaniment to most meals is *papas arrugadas*, literally 'wrinkled potatoes'. These are small Canary potatoes, cooked in their jackets in seawater or well-salted water, and boiled dry to leave a crispy coating of salt across the skins. Vegetables are comparatively rare, though *ensalada* (salad) is cheap and plentiful. Often two cold olive-oil based sauces will be placed on tables to accompany meals: red *mojo picón* (piquant sauce) and *mojo verde* (green sauce). The latter is a cool parsley and coriander sauce, perfect with fish; the former is a spicy vinaigrette-type mix of chilli, cumin, saffon, paprika and red peppers, generally served as an accompaniment to potatoes and red meat. Both can be bought ready-made in supermarkets in tiny bottles to take home as souvenirs. Less likely to appear in restaurants, but a staple of Tenerife home-cooking, is *gofio*, a crude doughy paste devised by the ancient Guanches. Composed of milled and toasted maizemeal (or wheat and barley), it is used to thicken stews, can be either sweet or savoury, and is often eaten in place of bread.

Puddings The Canaries' most famous *postre* (dessert) is *bienmesabe*, a mouthwatering confection of almonds, sugar, honey, eggs, lemon and sponge cake. Eaten with *nata* (cream) or ice cream it comes close to pudding perfection. In simpler restaurants, however, puddings may simply be a choice of *fruta* (fruit), *macedonia* (fruit salad) or *helado* (ice-cream). *Flan* is also extremely common, but don't be put of by its ubiquity: a simple cooked milk dessert (rather like crème caramel), it's usually home-made in any good local restaurant, and a source of some pride to the maker.

Crème caramel itself (*tocino de cielo*) is also common, as are *tarta de almendras* (almond tart), *nuezes garapiñadas* (walnut brittle) and *turrón*, a delicious almond-based paste that comes in two varieties: hard (like nougat) and soft (like the Greek *halva*). Bananas, inevitably, also feature among local puddings, most spectacularly as a flambé sweetened with honey and liqueurs. *Plántanos a la canaria* is banana fried in brandy sauce.

A tile sign advertising the health benefits of fish oils

157

Menus
All Tenerife restaurants are supposed by law to offer a *menú del día* (menu of the day), a low-price set meal often advertised on a board outside. Generally this is cheap but unexciting. Coffee (and sometimes wine) is extra. Go for the *especialidad del día* (speciality of the day). Canarian portions under any circumstances are usually generous.

Banana flambé: a Tenerife classic

Timeshare
You will be lucky to spend time on Tenerife without being approached by someone offering timeshare properties. These properties will be dressed up with all sorts of free offers, free gifts, the chance to win holidays and much more besides. Unless you are genuinely interested in property (as are 20,000 Britons a year) do not waste your time with any of these touts (officially known as OPCs – Off Property Contacts), their offers, or their persuasive sales patter. If you are interested be certain to deal only with licensed and long-established operators. On no account sign anything until you have taken good legal advice.

► **Playa de las Américas**   140B1

Accept Playa de las Américas for what it is – a vast purpose-built resort designed for the British and German package-tour market – and you will be able to enjoy yourself amidst its multitude of hotels, restaurants, bars and non-stop nightclubs. Some 40 years ago this flat stretch of coastline in Tenerife's southwestern corner was little more than a drab, desert-like expanse of sand, stone and the occasional banana plantation. What it did have in abundance was sunshine – almost 12 months a year of it – which is why the developers chose it as the site for what would become one of Europe's largest resorts. Work began in 1966 and continues to this day, more and more hotels and apartments being added to the resort's aimless sprawl. These days its amorphous borders mingle with those of nearby Los Cristianos.

Modern You should expect absolutely nothing by way of the old Tenerife in Playa de las Américas: everything here has been built from scratch. Many restaurants and bars actually make a virtue of the fact that they eschew all things Spanish: English and German breakfasts are widely advertised, English 'pubs' prevail (along with English beer and English punters) and some establishments go so far as to boast that 'no Spanish food is served here'. What the resort has in abundance, however, is nightlife, including some of Europe's biggest and brashest clubs and discos. Dancing and rowdy partying go on into the smallest of the small hours. You can also indulge in just about every watersport imaginable. Hotels have details of schools and rental companies: check they are reputable, and – most importantly – that schools are fully insured. Most hotels also have swimming pools and tennis courts.

Town Playa de las Américas is nothing like a town in the conventional sense. Rather it is an unfocused sprawl of *centros commerciales* (shopping centres) and *urbanizaciónes* (development zones). Some developers, however, to their credit, have softened the modern concrete jungle with wide tree-lined avenues, and squeezed pleasant gardens between the countless hotels and apartment blocks. The nicest central spot, in so far as there is a centre, is the **Puerto Colón**, a smart marina often filled with yachts awaiting the favourable trade winds that will take them across the Atlantic. This lies at the western end of the resort's seafront promenade, a route which has been extended to allow you, if the mood takes you, to walk all the way to Los Cristianos. At other points along the promenade you can settle down on artificial pale-sand beaches. The two best stretches of sand are probably Playa del Bobo and Playa de Troya, though the small beach near the Puerto Colón is also pretty. Protected by offshore breakwaters, these stretches of sand are attractively laid out and safe for children, though all can become horrendously

Fun for all the family: the Aguapark Octopus

crowded during peak periods. Be sure to arrive early to find space.

Waterpark Most people, if they are not headed for the beaches, make instead for the **Aguapark Octopus** (*Open* daily 10–6. *Admission charge* expensive; cheaper after 2.30), an excellent family waterpark with a huge water-chute, dolphin pool, wild water runs and several good swimming pools. Excursions run here from several points around the island, and there are free shuttle bus services from several major hotels in Playa de las Américas. The park is situated at San Eugenio, 2km north of the resort, just off exit 29 of the Autopista del Sur. Other attractions include the chance to go fishing, or to watch whales and dolphins. Windsurf boards can be hired, as can motor-boats, speedboats and – for the less speed conscious – pedaloes and sailing boats. Off the promenade, near the Puerto Canario, the Acuarío Atlántico offers visitors the chance to observe various Atlantic fish and marine animals in controlled surroundings.

Practicalities
The main information centre (Oficinas de Turismo) in Playa de las Américas is situated at Playa de Troya on Avenida Litoral (tel: 75 06 33). If you need emergency treatment, contact the Clinica del Sur (tel: 79 16 00). To call a taxi, tel: 79 14 07.

Puerto Colón marina, the most pleasant aspect of Playa de las Américas

LA GOMERA

REGION HIGHLIGHTS ◄◄◄◄◄◄

LA GOMERA

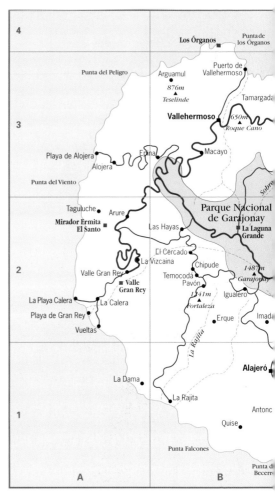

Above: a modern statue by César Manrique in the Valle Gran Rey
Previous pages: rugged scenery typical of La Gomera

La Gomera, or the Isla de Cordialidad, is the second smallest of the Canary Islands, surpassing only tiny El Hierro in size. Yet for all its modest proportions it is a beautiful and fascinating little enclave attracting ever greater attention from visitors. A peaceful and unspoilt paradise, it lies just 32km southwest of Los Cristianos on Tenerife, to which it is connected by ferry and hydrofoil.

It measures just 23km by 25km. This small size is misleading, however, for the great dome-shaped island – baked and barren on its fringes, gloriously wooded in its mountainous interior – is broken up by numerous deep ravines and gullies. This adds considerably to the time needed to get around by road – at least two days are needed to do the island justice.

Many people make day-trips from Tenerife to **San Sebastián**, the island capital, and several tour operators run all-inclusive coach trips from the 'mainland'. To see only San Sebastián, however, a relatively lacklustre point of entry to La Gomera, would be to miss the island's many highlights.

Festivals

La Gomera's villages, like their counterparts on the Tenerife mainland, need no excuse for a fiesta. The following are the most important:

6 Jan	Santos Reyes (Valle Gran Rey)
20 Jan	Fiesta de San Sebastián (San Sebastián)
Feb/Mar	Carnaval de San Sebastián (San Sebastián)
25 Apr	Fiesta de San Marcos (Agulo)
25 Jun	Fiesta de San Juan (Vallehermosa)
15 Aug	Fiesta de Candelaria (Chipude)
1–6 Sep	Seman Colombina (San Sebastián)
15 Sep	Virgen de Buen Paso (Alajeró)
1–6 Oct	Virgen de Guadalupe (Puntallana)

Hermigua is typical of many villages on La Gomera

LA GOMERA

Highlights Not least of these are two of the finest **hotels** in the Canaries, the Parador San Sebastián de la Gomera in San Sebastián and the Hotel Tecina in Playa de Santiago (see pages 177 and 172). Each provides added incentive for spending at least one night on the island.

Other attractions include the island's remarkable interior scenery, at its best in the **Parque Nacional de Garajonay** (see page 170), a national park which protects a beautifully lush forest of palms, laurels and tree ferns on the slopes of Mount Garajonay (1,487m), the island's highest point.

Walking is one way to explore the area, but you can enjoy the scenery almost equally as well from the tiny roads which twist through the interior. Much the same goes for La Gomera's other scenic set-piece, the **Valle Gran Rey** (see page 178), the most spectacular of the island's many majestic gorges and valleys.

Beaches La Gomera does have one small failing, in that it has only one 'proper' **beach** (at Playa de Santiago, see page 172). This *is* a shortcoming, though it is likely to save La Gomera from the worse side effects of mass tourism, a phenomenon that has yet to take hold on the island (one of its great charms).

This said, there are plenty of pebbly beaches and small dark-sand beaches, all the more appealing for their emptiness and lack of facilities. Only a handful are readily accessible by car, notably those at Playa de Gran Rey (see page 178), Agulo (see page 168) and Playa de Alojera (see page 178). If you're prepared to get off the beaten track, however, and explore some of the many rough roads that drop to the coast, you'll find not only a host of unspoilt hamlets, but also numerous secluded little beaches and coves.

Itineraries A rented car, a stout pair of walking boots and a week's stay are the best ways to see La Gomera. If time is short, however, the road route across the north of the island is the one to choose. This takes you from San Sebastián to the pretty village of Vallehermoso (see page 182), passing through Agulo (see page 168), Hermigua (see page 169) and other picturesque hamlets en route. It also offers the chance to admire part of the Parque Nacional de Garajonay and other of the island's wide variety of landscapes. The route is winding and spectacular, and has the advantage of being lower than the southern route across the island. This means it usually avoids the clouds which can form on the higher ground (though it is these clouds that provide the moisture to nurture the island's famous forests). Once at Vallehermoso you can drive to the sea and, weather permitting, take the popular boat trip to admire the cliffs at Los Órganos (see page 183).

If you have more time, continue on a circular route in an anticlockwise direction around the island, being sure to visit the Valle Gran Rey and the roads which return to San Sebastián by way of La Laguna Grande and the heart of the Parque Nacional de Garajonay. You may also want to head to the Playa de Santiago, which – along with the little collection of hamlets at Playa de Gran Rey – is the nearest thing the island has to a 'resort'.

Fishing boats tied up at Playa de Santiago

Vines growing in one of La Gomera's spectacular valleys

Christopher and Beatriz

■ **The name Christopher Columbus is evocatively woven into the history of La Gomera, not only because he used the island as a staging post before his famous voyage to the New World, but also because he became involved with Beatriz de Bobadilla, one of the Canary Islands' most colourful characters.** ■

Columbus' commission Columbus' route to the Canaries and thus to the New World was a tortured one. As early as 1476 he sought support for his venture – a western route to the Indies – at the Portuguese royal court in Lisbon. Spurned by the Portuguese, he then petitioned the Spanish court in 1486. Only in 1492 did Ferdinand and Isabella of Spain offer their support, granting him the title of viceroy to any lands he discovered, and a ten per cent share of any profits accruing from his voyage.

Invasion Little is known of La Gomera's early history or its early inhabitants. The first certain details of its story emerge in 1404, when Jean de Béthencourt, a Norman adventurer in the employ of Henry III of Castile, landed on the island as part of his mission to conquer the Canaries. He established a small settlement on the island, which was abandoned after sporadic fighting with local tribes. A Spaniard, Fernando Ormel de Castro, arrived on the island in 1438, but for reasons unknown left before making any lasting impression. Conquest was finally achieved in the mid-15th century by Hernán Peraza the Elder, a Spaniard who established himself as the island's seigneurial ruler, the self-styled Conde, or Count of Gomera. In time he was replaced by Hernán Peraza the Younger, husband of the infamous Beatriz de Bobadilla.

Bobadilla Beatriz was a woman of some renown – and not inconsiderable beauty – who made a name for herself at the Spanish court. She was also the mistress of the Spanish king, Ferdinand of Aragon, a role which not surprisingly failed to endear her to Ferdinand's queen, Isabella of Castile. When a chance came to rid herself of Beatriz, Isabella was quick to act. Hernán Peraza the Younger, it appears, was suspected of murder, and as a condition of his pardon was ordered to marry Beatriz and live with her on La Gomera. Once on the island, Beatriz and her husband proved tyrannical in their rule, their vicious treatment of the local Guanche population provoking a revolt in 1488 in which Hernán was killed (lured to a love-nest, it is said, and then ambushed). Beatriz subsequently installed herself in the Torre del Conde in San Sebastián, and it was here, so it is rumoured, that she enjoyed a dalliance with Christopher Columbus.

The Santa Maria, *Columbus' ship*

Columbus Columbus probably knew Beatriz from the time he spent at the Spanish court, especially as he embarked on his famous 1492 voyage of discovery under the patronage of Ferdinand and Isabella, rulers of Spain. Details of precisely when (and where) the explorer visited in the Canaries are still disputed, but it seems almost certain that in 1492 he visited both Gran Canaria and La Gomera. At Las Palmas and Gran Canaria he over-hauled his ships and took on supplies. Later he sailed past Tenerife, noting an eruption of Mount Teide in his log, an event his crew took as an inauspicious omen.

In August he put in to La Gomera, partly to take on water, and partly, it is said, to pursue a romantic dalliance with Beatriz. Some evidence of an affair may be provided by the fact that Columbus probably returned to the island on his second major voyage (1493–5), when Beatriz is said to have received the explorer with an artillery salute and a fireworks display.

Aftermath Columbus may have visited La Gomera again, this time during the third of his great voyages (1498–1500). However, he conspicuously failed to do so during his fourth (and final) voyage in 1502. One reason for his hesitation may have been Beatriz's altered marital state, for in 1498, wily as ever, she had managed to ensnare Alonso Fernández de Lugo, the Andalusian nobleman who had played a leading role in subduing the Canaries. It was probably no coincidence that he was, at the time, the most powerful man in the islands (see page 30). Such elevated connections cemented Beatriz's role as La Gomera's *de facto* countess. Similar strong-willed individuals ruled for generations to come, and the island remained a *señorio*, or seigneurial land, until as late as 1812.

Spain's King Ferdinand of Aragon and Queen Isabella of Castile bid farewell to Columbus

Mixed memories
Whatever the esteem in which Christopher Columbus is held in the rest of Spain and the Canaries, the Gomerians appear to have mixed feelings about him. Most know of his involvement in the slave trade, and virtually all view his relationship with Beatriz de Bobadilla with distaste. Beatriz, after all, is still remembered for the ferocity with which she put down the Guanche revolt on the island in 1488 – all the ring leaders were executed after being promised a free pardon (see panel, page 176). Hostile graffiti was even daubed around San Sebastián in 1992 during celebrations to mark the 500th anniversary of Columbus' famous voyage.

LA GOMERA

Agulo, with Mount Teide visible in the distance on mainland Tenerife

La Gomera wine
La Gomera's perfect climate and steep mountainous terrain make it ideally suited for the production of wine. Gnarled vines cling to the island's majestic ancient terraces, each protected by tiny dry-stone walls. Most are still tilled and tended by hand. The chief areas of production are the slopes around Agulo, the Valle Gran Rey and Vallehermoso. The end product is good but not of vintage quality. The best names to look out for are Listan Blanco, Marmajuelo and Forastera Gomera. The white wines of Vallehermoso, honey-coloured and strong, are particularly interesting.

▶▶▶ Agulo   163C3

Agulo, just 3km from Hermigua on La Gomera's northern shore, has the island's best coastal setting. From the main road above the village, which nestles at the foot of an amphitheatre of towering cliffs, you can enjoy lovely views over banana groves, centuries-old agricultural terraces and the tight-clustered village itself, raised high above the sea on a tiny domed hill. To the rear the distant mainland profile of Tenerife's Mount Teide provides a dramatic and frequently snow-capped backdrop. Trim cobbled streets lend the village centre a medieval air, the twisting thoroughfares converging on the Iglesia de San Marcos, a curious little grey-white church built in 1939 and topped with four bright white Moorish domes.

The village lies some 25km northwest of San Sebastián, providing a pleasant stop-off if you're following the main northern route across the island. Buses on the San Sebastián to Vallehermoso route (via Hermigua and Las Rosas) call in at the village anything between two or three times daily (once on Sunday). Various walks are possible onto the ridges and the Barranco Sobre, the gorge which strikes inland from the village.

A couple of kilometres west of Agulo lies the hamlet of **Las Rosas**, at the edge of which lies a large modern restaurant much frequented by tour buses. Most are drawn here by the reasonable food, fine views and various displays of local music and dancing. Occasionally demonstrations of La Gomera's famous *el siblo* (see page 173) are also laid on for visitors.

▶▶ El Cercado   162B2

En route for the Valle Gran Rey, one of La Gomera's highlights (see page 178), you may well pass through El Cercado, a tiny village located some 37km west of San Sebastián on the minor road across the island's southern margins. It is noted for its huddle of rustic cottages and

distinctive **pottery** (*alfarería*), made without the use of a potter's wheel in several little workshops around the village. Dark red Gomeran clay lends the ware its unmistakable colour. The designs are based on centuries-old Guanche originals and most pots are still finished in old-fashioned clay ovens.

A short hop by road (1km) over the nearby mountain pass lies El Cercado's near identical neighbour, **Chipude**, a one-church hamlet attractively framed against the large table-top basalt pinnacle known locally as Fortaleza (Fortress), which lies a couple of kilometres to the south. The soaring sentinel (1,243m) is visible from afar and was long believed to have been a Guanche holy site. Note that El Cercado's pottery is sometimes known as Chipude ware, the craft also being practised in surrounding local hamlets such as Pavón and Temocodá.

▶▶▶ Hermigua   163C3

Peaceful Hermigua is the largest settlement on Gomera after San Sebastián (20km away), and offers far more to distract the visitor than the island's modest capital. Ringed around by the vivid green of banana plantations, the slightly disjointed village ambles along the roadside above a pleasant tree-dotted gorge. The chief point of interest is the **Los Telares** *artesanía* (craft centre), an exhibition–shop, spread across several rooms, devoted to the region's spinning and weaving traditions. Women can be seen conjuring rugs and fabrics from ancient handlooms, most of their work being available for purchase upstairs. Other crafts include local pottery and basket work fashioned from banana leaves. Also worth a look is the 16th-century monastic church of the **Convento de Santo Domingo** almost opposite, known for its striking Moorish-style wooden ceiling and the image of the local patroness, Nuestra Señora de la Encarnación, the work of the 19th-century Spanish sculptor, Fernando Estévez.

An inhabitant of El Cercado pauses for thought

LA GOMERA

Date palms
The Parque Nacional de Garajonay is most famous for its large laurel trees, but another tree also prospers in the park (as well as in groves across the rest of La Gomera). This is the Canary date palm, or *Phoenix canariensis*, a tree which has spread from the Canaries across much of the Mediterranean. It is a cousin of the true date palm of northern Africa and the Middle East. But while it has more luxuriant foliage, it unfortunately produces only tough and unappetising dates.

The Parque Nacional de Garajonay protects the rugged landscape of central La Gomera

►►► Parque Nacional de Garajonay   *162B2*

The glorious forested heights at the heart of La Gomera were declared a national park in 1978 – the Parque Nacional de Garajonay – and a World Natural Heritage of Mankind Site by Unesco in 1996 (the highest award for a protected park). Extending over an area of some 4,000ha, the park covers much of the island's central high plateau – a region of crags, ravines and green-swathed slopes – and enjoys protected status as a result of the almost unique remnants of its Canarian *Laurasilva* forest. *Laurasilva* vegetation is a dense, dank and magical mixture of ferns, lichens, tree heaths and laurels, and thrives best in the type of high, damp conditions that prevail in the often mist-shrouded slopes of La Gomera's 'El Alto de Garajonay', or Mount Garajonay (1,487m).

Flora Rainfall in this region is relatively high (around 600mm a year), the result of the damp air of the trade winds meeting the hot air of the Sahara. Surface water, therefore, abounds, La Gomera being one of the few places in the Canaries which boasts year-round rivers and streams (it ranks second only to La Palma in the abundance of its water supply). After heavy winter rains, *cascadas* (waterfalls) plunge through the woods, creating tiny rivulets that water the forest floor's dense carpets of ferns, mosses and creepers. All manner of plants and flowers proliferate in the woods' silent depths, with some 400 floral species – many endemic – recorded in the park. Rare insects and spiders are also abundant, along with birds such as buzzards, blue tits, chiffchaffs and endemic white- and dark-tailed pigeons.

The park's most precious natural feature, however, is the key component of the *laurasilva* – the Canarian laurel (*Laurus canariensis*). Those in the park represent the world's largest and most complete examples of laurel woodland. The laurel's leaves, incidentally, can be used as culinary herbs. Note that much of the park's eastern forest is known as the Bosque del Cedro, a misleading name, for the *cedro* (cedar tree) is now largely conspicuous by its absence.

Ancient laurel rainforest such as this is today found only in the Canaries

Information The park's main headquarters lies to the north at **Juego de Bolas** (near Las Rosas), where there is an informative visitor centre (*Open* Tue–Sat 9.30–4.30. For further information, tel: 80 09 93). This has exhibits on the park and La Gomera's flora, as well as gardens (with well-labelled plants and shrubs) and a small ethnographic museum of crafts and displays relating to local peasant life. Craftspeople can also occasionally be seen demonstrating traditional methods of basketry, weaving, pottery and woodwork. The centre also carries details of the many **walks** possible in the park, as does a smaller information point at **La Laguna Grande**, where a clearing in the forest plays host to a café, toilets, barbecue grills, car park and a popular rough-and-tumble children's playground. A track from the centre leads to a newly created *mirador* (viewpoint), from where there are lovely views down to Agulo (see page 168) and across to Tenerife.

Walks La Laguna is also close to the starting point for several well-worn hikes that weave through the park's central uplands. Some 2.6km from La Laguna (on the road towards San Sebastián) a large car park on the left marks the start of signposted tracks to the **Bosque de Cedro** (the summit of Mount Garajonay). The Mount Garajonay track, which strikes off opposite the car park, takes around 30 minutes and – weather allowing – offers some superlative views. The other track, which drops into the stunning gorge of the **Barranco del Cedro**, is more demanding, and can be followed all the way to the road just above Hermigua (this is one of the best hikes on the island). A shorter stroll on this track would take you to the rustic hermitage of **Nuestra Señora de Lourdes** and back the same way, a distance of about 3km.

Tragic union
An ancient La Gomeran legend tells how Mount Garajonay, the island's highest point, got its name. Once upon a time, so the story goes, two star-crossed lovers took to trysting and walking in the woods on the mountain's slopes. Their dalliance was discovered by their respective families, each of whom forbade the couple to meet again. But meet they did, one last time, on the mountain, where they fixed two sharpened stakes to each another. In one last embrace they then pierced one another's hearts, binding themselves and their names – Garon and Jonay – in one final, lasting union.

LA GOMERA

Banana trees flank the beach of Playa de Santiago

▶▶ **Playa de Santiago** *163C1*

Those with an interest in developing tourism on La Gomera have high hopes for Playa de Santiago, a village and stony beach on the southern side of the island (34km southwest of San Sebastián). It is, according to statistics, the sunniest spot on the island, and as such has recently been earmarked as a resort. The proximity of La Gomera's new airport will doubtless bring this about, and lead to an influx of visitors, but at present the beach and small fishing village remain in the first throes of tourism. So far, just a handful of bars and restaurants line its new promenade. Most pleasure here is to be had watching fishing boats unload their catch in the deepwater harbour – usually *bonita* (tuna) – or dropping into the little fishermen's chapel to look at the seamen's knots and model boats, the latter left as votive offerings.

Leading the way in turning the village into a fully-fledged resort is the **Hotel Jardín Tecina**, which is almost as impressive as the sublime Parador San Sebastián de la Gomera in San Sebastián (see page 177). Its setting is magnificent, perched on a cliff above the village, with Mount Teide's evocative profile looming on the Tenerife mainland. Despite its gargantuan size – there are over 430 rooms – the hotel has managed to avoid spoiling its surroundings. Instead, the grounds resemble a typical Canarian village, with individual houses in a local style designed to offer accommodation on either ground or first floor. The gardens, too, are beautiful, providing a showcase for indigenous and exotic flora, all perfectly labelled. There is also a beautiful swimming-pool area.

For better or worse, hotel and similar local developments will help counter the effects of emigration, long a problem on La Gomera (see panel), bringing a source of employment to a village blighted over the years by the repeated failure of various fish-canning initiatives.

FOCUS ON

El siblo

■ **La Gomera is famous above all for its almost unique language, *el siblo*, or 'the whistle', a complex form of whistling which has evolved over the centuries and survives to this day, despite the march of progress. It was designed to allow shepherds and labourers in the fields to communicate with one another over great distances.** ■

Useful No one knows when La Gomera's extraordinary whistling 'language' originated, though it may date back to prehistoric times. It may also once have been practised right across Tenerife. Looking today at the island's tortured landscapes and twisting tracks and roads, it's easy to see how difficult communication must have been before the advent of cars and telephones. It's also easy to understand how a 'whistled' code might have evolved to circumvent the problem. An alternative (but probably fanciful) theory suggests that the language developed after rebel Guanche leaders had their tongues cut out by the invading Spanish *conquistadores* in the 15th century. Deprived of speech, so the story goes, they began using their mouths and fingers to produce different sounds and communicate with one another.

Loud The language as practised by La Gomera's skilled *sibadores* was far more than a few codified whistles and sounds. Rather it was a language in the truest sense, in which the different pitch, volume and modulation of a whistle were designed to represent different syllables and letters of the alphabet. Using the language required great skill on the part of both the sender and receiver, each of whom had to have an ear finely tuned to the subtle nuances of delivery. *El siblo* is the most far-reaching means of ordinary human communication and messages could be passed along in a chain, reaching from one end of the island to another in a short time. These days, with the advent of telephones and the creation of better roads, the old skills are inevitably dying out, though in an attempt to preserve a unique fragment of Tenerife's culture, Unesco has declared *el siblo* part of the World Cultural Heritage.

Whistling today La Gomera's whistling language is inevitably dying out, but you may still hear the strange sound – like the whooping or whistling of mynah bird – while walking in the countryside. Taxi drivers also sometimes use a simplified form as they 'talk' to friends while rattling through a village. Demonstrations of *el siblo* are held regularly for coach parties at the Las Rosas restaurant (see page 168).

Shepherds probably devised el siblo *in order to communicate across vast distances*

Loudest language
No one can quite agree precisely how far La Gomera's *sibadores* were (and are) able to communicate using their remarkable whistling language. Depending on wind conditions and the configuration of the landscape, distances of up to 8km are possible, though 3–6km is more usual. In any event, the language has earned an official listing in *The Guinness Book of Records* as the most far-reaching means of ordinary human communication.

►► San Sebastián de la Gomera *163D2*

Hermitage
Among the lesser sights on Calle del Medio, San Sebastián's main streets, is the Ermita de San Sebastián, a monastery built in the 15th century to honour St Sebastian, the town's patron saint. Local legend claims it was La Gomera's first religious building. Much of the building was destroyed during pirate attacks in 1571 and 1618, leaving only the side aisle and its pointed Gothic arches as monuments to the original foundation.

San Sebastián de la Gomera, usually known simply as San Sebastián, is La Gomera's capital and chief port. Celebrated primarily for its associations with Christopher Columbus (see page 166), it is a modest and easy-going place (population 6,000), located on the island's rocky east coast at the mouth of the Barranco de la Villa gorge. White, flat-topped houses, framed by the mountains beyond, straggle up the barren hillside above the harbour and its sheltered bay. A handful of yachts and fishing boats labour in and out of the port, giving way two or three times a day to the ferries and hydrofoils from Los Cristianos on the Tenerife mainland (virtually the only time the town's somnolent village-like atmosphere is disturbed). Fishing nets dot the stony beach near by, reached via a small tunnel cut in the rock, which provides a cheerful summer playground for children.

San Sebastián's sights can be easily seen, and most people leave the town quickly – if they stop at all. One or two churches are worth a pause, however, and in the Parador San Sebastián de la Gomera the town boasts one of the island's finest places to stay (see page 177).

San Sebastián also offers car-hire facilities and a reasonable selection of shops to stock up on provisions, both of which are harder to come by elsewhere on the island. Orientation is straightforward: a short walk from the port brings you to Plaza Calvo Sotelo, the town's main square (which is graced by a small laurel garden), while

The market
San Sebastián's daily market is held every morning except Sunday in the Avenida de Colón. Among the colourful array of stalls selling fruit, fish, flowers and vegetables you will find local specialities such as palm honey and local breads and cheeses.

two parallel streets – Calle del Medio (literally 'Middle Street') and Calle Ruiz de Padron – make up the town's principal thoroughfares.

A short distance from Plaza Calvo Sotelo, in Calle del Medio, lies the **Pozo de Colón▶**, or Pozo de la Aguada, (meaning Well of Columbus or Well of the Watering Place). An *aguada* in Spanish means somewhere a ship stopped to take on water before a long voyage, lending weight to the long-held Gomeran theory that it was water from this well which Christopher Columbus took with him to the Americas in 1492. True or not, a plaque alongside the well announces that 'with water from this well was America baptised'. It is known for certain that at least two other Spanish explorers and *conquistadores* did avail themselves of the well's water before voyages. One was Pizarro (conqueror of Peru), the other Nuñez de la Balboa, probably the first European to catch a glimpse of the Pacific Ocean.

Today the well is concealed within the cool courtyard interior of the old Casa del Pozo de la Aguada (House of the Well), also known locally as the Customs House, having served as the customs post until late this century. The house, a single-storey building with a Moorish-tiled pitched roof, and pretty courtyard probably date from before the 17th century. Its exterior bears the coats of arms of the Peraza family, the local Counts of Gomera. The building also incorporates the town's **visitor centre** (tel: 14 01 47, fax: 14 01 51) and Oficina de Turismo

175

San Sebastián, La Gomera's tiny capital and main port of entry

LA GOMERA

The Virgin of Guadalupe

The Virgin of Guadalupe, or La Virgen – or Nuestra Señora – de Guadalupe, is the patroness and protector of La Gomera. A fiesta in her honour is held in San Sebastián on the first Monday in October. The image of the Virgin, which is kept in a remote chapel on the Punta Llana promontory, is taken in procession from its chapel to the sea, where a waiting boat carries it to San Sebastián. As ever, the religious ceremonies are accompanied by Canarian wrestling, fireworks, singing and folk dancing.

Puerta del Pardón

The so-called Puerta del Pardón (Portal of Pardon), recalls the duplicity of the infamous Beatriz de Bobadilla, wife of Hernán Peraza, the despotic 15th-century ruler of La Gomera. After her husband's murder (see page 166), Beatriz organised a service apparently designed to effect reconciliation with the island's disaffected rebels. She promised a pardon and immunity to all who passed through the Puerta del Pardón, who in doing so would acknowledge their complicity in Hernán's death. In fact she broke her promise, and the insurgents were all executed.

(tourist office). Among other things, the centre provides information on walking possibilities on the island.

Beyond Columbus' well on Calle del Medio stands the ancient **Iglesia de la Asunción**►► (Church of the Assumption), a building to which Columbus is said to have repaired for a final session of prayers before setting sail for the New World. It was begun in the 14th century on the orders of Count Hernán Peraza the Elder, though much of the present building dates from four centuries later. The aisles and arcades alongside the nave were added in the 16th century. The imposing three-doored façade ushers you into a interior which still preserves traces of its Gothic origins. Much of the woodwork is outstanding, in particular the baroque altar, the heavily ornamented beamed ceiling and the balcony above the entrance doors. Make a point of seeing the crumbling wall painting, dated 1760, which depicts a naval attack made by the British against La Gomera in 1734.

Calle del Medio contains still more of historic interest, namely the **Casa de Colón**►, a two-storey town-house said to have been used by Columbus, though its connections with the explorer are unconfirmed. Today it is owned by the Cabildo Insular (Island Council), and run as a museum devoted to models of Columbus' ships, old maps and a selection of pre-Columbian ceramics. The building is the focus of the town's annual Columbus festival, the **Fiestas Colombinas**, when the town celebrates its associations with the explorer (first week of September). Special football matches are played, along with the usual excess of eating, drinking, singing and dancing. A more permanent memorial to Columbus is contained in the tiles of the town's harbour promenade, which depict the route of the explorer's most famous voyage.

San Sebastián's most important and most prominent sight, however, has little to do with Columbus: the Castilian-style **Torre del Conde**►► (Tower of the Count),

The Torre del Conde was once home to New World silver

stands in the Parque de la Torre next to the harbour front, a redoubtable pink and white brick tower built in 1447 by the first Count of La Gomera, Hernán Peraza the Elder. It was to be the home of Hernán's wife, the infamous Beatriz de Bobadilla after the murder of her husband (see page 166). Later it was used to guard some of the vast store of treasures that flooded back to Spain from the New World. Today it has the revered status of a Spanish Historical Monument. Despite its sturdy walls – well over a metre thick in most places – the interior is in a perilous state and has been closed for many years, though there are plans to reopen it and the tower's small museum of South American artefacts.

It is well worth trying to spend at least one night at the **Parador San Sebastián de la Gomera▶▶▶**, one of the most beautiful hotels in the Canary Islands. It stands perched on a cliff top just above San Sebastián astride the so-called Lomo de Horca (Ridge of the Gallows). To all intents and purposes, the long, low building resembles a classic Canarian mansion from centuries past. Beyond the plant-filled courtyard lies an aristocratic wood-panelled interior decorated with antiques and other precious *objets d'art*, while paintings of figures from La Gomera's past line many rooms and the impressive main staircase. There is also a lovely swimming pool, an excellent dining room and a patio filled with plants and chattering birds. Despite the hotel's persuasive historical appearance, however, it was only built in 1973, the whole thing being a skilfully presented architectural pastiche – even the entrance is a carefully copied version of a genuine doorway still preserved in San Sebastián's Ermita de San Sebastián (see panel, page 174). Even if you pass up the chance of staying here, it is still worth coming to eat in the **dining room**, open to non-residents, one of the best places on the island to sample Spanish and Canarian cuisine.

Way out beyond the parador, at Punta Llana, lies the hermitage containing the shrine of Nuestra Señora de Guadalupe, La Gomera's much revered patroness (see panel, page 176).

Old-style elegance and comfort at the splendid Parador San Sebastián de la Gomera

Paradors
Paradors (*paradores* in Spanish), are state-run hotels, set up to provide top-quality local-style lodgings in regions where accommodation was previously scarce. La Gomera's mock-colonial San Sebastián de la Gomera is one of the finest in the whole chain, while in Tenerife the Cañadas del Teide has recently been refurbished. Contact hotels directly, or for central bookings contact: Paradores de España, Central de Reservas, Calle Requena 3, 28013 Madrid (tel: 91/516 6666; fax 91/516 6657).

LA GOMERA

Palm honey

The delicious palm honey, or *miel de palma* of La Gomera and the mainland makes a unique souvenir of your trip to Tenerife. Miel is not honey in the true sense, but derives from a rich, sugary sap, or *guarapo*, tapped from the island's date-palm trees. Ladders leaned against the palms are a likely sign that the tree is being tapped for its sap, which is boiled – rather in the manner of maple syrup – to form a thick, black and very sweet syrup resembling honey. It can usually be bought directly from farms or smallholdings, or from outdoor markets such as that in San Sebastián.

Viewpoints

A short way west of Arure, easily reached along a short track, lies the Mirador Ermita El Santo, a viewpoint over a broad swathe of largely virgin countryside. In the distance, to the west, you should be able to make out the remote hamlet of Taguluche. Further down the road lies another recently built *mirador*, a discreetly fashioned viewpoint built by César Manrique, the late Lanzarote architect responsible for taming some of the wilder excesses of mass tourism in the Canaries (see panel on page 104).

Looking down on Valle Gran Rey from the Mirador Ermita El Santo

▶▶▶ **Valle Gran Rey** 162A2

Gomeran tourism in the modern sense had its beginnings in the Valle Gran Rey (Valley of the Great King), albeit in humble circumstances, for it was here, in La Gomera's most spectacular ravine, that hippies and other refugees in search of alternative lifestyles first set up camp in the 1970s. Most were attracted primarily by the valley's breathtakingly wild appearance, its rows of tiny white-washed houses, and its mountain crests and steeply terraced slopes. Others were drawn by the verdant spread of fields – full of vines and banana trees – and the region's evocative proliferation of palms and other exotic flora. Today the region boasts only one road to speak of, just as it did 25 years ago, but the arrival of more organised tourism has taken the edge off the valley's previously pristine appeal. This said, the area is still strikingly beautiful, and well worth a visit.

Should you approach from Vallehermoso and the north (see page 182), consider making the easy side detour to visit the villages of Epina and Alojera: to reach them take the junction off the main Vallehermoso–Valle Gran Rey road 10km southwest of Vallehermoso. Drink the water from the Fuente de Epina, the spring at **Epina**, 3km off the main road, and legend has it that you will return to La Gomera. Another 6km of twisting descent brings you to **Alojera**, a village ear-marked for tourist development, but at present made up of just a few houses ranged along the *barranco* (ravine) and a small group of immaculate terraces ending in a small cove and rustic restaurant. There's also a small black-sand beach, and – if you want a taste of the real Gomera – rough roads and tracks that push north to the remote old-world villages of Cubaba, Tazo and Arguamul.

Back on the main road, the descent into the Valle Gran Rey proper begins beyond **Arure**, believed to have been one of La Gomera's main pre-Hispanic settlements (the Valle Gran Rey almost certainly takes its name from the era of the Guanche kings). A short way west of the village, easily reached along a short track, lies the **Mirador Ermita El Santo**, one of several viewpoints on this stretch of road (see panel). Beyond the valley the road drops towards the coast, dividing at **La Calera**, a stunning hill village ringed by banana plantations. Side roads branch off here for La Playa Calera and Vueltas respectively, two small hamlets that form a connected cluster of grey-sand and pebble bays and beach settlements (including the beaches of Playa del Ingles and Playa de Gran Rey). **La Playa Calera** has La Gomera's only real sandy beach, while **Vueltas** is a fishing village clustered around a modest harbour.

The area offers little to do – one of its charms – apart from soaking up the sun, scenery and celebrated Gomera *calma* (tranquillity). Boats trips are available, however, notably to the celebrated Los Órganos around the coast to the north (see page 183). There are also a few basic local bars such as the Bar Restaurante del Puerto in Vueltas, a rough-and-tumble fisherman's bar and restaurant with rickety oilcloth tables. Great local food is available here and elsewhere, including dishes with tomatoes fresh from nearby terraces and a *parrillada del pescador* with fish just pulled from the sea.

Walk Vallehermoso

A simple walk from the village of Vallehermoso through classic Canarian landscapes (2.5km; allow 1 to 1½hrs)

This walk combines Gomeran landscapes of lush ravines, overlooked by volcanic rocks, and culminates at a charming reservoir. It is suitable for people of all ages and fitness levels, though the initial hill is quite steep. Much of the walk, though, can be followed in a car if necessary.

Start in the centre of Vallehermoso and follow the road uphill out of town, to the left of the Bar Restaurante Amaya.

Roque Cano

The large 'Dog Rock' which at some 690m soars above Vallehermoso and dominates many views locally is named after its resemblance to a canine tooth. Like so many other volcanic outcrops on the island, it is the central volcanic plug of a former volcano – the rest of the old cone has long been eroded away.

As you continue to climb, look back over your shoulder for fine views of Vallehermoso and its church. Down to your left, the fertile abundance of the lush valley is clear. Bananas, palm trees, sugar cane, orange groves and vines all jostle for space.

Continue your climb, which becomes steeper and after some 250m rounds a sharp bend.

The Valley of the 1001 Palms

It is unlikely that anyone has really counted the trees here, but it is possible that as many as claimed are on tap for Gomera's famous palm honey (see panel, page 178). Look for metal cups attached to the trunks, catching the 'honey' or palm sap ready to be boiled down to a rich syrup. This valley is a splendid sight, particularly in late afternoon, as the sun seems to sink towards its heart.

After about 20 minutes' walking you will see the dam wall holding back the reservoir which is your eventual destination.

Embalse de la Encantadora

Despite its function – which is supplying water to the village and valleys below – this reservoir has a mercifully natural, almost ornamental look, hence its romantic name: the Lake of the Enchanted Lady. Ducks are often to be found bobbing on its surface, and there is a statue of a man– perhaps a Guanche – stranded on a tiny island with just a pole for company. Walk all the way round the reservoir, being prepared to meet the odd goat en route, tethered and grazing. As you complete the circle, cross the metal bridge and (if you don't suffer from vertigo) look down the sheer wall of the dam, usually trickling water into the valley.

Walk down the hill and take the right turn downhill.

At the time of writing, a ramshackle smallholding of goats, chickens, pigeons, and rabbits is at the bottom of the hill. Beware barking dogs, and if there are any, check that they are attached to their tethers. The route descends all the way to the foot of the dam, where the running water usually forms a small stream. You can cross this to the orange grove on the other side but can go no further thereafter.

Return to the main road and follow in your own footsteps back down to the village.

181

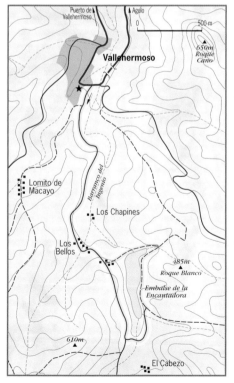

Unexpected companions on the mountain paths of La Gomera

▶▶▶ Vallehermoso   162B3

Vallehermoso is a neat and compact village located some 42km from San Sebastián, its picturesque outlook, hugging the valley side, providing a fine scenic climax to the northern road route across La Gomera. Just short of the village, to the west, the road passes a majestic *mirador* (viewpoint) at Tamargada, with sweeping views over the dense forest below. If you have time to extend your trip, roads lead south from the village to two other highlights: the Parque Nacional de Garajonay (see page 170) and the Valle Gran Rey (see page 178).

Vallehermoso takes its name from *hermoso* (Spanish for 'beautiful') – justifiably, for it is a pretty village – though it is also an important commercial centre, and has a population greater than San Sebastián. For all its commerce, however, it is also pleasantly somnolent. The main attractions for visitors are the chance to buy local crafts and to view the famous **Roque Cano** (Dog Rock), so called

Superb countryside can easily be reached on foot from Vallehermoso

because the 690m pillar of rock resembles a vast dog's tooth. The rock represents the remnants of a volcanic vent exposed by erosion over the millennia.

Many visitors also pass through the village en route for Puerto de Vallehermoso, 4km distant, a small harbour where you pick up boat trips for **Los Órganos►►**, a series of vast basalt columns rising from the sea a few minutes' boat ride to the west (they are only visible from the sea). The cliffs' thin and delicate-looking columns – named after their resemblance to organ pipes – rise along a 200m stretch of coast, some of the tightly packed pillars reaching heights of over 80m. Puerto de Vallehermoso is the closest point of embarkation if you want to see this natural wonder, though boat trips also run here from the Playa de Gran Rey (see page 178) and the Playa de Santiago (see page 172). Note that surf and undertow make swimming dangerous at Puerto de Vallehermoso.

Entry formalities Visitors from EU countries, North America, Canada, Australia and New Zealand need only a passport to enter Tenerife. Citizens of EU countries, including Britain, do not require a visa whatever the length of their visit. A visa is necessary for nationals of non-EU countries if you intend to stay longer than 90 days: contact the Spanish Embassy in your country of origin for further information.

By air Tenerife has two international airports. Reina Sofía, also known as Tenerife South, is the main airport and is used for most international charter flights. It lies near El Médano, 62km southwest of Santa Cruz, and goes by the full name of the Aeropuerto de Sur Reina Sofía (tel: 75 90 00 or 77 00 50). The older Los Rodeos Airport (Tenerife North) or Aeropuerto del Norte Los Rodeos,

lies 13km northwest of Santa Cruz and is used for scheduled and inter-island flights (tel: 63 58 00.

For general flight enquiries, tel: 77 13 75. Shuttle buses run from both airports to Santa Cruz and many of the larger resorts. A shuttle also operates between Tenerife's two airports.

A new airport has been built on La Gomera (near Playa de Santiago on the south of the island), but at the time of writing was still closed to inter-island flights. Most charters from Britain and other European cities are direct, but the majority of scheduled international flights involve a connecting flight from Madrid. Iberia, the national Spanish carrier, run a direct scheduled service from London. For details contact Iberia in London (tel: 0171-830 0011). Inter-island flights between Tenerife and the other Canary Islands are run by Binter (tel: 23 43 46, 23 48 22 or 26 01 01), a subsidiary of Iberia.

Regular ferries run between Tenerife and La Gomera

By sea The major sea route to Tenerife is from mainland Spain. Ships sail from Cádiz to Santa Cruz weekly: journey time is just under two days. You can also sail to the island from any other Canary Island and there is a hydrofoil service to and from Santa Cruz to Las Palmas on Gran Canaria that takes 80 minutes.

A passenger-only hydrofoil service (usually four daily) runs from Los Cristianos to San Sebastián on La Gomera (journey time is 35 minutes. Two shipping lines – *Ferry Gomera* and *Compañía Trasmediter-ránea* – offer regular car and passenger ferries on the same route (journey time of around 90 minutes).

For current times and prices of sailings contact *Ferry Gomera* in San Sebastián on La Gomera (tel: 87 10 07) or Los Cristianos on Tenerife (tel: 79 05 56); and *Compañía Trasmediterránea* in Santa Cruz (tel: 24 30 11; Los Cristianos (tel: 79 61 78) or San Sebastián (tel: 87 13 24). The UK agent for the *Compañía*

Taxis are a cheap way of getting around Tenerife's larger towns

Trasmediterránea is Southern Ferries, 1st Floor, 179 Piccadilly, London W1V 9DB (tel: 0171-491 4968).

Customs There are no limits on the amounts of alcohol and tobacco that can be brought into Tenerife, but given the extremely low prices of these products on the island it makes sense to buy them when you get there. As regards alcohol and tobacco taken out of the country, Tenerife and the rest of the Canaries has a special status despite their EU membership. This will almost certainly change, leaving limits at the following rates.

- EU tobacco limits: 800 cigarettes plus 400 cigarillos plus 200 cigars plus 1kg of tobacco
- EU alcohol limits: 10 litres of spirits plus 20 litres of fortified wine plus 90 litres of wine (not more than 60 litres sparkling) plus 110 litres of beer
- Non-EU tobacco limits: 200 cigarettes or 100 cigarillos or 50 cigars or 250g of tobacco
- Non-EU alcohol limits: 1 litre of spirits or 2 litres of fortified wine plus 2 litres of still table wine

Travel insurance Buying fully comprehensive travel insurance is highly recommended. If you are travelling on a package, check the details of any insurance cover with your travel agent or tour operator.

Climate Sunny days throughout most of the year are one of Tenerife's major attractions, though remember that year-round sun is only a feature of the southern part of the island: in the north and parts of La Gomera it can be rainy, particularly in winter, while in the mountainous interior, snow often persists late into spring (May) on high ground. January is the coldest month, August the hottest, though the average temperature difference between the two is only 6.4°C (11.5°F). Winds can be strong in winter. Hot, debilitating *sirocco* winds from the Sahara, known locally as the *calima*, may also blow for a few days during the year. Summer sunshine is guaranteed everywhere.

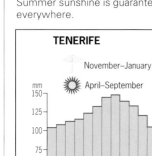

Religious festivals are often marked by public holidays

When to go Winter breaks make November to April one of the most popular times to visit the so-called 'Island of Eternal Spring', with Christmas and Easter the peak periods and the time when prices are highest. Spring (March to July, depending on altitude) is a wonderful time to enjoy the island's flora, while summer – a relatively quieter time – is a popular holiday period for mainland Spaniards. If you want the best of the festivals, come to Santa Cruz at Carnival time (February–March), but be sure to check dates and confirm accommodation.

National holidays Fixed Dates
1 January – Año Nuevo (New Year's Day); 6 January – Los Reyes (Epiphany); 2 February – La Candelaria (Candlemas); 19 March – San José (St Joseph's Day); 1 May – Día del Trabajo (Labour Day); 25 July – Santiago (St James' Day); 15 August – Asunción (Assumption); 12 October – Día de la Hispanidad (Discovery of America/Columbus Day); 1 November – Todos los Santos (All Saints' Day); 6 December – Día de la Constitución (Constitution Day); 25 December – Navidad (Christmas Day).

Movable Feasts Jueves Santo (Maundy Thursday); Viernes Santo (Good Friday); Pascua (Easter Sunday); Lunes de Pascua (Easter Monday); Corpus Christi (May/June); Concepción (Immaculate Conception) – usually 8 December.

Different autonomous regions within Spain can move public holidays a day or so at their discretion, particularly if the holiday falls on a Sunday, when the previous Friday or following Monday may be declared a holiday. They are also allowed to decree two additional holidays a year.

Time differences Tenerife maintains
Greenwich Mean Time (GMT) in the
winter, which is one hour behind
most European countries and in line
with the UK. As in the UK, the clocks
go forward one hour in the spring
(late March) and revert back one hour
in the autumn (late September).
Mainland Spain is usually one hour
ahead of Tenerife.

There is a brief period of a one-
hour discrepancy between the island
and the UK (from late September to
October) owing to the different end
dates of summer, though EU
changes may synchronise
changeovers.

Tenerife is five hours ahead of US
Eastern Standard Time (EST), and
eight hours ahead of Pacific Time.
Johannesburg is ahead by one hour,
Australia by 10 hours and New
Zealand by 12 hours.

Money matters The Spanish *peseta*
(pta) is the unit of currency in
Tenerife. Bank notes are issued in
denominations of 1,000; 2,000;
5,000; and 10,0000 pesetas: coins
are issued in denominations of 1, 5,
10, 25, 50, 100, 200 and 500 pesetas. There is no limit to the amount
of money you can bring into Tenerife,
though limits – too high to trouble
most casual visitors – apply on the
amount of money that can be taken
out of the island.

*Shoppers enjoying a leisurely
stroll on the Calle Castillo, in the
heart of Santa Cruz de Tenerife*

Foreign exchange Banks are generally open Monday to Friday 9–2 and
Saturday 9–1, but closed Saturdays
from 1 June to 31 October. They
often charge a sizeable commission
for changing money, so change large
amounts if possible, and be sure to
take your passport. Outside bank
hours, many travel agents and *cambio*
(bureaux de change) change money.
Double check for deductions, which
may not be clearly advertised.

Do *not* change money at tourist
shops. Even if the rates on offer
appear attractive, there are usually
many hidden deductions. Hotels will
often change money, but at poor
rates. Credit card and Eurocheque
cash dispensers are becoming
increasingly common in Santa Cruz
and the main resorts.

Credit cards Most hotels, many
restaurants, shops and all car-rental
firms accept major credit cards. Not
all petrol stations do. Travellers'
cheques and Eurocheques (made
out in pesetas to a maximum of
30,000), are widely accepted, but it
makes sense to buy some pesetas
before you travel for first-day
expenses, particularly if you may be
arriving late at night.

By car

Car rental You can take your car by ferry to Tenerife via mainland Spain, but as the island provides extremely reasonable car-hire rates, it is rarely worth the effort or expense. Most leading international rental firms have offices at the airports, cities and major resorts in Tenerife and La Gomera. There is also a plethora of local firms, most of them reliable and reasonably priced, but cast an eye over the age and quality of the cars before committing yourself. The cheapest rental arrangements can usually be made before you travel, either as part of a package arranged through your tour operator, or as part of a 'Fly-Drive' deal.

Driving conditions The standard of roads in Tenerife is high, with many newly built and smooth-surfaced carriageways. A motorway runs along part of the north coast and down the east coast, from Puerto de la Cruz to Playa de las Américas. The first stretch, to Santa Cruz, is known as the Autopista del Norte (north); thereafter it is called the Autopista del Sur (south).

Expect to encounter traffic jams in Playa de las Américas, Puerto de la Cruz and Santa Cruz. The lack of parking and complicated one-way

Roads are generally good: many are newly built

systems also make driving something of a challenge in these towns.

The standard of driving is reasonable, though accident rates have increased alarmingly: beware impatient drivers in oncoming traffic, particularly on bends on mountain roads. Never stop on narrow, winding mountain roads to admire the view, unless you can safely pull off the road. *Miradores* (viewpoints) are placed every few kilometres specifically for this purpose.

Parking In areas marked with blue lines – *zonas azul* (blue zones) – you must buy a parking ticket during the designated hours, usually between 9 and 2 and 4 and 8. If you forget, or exceed your time, you receive a fine to be paid on the spot. Press the button marked *anulación de denucia*, insert the sum required, then enclose this ticket with the fine and put it in the box below the machine. Remember that even if you are in a hire car, any unpaid tickets will eventually catch up with you.

Petrol Petrol is quite expensive, and often cash is required, as not all petrol stations accept credit cards.

Garages are relatively numerous along the main roads, with 24-hour opening in the larger resorts and towns. Many garages, though, close on Sundays and public holidays. Don't drive into the mountains on a near-empty tank. There are few, if any, filling stations in remote upland areas. Diesel is *gasoleo*, unleaded *sin plomo*.

Rules of the road The same rules of the road apply in Tenerife as on mainland Europe – drive on the right, overtake on the left and give way to traffic approaching from the right. Use of seat belts is compulsory in front seats and in rear seats where fitted: children under 12 must travel in the back seat. In towns, cars should be parked facing the direction of the movement of traffic. Speed limits are 120kph on motorways; 100kph on roads with two or more lanes in each direction; 90kph on other roads; 50kph in built-up areas; and 20kph in residential areas.

Documents All European, American and Australian driving licences are valid, though it may be advisable to take a Spanish translation with you (contact a driving organisation in your own country before travelling for the latest information). An International Driving Permit is not necessary.

By taxi

Taxis are recognisable by a green light in the windscreen or on a white roof and an official plate with the letters 'SP', which stands for *Servicio Público* (Public Service). The light shows *libre* (free) when cars are available for hire. For short trips within tourist areas, many taxi drivers won't bother to put their meters on, though you will rarely be cheated (confirm a price or ask for the meter to be turned on if you are concerned). Supplements are levied for luggage and waiting time. Boards by the main taxi ranks display the latest fixed prices between the most popular destinations. Taxis are still good value by northern European standards, and can be useful for longer journeys that you might usually think twice about before

taking a taxi. Be sure, though, to fix a price for longer trips before you start. You might also take one of the various 'taxi tours' available.

By bus

Tenerife's distinctive *guaguas* (green buses) are operated by TITSA, and are cheap, fast, safe, popular and reliable. Most towns and villages are connected by frequent services. Bus stops are marked by a red-white-blue sign with a 'P' for *parada* (bus stop). If you intend travelling a lot on buses, consider buying a *bono* (voucher), which for around 2,000–2,500 pesetas entitles you to buy tickets at a 25 per cent discount.

By boat

Ferries and hydrofoils run between Tenerife and La Gomera, and from Tenerife to several of the other islands of the archipelago. See 'Arriving' on page 187 for more details.

Most Tenerife towns and villages are connected by regular bus services

Media

The free publication, *The Island Gazette* comes out monthly and provides a useful source of listings and general information. Pick up a copy from local tourist offices. Another English-language publication, *Island Connections*, available from most newsagents, covers all the Canary Islands and is worth buying. A third tourist-oriented newspaper is the *Island Sun*, which also covers all the islands of the archipelago. Such publications are notoriously difficult to maintain, and have a tendency to cease publication at short notice: those listed above have been established longer than most.

The BBC World Service and Voice of America can be picked up in Tenerife on short wave, and there is usually at least one radio station on the island broadcasting in English at any time. Consult tourist offices for details of current stations and their wavelengths. Many hotels and bars offer a bewildering selection of cable and other television channels. Full listings are published in most local and English-language newspapers.

In the larger resorts of the south, British and other European-language newspapers are usually available on the day of publication, as are European editions of the *International Herald Tribune*, *Financial Times* and *The Guardian* (these last three are often more widely available).

Rangers keep a watchful eye in Teide National Park

Caja Postal
ARGENTARIA

Correos y Telégrafos

Post offices
- *Correos* (post offices) are open Mon–Fri 8.30–2 in summer; 9–1 in winter; Saturday 9 to 1.
- *Sellos* or *timbres* (stamps) can also be bought at *tobacos* and in most shops which sell postcards.
- Post boxes are painted yellow. Use the slot marked *extranjeros* (foreign) for post being sent abroad.
- There are rarely telephones in post offices.

Telephones
You can make international calls from virtually any telephone on Tenerife. Public phones all have clear instructions in English, French, German and Spanish. The best way to phone long-distance is from a *telefónica* cabin, which comprises metered booths where you pay after your call. This works out as not much more expensive than a street telephone. It is also less noisy and more convenient, as you do not need large amounts of change to hand. Be aware the LED indicator above your phone is not the amount in pesetas you are spending, but the unit charge of a call (much less than the price of the call). *Telefónicas* are usually in central locations and open late. Remember that hotels often levy a surcharge on calls made from rooms, making this an expensive way of phoning home.

- The code for Tenerife and La Gomera is 922. When you are calling from outside either island (or the Canaries in general), omit the 9. Thus calling from the UK you would dial 00-34-22 and then the number.
- For international calls from Tenerife dial 07, wait for the tone to change to indicate you have a line, then dial your country code: Australia (61), Canada and the USA (1), Germany (49), France (33), Ireland (353) and the UK (44). Follow this with the local code minus the first 0 (if there is one) and then dial the number.
- To call the operator dial 003.

Island paradise: the view from La Garañona in El Sauzal

Emergencies

Crime The sheer number of visitors to Tenerife makes them a target for the unscrupulous. While serious crime is comparatively rare, petty crime is on the increase. If you are the victim of crime, report it to your hotel, travel rep and to the police. If you intend to claim against your travel insurance, the police should be able to issue a signed statement for this purpose. Generally common sense and a few precautions should keep you safe.

- To contact the police in an emergency, telephone **091**.
- Theft from cars is the most common form of crime on Tenerife, so always lock your car, and never leave luggage, cameras or valuables inside.
- Try to avoid parking in secluded places.

Law enforcement on the streets of Tacoronte

- Always carry cash in a belt or pouch – never in a pocket. Leave large sums in hotel safes.
- Do not carry large amounts of cash. Use credit cards or travellers' cheques.
- Wear your camera and never put it down on café tables. Beware of strap-cutting thieves.
- Do not flaunt valuables. Better still, leave them at home.
- Leave jewellery in the hotel safe (not in rooms), especially items like chains and earrings which can easily be snatched.
- Remember to close windows and lock doors to hotel room balconies.
- Do not take more than necessary to the beach.
- Carry bags across your front – not hung over one shoulder where they can be rifled or grabbed.
- Be aware of pickpockets on crowded buses, in street markets or anywhere that large groups of tourists congregate.
- After dark, avoid non-commercial parts of towns and cities.

Police
Police responsibilities are split three ways on Tenerife. The *Policía Municipal* (blue uniform) direct traffic and other municipal duties; the *Policía Nacional* (brown uniform) deal with crime in the towns; the *Guardia Civil* (pea-green uniform) deal with crime and patrol highways in rural areas. To summon the police, telephone **091**.

Consulates
Republic of Ireland La Marina 7, Santa Cruz (tel: 24 56 71)
United Kingdom Plaza Weyler 8, 1st Floor, Santa Cruz (tel: 28 68 63)
United States Alvarez de Lugo 10, Santa Cruz (tel: 28 69 50)

Emergency telephone numbers
Police 091
Ambulance/Cruz Roja (Red Cross) 28 18 00 in Santa Cruz; 78 07 59 in Playa de las Américas; 38 38 12 in Puerto de la Cruz
Fire 60 00 80 in Santa Cruz; 71 08 80 in Playa de las Américas; 33 00 80 in Puerto de la Cruz

Lost property

Lost property offices in Tenerife are few and far between. The local police station in any town is a good place to start. Alternatively ask at the tourist office where to go locally. Report loss of valuables to the Policía Municipal or Guardia Civil and obtain a form for your own holiday insurance purposes. Report lost passports to your consulate.

Health

The main ailments visitors are likely to suffer are stomach upsets brought on by a sudden change of diet (often combined with too much sun). Break yourself in gradually to sunbathing and always use suntan lotions and blocks. Do not spend too long in the sun, and never fall asleep in the sun. Children are particularly vulnerable to too much sun. Always drink bottled water where possible.

Pharmacies Minor ailments can usually be treated at a *farmacia* (pharmacy), which can be identified by a green cross. Don't confuse them with a *droguería*, which sells perfumes and toiletries. Normal opening hours are Mon–Fri 9–1, 4–8;

All aboard the famous yellow submarine at Las Galletas

Sat 9–1. At least one pharmacy in each town stays open after hours on a rota basis (known as a *farmacia de guardia*). Its location is posted in the windows of all the other pharmacies, and is also available from the tourist office and local newspapers.

Doctors There are many English-speaking doctors and dentists dotted around Tenerife (some are British nationals). If you need a doctor (*médico*), first try contacting your hotel. Alternatively enquire at tourist offices for details of local bilingual doctors. The Centro Medicas Salus Canarias offers private medical treatment, with centres in Puetro de la Cruz, Los Gigantes, Playa de las Américas and La Orotava (freephone 900 10 01 44 for details).

Vaccinations Vaccinations are not generally necessary for entry into Tenerife unless you are travelling from a known infected area. Check current requirements if you are travelling from the Far East, Africa or South America.

The Iglesia de Nuestra Señora de la Concepción, one of several fine churches in La Orotava in Tenerife

Camping

Tenerife has just one major year-round official campsite, the well-equipped 700-pitch Nauta Camping and Caravanning at Carretera 6225, Cañada Blanca, Las Galletas, Arona (tel: 78 51 18). If you do see back-packers in southern Tenerife it is likely that they are off to La Gomera – probably to the Valle Gran Rey, which is particularly popular with campers.

There is also one major designated site on La Gomera, at Caserío del Cedro on the edge of the Parque Nacional de Garajonay. This is administered by the island government, so if you wish to camp here contact their office in San Sebastián at Carretera General del Sur 20 (tel: 87 01 05). Camping within the national parks is strictly forbidden on both Tenerife and La Gomera.

CONVERSION CHARTS

FROM	TO	MULTIPLY BY
Inches	Centimetres	2.54
Centimetres	Inches	0.3937
Feet	Metres	0.3048
Metres	Feet	3.2810
Yards	Metres	0.9144
Metres	Yards	1.0940
Miles	Kilometres	1.6090
Kilometres	Miles	0.6214
Acres	Hectares	0.4047
Hectares	Acres	2.4710
Gallons	Litres	4.5460
Litres	Gallons	0.2200
Ounces	Grams	28.35
Grams	Ounces	0.0353
Pounds	Grams	453.6
Grams	Pounds	0.0022
Pounds	Kilograms	0.4536
Kilograms	Pounds	2.205
Tons	Tonnes	1.0160
Tonnes	Tons	0.9842

MEN'S SUITS

UK	36	38	40	42	44	46	48
Rest of Europe	46	48	50	52	54	56	58
US	36	38	40	42	44	46	48

DRESS SIZES

UK	8	10	12	14	16	18
France	36	38	40	42	44	46
Italy	38	40	42	44	46	48
Rest of Europe	34	36	38	40	42	44
US	6	8	10	12	14	16

MEN'S SHIRTS

UK	14	14.5	15	15.5	16	16.5	17
Rest of Europe	36	37	38	39/40	41	42	43
US	14	14.5	15	15.5	16	16.5	17

MEN'S SHOES

UK	7	7.5	8.5	9.5	10.5	11
Rest of Europe	41	42	43	44	45	46
US	8	8.5	9.5	10.5	11.5	12

WOMEN'S SHOES

UK	4.5	5	5.5	6	6.5	7
Rest of Europe	38	38	39	39	40	41
US	6	6.5	7	7.5	8	8.5

Electricity

The current in Tenerife is 220 volts AC, as in the UK, but sockets take the circular two-pin continental-style plug, so you will need an adapter for appliances brought from the UK. Very occasionally you may still find 110 or 125 volts supply, but this is rare. Power cuts are not infrequent, so pack a torch.

Opening times

- Traditional shop opening hours are Monday to Friday 9–1 and 4–8, Saturday 9–2. In the main tourist areas, shops may open every day.
- Museum opening hours vary and are liable to change from year to year: check individual entries, but also double check at tourist offices if you have the chance.
- Offices and businesses usually open Monday to Friday 9–1 and 3–7, Saturday 9–1.
- Churches are usually open from early in the morning until 11am or noon, reopening in late afternoon. Morning and evening service times will usually find them open.
- Pharmacies open Monday to Friday 9–1 and 4–8; Saturday 9–1 (see also page 195).
- Post offices open Monday to Friday 8.30–2 in summer; 9–1 in winter; Saturday 9–1.
- Banks open Monday to Friday 9–2; Saturday 9–1, but are closed on Saturday between 1 June and 31 October (see also page 189).
- Petrol stations remain open until 8 or 10pm, though most are shut all day on Sunday.

Places of worship

Tenerife is a predominantly Catholic island, so Mass can be celebrated in various languages at most of the major resorts. Many of these resorts also have at least one church of other major denominations, as well as Jewish and Evangelical services. Contact your hotel or local tourist offices for further details. Details of services are also sometimes given in the local press.

Senior citizens

Senior citizens are well catered for in most Tenerife hotels and resorts.

Many holiday packages are specifically aimed at older travellers, and off-season discounts are often available. However, note that getting around is not always easy for holidaymakers who are infirm or need a wheelchair (see below).

Tipping

Most hotel and some restaurant bills include a service charge. A small tip, however – around 10 per cent – for a well-served meal, a friendly taxi driver, the hotel maid, or hotel staff who have been particularly helpful, will be appreciated.

Toilets

Public toilets are very rare and recommendable public toilets are rarer still. In order of preference, use those in hotels, restaurants and bars. It helps to buy a drink in the last as a matter of courtesy. There are several terms for toilets that are commonly used: *servicios*, *WC*, *aseos* or *retretes*. The doors are usually marked *Señoras* (ladies) and *Caballeros*, *Señores* or *Hombres* (gentlemen), or will use a familiar pictogram.

Visitors with disabilities

The most wheelchair-friendly part of Tenerife is the south. Los Cristianos has a good reputation for its facilities, with ramps provided throughout the town. The Mar y Sol resort has been purpose built for holidaymakers with disabilities. For direct information, tel: 79 54 73. The resort also has a comprehensive range of disability appliances for hire. Newer hotels invariably have better facilities, so matters are improving, at least in the major resorts.

Away from the resorts, however, general facilities are poor to non-existent. There are few adapted toilets, few adapted public transport facilities, and very few adapted taxis or hire cars. Kerbs are generally high and blocked by parked cars. There are cobbled streets in the older towns, while the hilly nature of much of the terrain makes it more difficult to access. There are, however, wheelchair facilities at both Tenerife's main airports.

Language guide

The Canary Islanders speak Spanish and the only major difference from the mainland is that the letters c and z are pronounced softly, instead of lisped with a 'th' sound. There are a few indigenous words still in use, the most notable: *papa(s)* for potato(es) and *guagua* (pronounced 'wah-wah') for bus.

Pronunciation

Vowels

a is a short 'ah' sound in *gracias* (thank you).

e is a cross between the short English e (as in get) and the long English a (as in grace), eg *de* (of/from) is pronounced 'day' but in a clipped way.

i is a long 'ee' sound as in *sí* (yes) pronounced 'see'.

u is like 'oo' in boot eg *una* (one).

198

Consonants

c is soft before e and i (eg Barcelona) but hard at any other time.

g at the start of a word is a hard sound (as in get). In the middle of a word however it is like the throaty ch as in the Scottish loch, eg *urgencia* (emergency) is pronounced 'ooer-chensee-ah'.

In *agua* (water) it is hardly pronounced at all ('ah-kwa').

h is always silent.

j is also pronounced like the ch in loch, eg *jamón* (ham) is pronounced 'ch-amon'.

ll is like 'll' in million eg *lleno* (full) is pronounced 'lyay-no'.

ñ is like 'ni' in onion, eg *España* (Spain) pronounced 'ay-spanya'.

qu is like k in key, eg *cuánto?* (how much?) is pronounced 'kwan-toe'.

r is rolled, rr is rolled even harder.

v is like b in bottle, eg *vino* (wine is pronounced 'bee-no'.

x is like s, eg *excelente* (excellent) is pronounced 'ess-say-len-tay'.

Useful words and phrases

yes/no	sí/no
hello	hola
good morning	buenos dias
good afternoon	buenas tardes
goodnight	buenas noches
goodbye	adiós
see you later	hasta luego
please	por favor
thank you	gracias
you're welcome	de nada
sir, madame, miss	señor, señora, señorita
excuse me	perdóneme
sorry!	¡lo siento!
today	hoy
tomorrow	mañana
yesterday	ayer
last night	anoche
tonight	esta noche
how are you?	¿cómo está?
very well/good	muy bien/vale
can you help please?	¿me podriá ayuder por favor?
I am English	soy inglés
I am sorry, but I do not speak Spanish	lo siento, pero no hablo español
do you speak English?	¿habla inglés?
is there someone who speaks...?	¿hay alguien que hable...?
I don't understand	no comprendo
what is your name?	¿cómo te llamas?
my name is...	mi nombre es.../ me llamo...
what do you call...?	¿cómo se llama...?
what time is it?	¿qué hora es?
can I get past?	¿podría pasar?
can you...?	¿puede usted/ puedes...?
how much is...?	¿cuánto vale/ cuesta...?
is there?/there is...	¿hay?/hay...
I would like...	quiero/quisera...
where is...?	¿dónde está...?
what/when	qué/cuándo
why/how	por qué/cómo
near/far	cerca/lejos
here/there	aquí/ahí
old/new	viejo/nuevo
cheap/expensive	barato/caro
open/closed	abierto/cerrado
right/left	derecho/ izquierdo
for, to	por/para, a/para
large/small	grande/pequeño
more/less	más/menos
the key	la llave
bathroom/toilet	(cuarto de) baño/servicio
the bill	la cuenta
ticket(s)	billete(s)
stamp(s)	sello(s)
bus station	estación de guagua
church	iglesia

Days of the week

Monday	lunes
Tuesday	martes
Wednesday	miercoles
Thursday	jueves
Friday	viernes
Saturday	sábado
Sunday	domingo

HOTELS AND RESTAURANTS

HOTELS AND RESTAURANTS

ACCOMMODATION

The prices listed below, which are based on the cost of a double room with an en-suite bathroom, have been divided into three categories:
- budget (£)   under 7,000 pta
- moderate (££)   7,000–12,000 pta
- expensive (£££)   over 12,0000 pta

The telephone code for all listings is 922.

SANTA CRUZ DE TENERIFE
Atlántico (££) Calle del Castillo 12 (tel: 24 63 75; fax: 24 63 78). Attractive two-star hotel at the heart of the city. 60 rooms.
Horizonte (£) Santa Rosa de Lima 11 (tel: 27 19 36/27 53 59). Simple fittings and friendly welcome: convenient for local shops and restaurants. 45 rooms.
Mencey (£££) Avenida Doctor José Naveiras 38 (tel: 27 67 00; fax: 28 00 17). The best luxury hotel in the city, extensively renovated and situated in a peaceful residential district in the north of the city. Graceful and luxurious atmosphere, with many facilities. 300 rooms and suites. Book at Christmas and during Carnival.
Océano (££) Castillo 6 (tel: 27 08 00; fax: 24 63 78). Slightly smaller, similarly appointed and equally central alternative to the nearby Atlántico (see above). 28 rooms.
Plaza (££) Plaza de la Candelaria 10 (tel: 27 24 53; fax: 27 51 60). Three-star business hotel at the heart of downtown. 95 rooms.
Príncipe Paz (£££) Valentín Sanz 33, Parque Principe (tel: 24 99 55; fax: 28 10 65). Reliable four-star hotel northwest of the city centre. 80 rooms.
Taburiente (££) Doctor José Naveiras 24A (tel: 27 60 00; fax: 27 05 62). Well-known three-star hotel with swimming pool to the north of the city centre in a cluster of hotels. Close to the Parque Municipal García Sanabria. 16 rooms.
Tanausú (£) Padre Anchieta 8 (tel: 21 70 00/ 21 72 11; fax: 21 60 29). Two-star hotel south of the city centre. No restaurant. 18 rooms.

ANAGA AND NORTHEAST TENERIFE
Bajamar
Delfín (££) Avenida del Sol (tel: 54 02 00/54 02 04; fax: 54 02 00). Modern three-star hotel residence near the sea with tennis courts and swimming pool. 66 rooms.
Neptuno (££) Calle Punta Hidalgo (tel: 456 04 61). Three-star hotel close to Bajamar at Punta Hidalgo. There are 75 two-bedroom apartments or small bungalows. Sea- and mountain views, bowling, tennis courts, solarium and two seawater pools.

Candelaria
Gran Hotel Punta del Rey (££) Avenida Generalisimo 165, Las Caletillas (tel: 50 18 99). Modern hotel with swimming pool, tennis courts and seaviews. 424 rooms.

Tenerife Tour (££) Avenida Generalísimo 170, Las Caletillas (tel: 50 02 00; fax: 50 23 63). A low-rise three-star hotel situated on the coast with swimming pool and tennis courts. 95 rooms.

La Laguna
Aguere (£) Calle Obispo Rey Redondo 57 (tel: 25 94 90/63 02 74; fax: 63 16 33). Pleasant one-star hotel with reasonably priced rooms on the main street through the heart of the old town. 20 rooms.
Nivaria (££) Plaza del Adelantado 11 (tel: 26 42 98; fax: 25 96 34). Three-star apartment hotel (HA) with 73 good-value self-catering units on the main square at the southern edge of the historic old quarter. No restaurant, but the bar serves snacks.

VALLE DE LA OROTAVA
Puerto de la Cruz
Botánico (£££) Avenida Richard J Yeoward (tel. 38 14 00; fax: 38 15 04). A luxurious, modern five-star hotel 2km from the centre with delightful gardens. Often available as part of a package deal. 282 rooms.
Condesa (£) Calle Quintana 13 (tel: 38 10 50; fax: 38 69 50). Three-star hotel at the bustling heart of the old town close to the Marquesa (see below). A pleasant atmosphere with some nice old-world touches. 45 rooms.
Chimisay (£) Calle Agustín de Bethencourt 14 (tel: 38 35 52; fax: 38 28 40). Three-star hotel well situated in the older part of town west of Playa de la Iglesia. Swimming pool but no restaurant. 57 rooms.
Don Manolito (£) Calle Doctor Madán 6 (tel: 38 50 40; fax: 37 08 77). Modern three-star hotel at the western edge of town, but within walking distance of the centre. Sports facilities. 79 rooms.
Gran Hotel Tenerife Playa (£££) Avenida Colón 16 (tel: 38 32 11; fax: 38 37 91). Four-star hotel (built in 1959) at the lower end of its price range. Central and well-established for package tours, and very conveniently situated for the waterfront lidos. Tennis courts and swimming pool. 337 rooms.
Maga (£) Calle Iriarte 9 (tel: 38 38 53). Welcoming one-star hotel in the old part of town a few minutes' walk from the harbour. Rooms are simply furnished but clean and have private bathrooms. 24 rooms.
Marquesa (£–££) Calle Quintana 11 (tel: 38 31 51; fax: 38 69 50). Three-star hotel dating from 1712, but much altered and restored since. Retains old-world charm and character, though rooms are relatively simply furnished. Swimming pool and popular restaurant with outdoor terrace. 88 rooms.
Monopol (£–££) Calle Quintana 15 (tel: 38 46 11; fax: 37 03 10). Rivals the Marquesa (see above) as one of Puerto's 'historic' hotels. Much renovated over the years, it retains old-world charm, with a patio,

plants, cane furniture and wooden balconies. Swimming pool. 94 rooms.

NH Semiramis (£££) Leopoldo Cólogan Zulueta, La Paz (tel: 38 55 51; fax: 38 52 53). The second five-star choice after the Botánico (see above). Away from the centre (but near the seafront) with fine views from some rooms of the coast and the gardens. Swimming pool and tennis. 290 rooms.

San Telmo (££) Calle San Telmo 18 (tel: 38 58 53; fax: 38 59 91). A family-run three-star hotel which is situated on the waterfront. Convenient for the harbour, old town and celebrated Lido San Telmo. Rooftop swimming pool. 91 rooms.

Tigaiga (£££) Parque Taoro 28 (tel: 38 35 00; fax: 38 40 55). Popular and well-run four-star hotel in a lovely garden setting above the town. Tennis courts and swimming pool. 80 rooms.

NORTHWEST TENERIFE
Garachico
Hotel San Roque (£££), Esteban de Ponte 32, San Roque (tel: 13 34 35; fax: 13 34 06). Recently opened three-star hotel in one of the town's narrow streets. An attractive old building, it is based around a plant-filled courtyard.

Parque Nacional del Teide
Parador Las Cañadas del Teide (£–££), Parque Nacional del Teide (tel and fax: 38 64 15). Two-star *parador* at the heart of Tenerife's national park in the shadow of Mount Teide. Excellent base for walking and exploring. Swimming pool. 37 rooms.

Los Gigantes–Puerto de Santiago
Barcelo Santiago (£££) La Hondura 8 (tel: 10 09 12; fax: 10 18 08). Huge but well-run four-star hotel. Tennis courts, swimming pool and numerous other facilities and entertainments. 406 rooms.

Los Gigantes-Still (££–£££) Flor de Pascua 12 (tel: 10 10 20; fax: 10 04 75). Excellent four-star hotel with excellent views of the sea and Los Gigantes cliffs. Swimming pool, tennis courts and many other facilities. 225 rooms.

THE SOUTH
Adeje
Colón Guanamani (£££) Playa de la Fañabé (tel: 71 20 46; fax: 71 21 21). Pleasantly quiet four-star hotel with tennis courts and swimming pool close to the sea. 154 rooms.

Gran Hotel Bahía del Duque (£££) Playa del Duque-Fañabé (tel: 71 30 00; fax: 74 69 16). The most luxurious five-star hotel on Tenerife. Swimming pool and every comfort and facility necessary. 362 rooms.

El Médano
Atlantic Playa Suite (££) Avenida Europa 2 (tel: 17 62 52; fax: 17 61 14). Self-catering units, of which 67 are multi-room suites. Swimming pool. 90 units.

El Médano (£) Playa del Médano (tel: 17 70 00; fax: 17 60 48). Three-star hotel built in 1960 and jutting out to sea: the sun terrace is directly over the water and the hotel is generally peaceful and pleasant, if a little dated. 90 rooms.

Playa Sur Tenerife (££–£££) Playa del Médano (tel: 17 61 20/17 61 80; fax: 17 63 37). Three-star hotel over three floors. Its position, set a little back from the dunes, plus its sports school and rental facilities, makes this a popular base for windsurfers. 70 rooms.

Los Cristianos
Andrea's (£) Avenida Valle Menéndez (tel: 79 00 12; fax: 79 42 70). Pleasantly small-scale two-star hotel-residence close to the old town and just a few minutes' walk from the harbour, shops, restaurants and most other amenities. 42 rooms.

Arona Gran Hotel (£££) Avenida Maritima (tel: 75 06 78; fax: 75 02 43). Modern hotel stretching along the seafront with fairly luxurious rooms in a quiet part of the resort. Rooms have balconies and sea views. Three pools, sauna, tennis courts, nightclub and many other facilities. 399 rooms.

Paradise Park (£££) Urbanizacion Oasis del Sur (tel: 79 47 62; fax: 79 48 59). One of many four-star big 'white' modern hotels at the eastern end of the resort with courtesy bus to beach and shops. Nightly entertainment, as in most hotels in the region, plus pool, solarium, gymnasium, sauna and squash courts. 280 rooms.

Princesa Dacil (££) Camino Penetración (tel: 75 30 30; fax: 79 06 58). Big three-star hotel looking over the harbour. Adequate rooms, but like most local hotels, geared largely to package tours. 366 rooms.

Playa de las Américas
Bitácora (£££) Avenida Antonio Domínguez Alfonso 1 (tel: 79 15 40; fax: 79 66 77). Four-star efficiently run establishment largely aimed at the package-tour market. Located at the southern end of the resort. Tennis courts and swimming pool. 314 rooms.

La Siesta (£££) Avenida Marítima (tel: 79 23 00; fax: 79 22 20). Four-star hotel set back around 300m from the sea. Boasts attractive gardens and grounds, three swimming pools and two tennis courts. 280 rooms, with 80 suites equipped with self-catering facilities.

Mediterranean Palace (£££) Avenida Litoral (tel: 79 44 00; fax: 79 36 22). Luxury five-star hotel with a striking appearance and decidedly more sophisticated than most of the resort's hotels. Many excellent facilities. 536 rooms including 42 suites.

Park Hotel Troya (££–£££) Playa de la Troya (tel: 79 01 00; fax: 79 45 72). Busy and central four-star package-tour hotel opposite the Troya beach. Pool and tennis courts. 318 rooms including suites, apartments and family rooms.

HOTELS AND RESTAURANTS

Torviscas Playa (£££) Urbanización Torviscas (tel: 71 23 00; fax: 71 31 55). Newly built four-star hotel at the relatively more peaceful and attractive western fringe of the resort close to some of the new artificial beaches. Three pools, tennis and squash and roomy sun terraces. 472 rooms.

LA GOMERA
Playa de Santiago
Jardín Tecina (£££) Lomada de Tecina (tel: 14 58 50; fax: 41 58 51). Excellent hotel perched on a cliff edge with lovely gardens, swimming pools and views across the water to Mount Teide.

San Sebastián
Garajonay (££) Ruiz de Padrón 17 (tel: 87 05 50; fax: 87 05 50). Central, convenient and friendly two-star hotel that makes an ideal base. No restaurant or bar. 29 quiet, simple and clean rooms, with or without private bathroom.
Parador de San Sebastián de la Gomera (£££) Balcón de la Villa y Puerto (tel: 87 11 00; fax: 87 11 16). Magnificent four-star *parador* – one of the best in the Canaries – and the undoubted first-choice hotel in the island's capital. Panoramic position, swimming pool and lots of old-world style. 58 rooms.
Villa Gomera (££) Ruiz de Padrón 68 (tel: 87 00 20; fax: 87 02 35). Pleasant one-star hotel in the town centre. One of many small hotels on this street. 16 rooms.

RESTAURANTS

The prices listed below are for a basic three-course meal for one with wine.
- budget (£)   under 2,000 pta
- moderate (££)   2,000–3,500 pta
- expensive (£££) over 3,500 pta

SANTA CRUZ DE TENERIFE
Café del Príncipe (£) Plaza del Príncipe de Asturias (tel: 27 88 10). Nice place for a simple *al-fresco* lunch, coffee or *tapas* in a pretty garden square.
El Coto de Antonio (£££) Calle General Goded 13 (tel: 27 21 05). Prestigious establishment located in the northwest of the city just off Rambla del General Franco, one of the main areas for restaurants serving the city's monied locals and business community.
Los Troncos (££) Calle General Goded 17 (tel: 28 41 52). Probably the best restaurant in the city for the evening, with Canarian and Basque specialities at surprisingly modest prices. Outlying location. Closed Sunday evening, Wednesday and from mid-August to mid-September.
Mesón Los Monjes (££) Calle La Marina 7 (tel: 24 65 76). This restaurant's name means 'The Monks'. A good central choice located just north of the Plaza de España.

Olympo (£) Plaza de España-Plaza de Candelaria (tel: 24 17 38). Cheap and popular café-restaurant with good harbour views from its first floor location at the corner of the city's main square. Particularly good and busy at lunch.

ANAGA AND NORTHEAST TENERIFE
Candelaria
Carlo's (£) Calle Obispo Pérez Cáceres 49. Great spot for ice-cream in Candelaria's main street.
Sobre El Archete (£££) Lommo de Aroba 2 (tel: 50 01 15). One of the smarter restaurants on this part of the coast, and perfect for lunch after a visit to the sanctuary.

El Sauzal
Casa del Vino (££) La Baranda (tel: 57 25 35). Attractive setting and interesting wine museum combined with an often busy but appealing restaurant (also see page 63). Boasts a terrace with a sea view for outdoor eating. Closed Sunday evening, Monday and mid-May to mid-June.

La Laguna
Casa Maquila (£) Callejón Maquila 4 (tel: 25 70 20). Simple and pleasant restaurant serving local specialities.
La Alacena (£) Barcelona 3 (tel: 63 20 58). Reliable establishment located in a street two blocks west of the old town and the main Calle Obispo Rey Redondo.
La Hoya del Camello (££) Carretera General del Norte 118 (tel: 26 20 54). One of La Laguna's best restaurants.

Tacoronte
Los Limoneros (££–£££) Los Naranjeros (tel: 63 66 37). Quite smart restaurant about 3.5km east of Tacoronte in the hamlet of Los Naranjeros. Closed Sunday evening.

VALLE DE LA OROTAVA
La Orotava
Casa Gabriel (££) Camino de los Rechazos 5 (tel: 33 55 91). Reliable standby for good local cooking at reasonable prices.

Puerto de la Cruz
Casino Taoro (££–£££) Parque Taoro (tel: 38 05 50). Smart restaurant located in the famous casino in the park above town. Formal atmosphere and international food with good views from the dining room.
Magnolia (££–£££) Carretera del Botánico 5-Avenida Marqués de Villanueva del Prado (tel: 38 56 14). Acclaimed, elegant and award-winning restaurant outside the centre on the main road to the Jardín de Aclimatación. Catalan and international cuisine with an emphasis on fish and seafood. Outdoor dining possible.
Mario (£–££) Edificio Rincón del Puerto, Plaza del Charco 14 (tel: 38 55 35). One of several restaurants in this renovated central courtyard development. Specialises in fish.

Mi Vaca y Yo (££–£££) Calle Cruz Verde 3A (tel: 38 52 47). Charming rustic Canarian setting for excellent local and international cuisine, particularly seafood. Centrally situated in the little grid of streets west of the harbour and Plaza del Charco. Open evenings only.

Patio Canaria (£) Calle del Lomo 4 (tel: 38 04 51). Good standard restaurant with typical Canarian décor: you might also try the similar and equally good La Papaya (tel: 38 28 11) at Calle del Lomo 10.

Régulo (££) San Felipe 16 (tel: 38 45 06). A pleasant plant-festooned patio makes this an atmospheric and pretty place at which to dine. Centrally situated, close to Mi Vaca y Yo (see above). Closed Sunday and July.

NORTHWEST TENERIFE
Garachico
Bodegón Plaza (£) Calle Esteban de Ponte (tel: 83 09 77). Located in an old-style Canarian house with several rooms where typical island food is served in a quiet, friendly atmosphere.

Casa Ramón (£) Calle Esteban de Ponte (tel: 83 00 77). Similar in character and cuisine to the Bodegón Plaza (see above).

Isla Baja (££–£££) Calle Esteban de Ponte 5 (tel: 83 00 08). A long-established restaurant situated on the seafront. Specialises in fish dishes.

Icod de Los Vinos
Carmen (££), below Plaza de la Iglesia (tel: 81 06 31). Probably the best restaurant in the central part of town: a beautifully restored traditional house serving Canarian and Spanish food.

Plaza la Pila (£) Plaza la Pila (tel: 81 34 28). Good local food in humble but appealing surroundings. Try also the nearby bar-restaurant Marítimo (tel: 82 27 02) for snacks and cheap meals.

Los Gigantes–Puerto de Santiago
Asturias (£–££) Acantilado de los Gigantes, Guía de Isora (tel: 10 14 23). A reliable choice in Los Gigantes with the option of outdoor eating.

Casa Pancho (£££) Playa de la Arena (tel: 10 13 23). In a resort largely dominated by bland international and British-oriented establishments, this excellent restaurant is an oasis of high-quality local cooking at good prices. Worth a special journey even if you are staying elsewhere.

THE SOUTH
Adeje–Barranco del Infierno
Otelo (£–££) (tel: 78 03 74). Close to the entrance of the Barranco del Infierno gorge and something of an attraction in its own right. Nonetheless it remains an unassuming and friendly place, serving excellent Canarian food with surprisingly good prices given its location. Especially famous for its chicken and rabbit. Closed Tuesday.

El Médano
Avencio (£–££) Chasna 6 (tel: 17 60 79/70 43 95). Fish and seafood specialities.

Los Cristianos
La Cava (££–£££) El Cabezo (tel: 79 04 93). A rustic setting and the chance to eat outdoors make this a good place for dinner, as well as a welcome antidote to the plethora of foreign-oriented restaurants that fill this resort.

Playa de las Américas
Casa Vasca (££–£££) Apartamentos Compostela Beach (tel: 79 40 25). One of the resort's more appealing places to eat outdoors.

El Patio (£££) Jardín Tropical Hotel, Urbanización San Eugenio (tel: 79 41 11). The first choice for a special occasion: book a table outside on the patio if possible and enjoy a menu which combines Andalucían and Canarian influences. Very expensive.

LA GOMERA
Las Rosas
Las Rosas (££) Las Rosas (tel: 80 09 16). Enjoying a stunning setting on the edge of the village, perched precariously on the edge of a ravine, with magnificent 180-degree view. Food is typically Canarian, but the establishment is partly tailored to suit the coach parties who come here to witness demonstrations of *el siblo* (see page 173). Open for lunch only.

Parque Nacional de Garajonay
La Laguna Grande (£–££) at the La Laguna Grande picnic area and viewpoint (tel: 89 54 45). A small bar-restaurant which serves snacks and meals during the day.

Playa de Santiago
Jardín Tecina (££–£££) Playa de Santiago (tel: 14 58 50). Gardens, the sea and Mount Teide provide the spectacular backdrop for a romantic setting in the balcony dining area of this fine hotel (see page 200). Excellent cuisine.

San Sebastián
Casa del Mar (£–££) Calle del Medio 61–Calle Fred Olsen (tel: 87 12 20). Airy bar-restaurant near the seafront serving snacks and robust Canarian meals.

El Pajar (£) Calle Ruiz de Padrón 44 (tel: 87 11 02). Lively and atmospheric bar-restaurant for snacks and meals. Often frequented by locals.

Marqués de Oristano (£) Calle del Medio 24 (tel: 87 00 22). Another atmospheric local place with an attractive dining terrace.

Parador de San Sebastián de la Gomera (££–£££) Balcón de la Villa y Puerto (tel: 87 11 00). This famous hotel (see page 200) serves the best Spanish and Canarian food on the island. It has a wonderfully atmospheric dark-wood dining room.

Index

Principal references are shown in bold

INDEX

ACKNOWLEDGEMENTS

Picture credits

The Automobile Association would like to thank the following photographers, libraries and associations for their assistance in the preparation of this book.

BRIDGEMAN ART LIBRARY, LONDON 28a and 29 Eg. 2709 f.2 Frontispiece; Conquest of the Canary Islands, a ship crowded with armed men by Gadifer de la Sale et Jehan de Bethencourt Le Canarien, (c. 1420-30) British Library, London; 31 The reception of Christopher Columbus by Ferdinand and Isabella by Eugene Deveria (1808-65) Musée Bargoin, Clermont-Ferrand/Giraudon; 44 Nelson on the 'Theseus' with the Inshore Squadron off Cadiz, July 1797, (oil on canvas) by Thomas Buttersworth (1768-1842) Christie's Images; 166a and 167 Illustration of Ferdinand and Isabella seeing Christopher Columbus off from the Dock at Palos on Friday 3rd August 1492 by Victor A. Searles. Library of Congress, Washington D.C. **BRUCE COLEMAN LTD** 16a (H. Lange); DIGITAL WISDOM PUBLISHING LTD top map on back cover. MARY EVANS PICTURE LIBRARY 22a, 22b, 24, 28b, 34b, 166b; ROBERT HARDING PICTURE LIBRARY 26a, 163, 170, 171, 172; HULTON GETTY 27; MAGNUM PHOTOS LTD 34a (M Riboud), 37 (G Peress); MUSEO DE HISTORIA DE TENERIFE 25, 30/1, 30; NATIONAL MARITIME MUSEUM , LONDON 45; NATURE PHOTOGRAPHERS LTD 17 (M Bolton); PICTOR INTERNATIONAL, LONDON front cover; POWERSTOCK PHOTO LIBRARY 79; SPECTRUM COLOUR LIBRARY 18b, 50a; WORLD PICTURES LTD 160/1, 164, 174/5.

All remaining pictures are held in the Association's own library (AA PHOTO LIBRARY) and were taken by James A Tims with the exception of the following pages:

Kirk Lee Aeder 33; Philip Enticknap 173a; Robert Holmes 130; Rob Moore spine 3, 14/5, 18a, 19, 23b, 35, 42, 49, 50b, 51, 61, 76, 78, 86/7, 89, 108, 112/3, 117, 119, 123, 127, 128/9, 131, 136a, 141, 143, 148/9, 152, 152/3, 154, 159, 188, 189, 190, 192, 195, 198a, 198b; Clive Sawyer 2, 4, 5b, 6, 12/3, 13, 21, 23a, 38/9, 47, 48, 53, 56/7, 64, 66, 69, 73, 74, 75, 77, 83, 100, 103, 104, 105, 106, 107, 110, 111, 120, 125, 132, 133, 134, 135, 137, 146, 147, 148, 155a, 156, 157a, 158, 162, 165, 168/9, 169, 173b, 176, 177, 179, 180, 181, 182/3, 186/7; Rick Strange 68/9.

Acknowledgements

The author and the Automobile Association would like to acknowledge the contribution of Paul Murphy, author of Thomas Cook Travellers *Canary Islands* and AA Essential *Tenerife*.

Contributors

Copy editor: Sarah Hudson **Verifier**: Colin Follett
Designer: Jo Tapper **Indexer**: Marie Lorimer